The Story of
Handball

Handball in action (Tommy O'Rourke, Kildare. Photo *Sportsfile Ltd.*)

The Story of
Handball
The Game, The Players
The History

Tom McElligott

WOLFHOUND PRESS

By the same author

Secondary Education in Ireland 1870-1921
(Irish Academic Press, 1981).

Education in Ireland
(Institute of Public Administration, 1966)

The European Teacher — a journal, editor 1962-1977.

Published by
WOLFHOUND PRESS
68 Mountjoy Square, Dublin 1.

British Library Cataloguing in Publication Data
  McElligott, T. J.
  The story of handball in Ireland.
  1. Handball
  I. Title
  796.3'09415   GV1017.42

ISBN 0-86327-018-2

Cover illustration Geraldine Garland. Cover typography Michael O'Brien. Detail of print on back cover reproduced courtesy Monaghan County Museum *(See caption on page 8 for full details).* Production — Typesetting by Leaders, Swords, Co. Dublin. Cover printed by Fine Arts, Tallaght, Co. Dublin. Text and illustrations layout by Redsetter Ltd., Dublin. Text printed by Billings & Co., Great Britain.

Publisher's Acknowledgement
The publisher wishes to acknowledge with thanks the contributions and assistance of: Ray McManus and Pat Maxwell; the staff of the Handball Council of the GAA at Croke Park for generous access to records and information; the Secretary of the Irish Ladies Handball Association, Ann Coady, for research into and compilation of records; Anthony Farrell for introducing the project to Wolfhound Press. In the few instances where we have failed to locate copyright holders, or if we have inadvertently used other copyright material, we would be grateful if the owners would write to the publisher. Finally, we wish to thank the author for his every co-operation and assistance throughout the publishing process, and to express the hope and opinion that this book will contribute to the continued growth of the game and give added enjoyment and understanding of handball to both players and non-players.

Contents

Acknowledgements

Anyone who has ever written anything, whether a railway timetable or a dissertation on scientific philosophy, knows what a myriad unforseen obstacles have to be faced. It was so with me. That I have surmounted most of them is due to the immensity of help I received. I acknowledge in particular the help of the following, but in doing so realise that there will be omissions for which I take responsibility and crave forgiveness. At the outset I must thank the Director of the National Library and his staff for their patience with the many demands I made on them. Joe Lynch, the present Administrator of the Irish Handball Council, put his files and records at my disposal and both himself and his Secretary, Irene Galvin, answered the scores of questions which I sent them almost daily. A special word of thanks also to Sean and Eugene McCarthy of the Foundry, Mountrath, to whose generosity I owe a debt for enabling me to publish a very old photograph of the first world champion. Many evenings spent in the company of John K. Clarke gave me an insight into the past and an appreciation of his love for the game. Finally, without the editorial guidance of Antony Farrell, the author would have abandoned the work long since.

I also gleaned much of value from correspondence and conversation with each of the following:- Eoghan Corry, Walter McGrath, Peadar de Bairtsibéal, Mick Dunne, Sean Kilfeather, Dick Murphy, Maurice Hayes, Pauline Caslin, Rev. Sean Farragher, Dave Guiney, John Healy, Colin Jenkins, Trevor West, Norman Lush, Joe McTernan, Sam MacAughtrey, Robert Maguire, Séamus Ó Buachalla, Tom Higgins, David Rose, M. O'Gara, Lord Killanin, Pat Maxwell, Mr. & Mrs. T. Duggan, Comdt. Joe Young, Kevin O'Donovan, Áine Nic Oda, Denis Weldon, Pakey Glennon.

Handballers in action today:
Top left: Brendan O'Brien, Kerry. *Top right:* John Sabo, USA. *Bottom left:* Dick Ling, Wexford. *Bottom right:* Francis McCann of Sligo plays John Sabo of the USA.

"Castle Blaney" painted in 1785 by John Nixon. This is the earliest known depiction of the game of handball in Ireland. Reproduced courtesy Monaghan County Museum.

Chapter 1

The Early Game

Handball is an old game of uncertain age: 'old' because references to it occur in writings that date back to the eighteenth century; 'of uncertain age' because no one can say when someone first struck a ball against a wall. It has survived in various forms but is always confined to two or three players. The ball was not always of rubber, the ballcourt did not always have four walls or even two, the players rarely wore any special attire. Local custom often decided the side to which the ball was to be served and if it were to be allowed to bounce more than once. Even the number of aces or points which constituted a game differed; some players favouring a 15-ace game and others a 21-ace game.

It may, indeed, have been because of such differences that the game appealed to the 'characters' who, more than in any other sport that I know, abounded in handball. Unlike the team games of hurling and football with their claim on the support of entire parishes, handball was ever a game for the individual. Only in a doubles game did he have to consider his partner and so he could, if he chose, play a distinctive game that differed from anyone else's. As a result, in handball there have always been players who were technically skilled and, of much more interest, others who displayed individual characteristics, amiable eccentricities, which made them remembered and their achievements recalled. The ballplayer in a singles match could indulge his temperament as he had no partner, no team-mates to consider. He could attempt the spectacular 'kill' or essay the impossible return; he could command the occasion like a great actor within the proscenium arch of the ballcourt walls.

The setting, too, was simple, with little to distract the eye from 'the stage'. A sloping hillside where spectators sat, a clay or flagged floor, a front wall with or without side-walls or wing-walls as they were sometimes called. Gerald Griffin describes such a scene in the first chapter of *The Collegians* when he talks of 'the young playing at ball, goal or other athletic exercises on the green while the old people drank together under the shade of trees'. That was in 1830 at a time when, in summer, Limerick people went up the river towards Castleconnell or Plessey to picnic in the meadows sloping down from the Clare hills.

When, almost 100 years later, I came to live in County Wexford, the Sunday afternoon scene at Ballyanne was little different. There the people from New Ross and the surrounding countryside gathered on a Sunday afternoon beside a creek on the River Barrow. The old rough-stone ballcourt which formed part of a disused limekiln had a tree-shaded hillside as a natural gallery where, while waiting their turn to play, the local lads threw the 56-lb weight or wagered a few pence on a game of 'brag'.

Unlike team games, handball did not require any special dress and it was not unusual to find priests in their soutanes and RIC men in their heavy uniform trousers playing ball with shirtless, barefooted lads. But, inevitably, cotton and other lightweight materials came to replace the linen shirts and frieze coats, and the players came to discard long trousers and wear knee-length breeches and, later, shorts.

Pictures of such players as Phil Casey, John Lawlor and Mike Egan show them wearing ankle-length drawers or trousers in the ballcourt. A change seems to have come about in the time of J. J. Bowles, who appears in every photo togged as though for a present-day match. The game had become a spectator sport and the television cameras were to follow!

The spectators, too, were changing. The crowds that came to back their fancy – noisy, turbulent and often quarrelsome – were giving way to a more specialised, more interested audience. While match-makers and stake-holders were still very much part of the game in my youth, gradually they dropped out as the influence of the GAA increased.

The social side of the game has also changed. Gone are the after-match gatherings; gone, too, the ceremony attached to the signing of the contract when a big match was being arranged. It may be that with whiskey at 18 shillings a gallon and light ale at 1 s 6d per dozen (1880 prices), conviviality and good fellowship were then more easily engendered. In Dublin the 'socials' were usually held in Dougherty's Hotel, Lower Bridge Street, and Conarchy's Hotel in what used to be Rutland Square. The meeting-place for American ballplayers who came so regularly to take part in or attend the Cork Tournament was invariably the Queen's Hotel in Parnell Place.

To go back even to the handball played when I was growing up is to recall a lost world. It was peopled by bare footed lads who, with skin and thread and elastic, made the hardballs with which they played and who knew no competitions except those for which the prize was money, often no more than a few pence. Within the ballcourt, the old cries of the handball world were still in use, and the 'let' of Shakespeare's day was used to mark an obstruction, i.e. a hinder ball. Level scores were indicated by the marker calling 'Horsemen', and when the game reached 18 the shout of 'Tally' was followed by 'Tally one' at 19, before 'Look sharp' and 'Game ball' signalled the end. Each game was scored in 'legs' so that a passer-by might hear the unexpected shout of 'One leg off' as he went his way. And, at the end, the marker rarely failed to make clear the urgent need for liquid refreshment when he called 'Game and match and the marker spitting ink for a drink'.

The role of referee was one of considerable importance. He was usually someone whose long association with the game gave him a certain status among followers and players. The name of the referee for a home-and-home match was usually released one week before the first half was played. On the day of the match he was introduced to each player and given formal possession of the balls to be used. Then, calling the players to him, he would point to any peculiarities in the construction of the ballcourt, present each player to the 'gallery' and toss the coin to decide 'first hand'.

As matches were usually played on a Sunday, a town-crier was sometimes employed to do the rounds of the town on the previous evening. I remember hearing one in the 1930s in Hospital, County Limerick, where Dobell's Theatrical Company were playing on the same day as the Munster handball finals. He was paid to publicise both events but the manner in which he did so must have caused surprise both to those interested in the drama and to those whose concern was to see Jimmy O'Toole and Tommy Downes winning a title. He simply announced, 'Come and see *The White Sister* and *East Lynne* at the ballcourt tomorrow at 3 pm!'

In those days when employment usually meant a 6-day, 48-hour working week, there were in Ireland, as elsewhere, certain carefree, loosely organised pleasures that brought relief from it. The bicycle had been invented, trains had opened up the countryside, and long cars and charabancs brought followers to venues not only for the 'goaling' and the 'hurling' but for a great variety of other sporting activities. A newspaper correspondent describes a gathering at Ballymun, in north county Dublin, which we may be sure was little different from that to be found elsewhere in Ireland at the time:

> Ten or twenty years ago there was a crowd of genuine 'sports' frequenting Ballymun – horse racing, hunting men, greyhound, terrier and bulldog followers, cock-fighting men, shooting and fishing, and boys that used to sing and dance – in fact, there were characters and tit-bits of all branches of sport, and everyone who wanted sport made for 'The Boot'! (*Sport*, 15 September 1917)

'The Boot', mentioned by Sir William Brereton in his *Travels* (1634-5), was and is a famous inn, once the site of the ballcourt designed by Irish handball champion, John Lawlor, and opened in 1909.

This pleasant image of week-end sport was to change with the gradual movement of people towards towns and cities. Teams were more easily organised and team games prospered as cars came to collect players either at some central point or at their homes, and parishes tended to amalgamate in order to meet the challenge of stronger teams from the towns. Handball was at first largely unaffected by the drift but it began to suffer as field games came to demand the allegiance of the young men for hurling and football. What psychologists call 'group rivalry' found expression in team games and many handball courts were deserted by all but schoolboys who, on their way from school, put their satchels away and had a 'dodge'.

The revival of interest may be said to date from the time when newspapers, radio and, later, television came to focus attention on a range of sports of which hurling and football were no more than two among many. As the emphasis shifted from the traditional sports and as games such as squash caught the imagination of the individual to whom team games meant a certain unwelcome anonymity, handball prospered.

Its advance was hastened by developments in air travel which brought the United States of America, the other great centre of the game, within a few hours' flying time of Ireland. The players who came here in the 'fifties were surprised by what appeared to them the great size of Irish courts, while Irish players found that the visitors had introduced many refinements necessary in what was for them a spectator sport. Among these was the abolition of kicking, the playing of the ball against the backwall and the introduction of the ceiling shot. Inevitably, as the governing bodies on both sides came to exchange ideas, the game itself underwent many changes.

From being a test of strength, stamina and, above all, skill, the game became less dependent on stamina as the length of rubbers was shortened, and more a test of skill. But the switch from the old Irish hardball to rubber was fatal to stroke play. The placing of the ball with all the deliberate artistry of a painter applying colour to a canvas was forever gone. The graceful curve of the arm following the line of the shot was replaced by the clouting of the rubber ball often with the closed fist.

The age of the game is a question to which it is difficult to give a precise answer. One of the great dandies of eighteenth century Dublin was Buck Whaley of whom many tales are told. He is said to have left his town-house in St. Stephen's Green, Dublin, in 1784 to win a purse of 100 sovereigns by playing handball against the walls of Jerusalem. The very absurdity of the wager and the amount of the purse has a ring of authenticity about it that leads me to believe that the walls may well have echoed to the sounds of the alley-cracker.

Of the few written records of the existence of the game before the nineteenth century, that of William Farrell of Carlow is by far the most detailed. William Farrell was a gate-keeper in Carlow who benefited from a good teacher and who later wrote a very complete account of life in the county during his youth. He was born in 1772 and the Ireland he grew up in was still rich in simple pleasures and pastimes. In describing those of his native Carlow, he wrote:

> . . . if anything was wanting to show the easy circumstances of the people, it would be found in the numbers in every town and in every part of the country that could afford time to practise all the manly exercises so well known to Irishmen as hurling, football, cudgelling, tennis or handball, leaping, wrestling, vaulting, throwing the sledge or bar or grinding-stone; and at every outlet of Carlow there were fields like commons, free to everyone that chose to amuse themselves, and one of the best ballcourts

in Ireland within ... (*Carlow in '98*, Roger J. McHugh [London, 1949])

Of those whose play in the ballcourt he most admired, Mr John Bagot, a gentleman from Rufflin about three miles distant from the town, might be placed foremost. Then there was Joe Dowling and his brother Jim, Paddy Foley – one of the greatest players I ever saw standing in a court – every blow from his right or left like clockwork and no matter how hard the ace was or if it even went against him, he was always good-humoured and came out laughing. Tom Nowlan comes next, a powerful player ...

He rated Jack Fogarty of the Castle Mill as the best of all those whom he had seen. Fogarty lived near the ballcourt, then kept by Bob Rankin, and he achieved great fame when he defeated Kearns, a wealthy Dublin businessman, who had no equal in the Patrick Street ballcourt.

If written records are scarce so, too, are illustrations of the game and its exponents. However, a watercolour dated 1782, in the possession of Monaghan County Museum, shows two boys playing handball against a wall of the old castle in Castleblaney. The players are in kneebreeches, as is the sole onlooker who may have been combining the duties of referee and marker. He is shown standing well to the side of what was probably the playing area and appears to be following closely the flight of the ball. This may be the earliest picture of the game which was known to be played at least by the end of the eighteenth century.

In the years prior to the Rebellion of 1798, many of the meetings of the United Irishmen in Kildare were held in ballcourts throughout that county. A young farmer, Michael MacRandall from Johnstown, known to be a United Irishman, played frequent challenge matches which were said to have been the occasions for his meeting other members of that organisation. One of the centres of rebellion was Rathangan, and the old ballcourt which stood in Doran's demesne near the canal bridge had the date '1790' roughly cut in stone at the corner of the front wall. In county Louth a young man named Michael Boylan of Blakestown, Ardee, was a leader in the United Irishmen:

He was arrested while playing handball in the village of Collon and shortly afterwards hanged in the most public spot in Drogheda, opposite the Tholsel, on 22nd June, 1798, one hour after receiving his sentence. There was some delay in getting possession of his body and his funeral took place from Pitcher Hill, Drogheda, to Kildemock, Ardee, arriving in the early morning, the coffin being carried all that distance on the shoulders of his sympathisers, Peter Boylan, father of Michael, being one of them. (*The Drogheda Independent*, 2 July 1960)

Close on a century later, T. F. O'Sullivan writes in *The story of the G.A.A.* 'that prosecutions took place in May, 1886, against persons in Ballintogher, Co. Sligo, for playing handball on Sunday'. Later still, the Irish Volunteers drilled in ballcourts, many of which were by then four-wall (i.e. enclosed) courts. Knowing this, the British authorities insisted on permits for handball matches even as they did for hurling and football matches. It may have been this which prompted an Irish MP, Mr Flavin, to ask the Chief Secretary 'whether it is a criminal offence, punishable by arrest or prosecution, in the eyes of Dublin Castle for boys in schools and colleges, and in handball courts, to play the game of handball in any part of Ireland?' (*Hansard*, 1 August 1918) The Home Secretary, Mr Shortt, replied that the answer was in the negative.

Despite his assurance, the RIC took possession of ballcourts in many parts of the country when matches were due to be played. They did so largely because the organisers refused to apply for the necessary permit. At Laffansbridge, county Tipperary, in July 1919, two District Inspectors with a force of armed police took possession of the ballcourt. A report in *The Nationalist* (Clonmel) says that while the matches as advertised were not permitted to take place, players were allowed to play provided that they left their coats on!

Despite official opposition, the game was immensely popular with the police and to this day ballcourts may be seen beside many of the older police barracks. One reason for this popularity was the refusal of the GAA to admit members of the British forces in Ireland (and this included the police) to its ranks. Denied the opportunity of playing the team games such as hurling and football, policemen could scarcely be prevented from playing handball on their own property. For over 20 years, beginning in 1890, the RIC Championships were played at the Mount Pottinger ballcourt in Belfast. These seem to have lapsed after 1912 perhaps because of internal troubles and the imminence of the First World War. A writer in the *Newry Sentinel* (1962) describes a handball final at the police station in Irish Street, Newry, in his youth. The four contestants were policemen: Head Constable Twamley, Sergeant Summers, Sergeant Ledwith and Constable Blaney. The writer adds that 'hundreds turned out to see the game'.

The ballcourts attached to police barracks were usually built of brick, sometimes though not always faced with cement. They were rarely enclosed and the side-walls seldom ran for more than half the length of the playing area.

The eagerness with which any suitable gable-end was used for handball may be seen from the way in which the walls of some old monasteries were converted into rough and ready ballcourts. The champion ballplayer of Ireland in 1854 was a Kilkennyman, Martin Butler, who learnt the game in the nave of St Francis' Abbey which is now part of Smithwick's Brewery.

Farther south in the same county, the chancel of the priory of the Augustinian Canons of Kells has been used for ballplaying for many years. Some thirteenth century inscribed tombstones in the floor are well worn by the feet of the players and the incised floriated crosses with which they were ornamented have almost disappeared. Some miles away, at Ullard, the old abbey of St Fiachra is used by the local club as their headquarters and it has long been recognised as a suitable venue for challenge matches! When it was first used for ballplaying is hard to say, but as far back as 8 October 1854 we find Sir Samuel Ferguson writing to his friend, Dr George Petrie, and telling him of the 'ball-alley' in the ruins. Part of his letter runs, 'My Dear Petrie – Only think of my being in sight of Ullard and knowing no more of it than that one end has been converted into a ball-alley. I crossed the Barrow in half an hour after receiving your letter and poked away at the ruins till five o'clock.'

Such use of old ruins is not unusual in at least one neighbouring country. Writing of Welsh sports, Edmund Hyde Hall has this to say: 'Quoits and skittles I have sometimes, though not often observed: but fives may be almost termed a national pursuit, in which both boys and men very generally and eagerly engage. To this sport the churchyard is commonly resorted to, and on this account it is that the windows of the churches are to be so frequently secured with shutters' (*A Description of Caernarvonshire*, 1809-11).

The game of fives which the author mentions never seemed to have reached the same degree of popularity in Ireland that it did in England and Wales. Yet, it is an attractive game retaining features such as the buttress or pepper-pot and the step, which may derive from its association with the cloisters of old monasteries, and, if we are to believe the essayist William Hazlitt, the most famous fives player in the world was from Cork! His skill as recorded in Hazlitt's obituary makes the achievements of other famous sportsmen seem very modest indeed:

Died at his house in Burbage Street, St. Giles', John Cavanagh, the famous hand fives player. When a person dies who does one thing better than anyone else in the world, which so many others are trying to do well, it leaves a gap in society. It is not likely that anyone will now see the game of fives played to its perfection for many years to come, for Cavanagh is dead and has not left his peer behind him ... Whenever he touched the ball there was an end to the chase. His eye was certain, his hand fatal, his presence of mind complete. He could do what he pleased and he always knew exactly what to do. He saw the whole game and played it; took instant advantage of his adversary's weakness, and recovered balls as if by a miracle and from sudden thought that everyone gave for lost. He had equal power and skill, quickness and judgment. He could either outwit his opponent by fitness or beat him by main strength. Sometimes when he seemed preparing to send the ball with the full swing of his arm, he would, by a slight turn of the wrist, drop it within an inch of the line. In general, the ball came from his hand, as if from a racket, in a straight horizontal line, so that it was in vain to attempt to overtake or stop it. He was the best uphill player in the world, even when his adversary was fourteen he would play on the same or better, and, as he never flung away the game through carelessness or conceit, he never gave it up through laziness or want of heart. The only peculiarity of his game was that he never *volleyed*, but let them hop; but if they rose an inch above the ground he never missed them. There was not only nobody equal but nobody second to him. It is supposed that he could give any other player half the game or beat them with his left hand. His service was tremendous. He once played Woodward and Meredith (two of the best players in England) together in the Fives Court, St Martin's Street, and made seven and twenty aces following off service alone – a thing unheard of (Extract from *Examiner*, 17 February 1819, of obituary on John Cavanagh of Cork. *The Badminton Library* [London 1891] pp. 420-21).

Fives, so popular in English public schools particularly in the last century, never seemed to catch the imagination of Irish schools and schoolboys. It was handball that was played most extensively, while team games such as football and cricket did not begin to prosper until trains made travel easier. John Jameson, author of *The History of the Royal Belfast Academical Institution* (1969), writes that for years after the opening of the school in 1814, the one game played was 'alley-ball':

A ball-alley of sorts had been made in 1815 after the boarders had petitioned the Joint Board to allow them to 'raise the walls of the outer offices' at their own expense, and some improvements in the form of paving had been made to it in 1824. The students of the Collegiate Department caused a certain amount of trouble by playing alley-ball while school classes were being held, and in 1838 they had a ball-alley of their own provided, which they were strictly enjoined to keep to. In 1864 William Dunville, who ten years earlier had been a hundred-guinea subscriber, offered to build a covered ball-alley at a cost of £200. His generous offer was naturally accepted with gratitude. Thirty years later alley-ball was still one of the most popular games – as a variation of it still is – and in addition to another new alley, it was reported in 1893 that the gables of the new Mathematical School – the present Common Hall – were being regularly used for play – as they still are to-day.

It is of some slight significance that it was in one of Ireland's few public schools, St Columba's College, Rathfarnham, that fives continued to be played until fairly recently. The court was built in 1855 by an Old Etonian, Warden Williams, with money provided by Archbishop Beresford. The game existed side by side with handball and Mahaffy on his rounds of inspection of Irish grammar schools in 1879 commented on 'the excellent racquet-court and two Eton five-courts' to be found there.' Eton Fives' originated at Eton College which in 1981 played host to the first-ever international Eton Fives Championships.

When the French College, Blackrock, was opened in 1860 handball was one of the first games played there, largely because of the simplicity of its requirements and also because the members of the Congregation who came here were completely unfamiliar with such games as hurling and football. The first ballcourt was built of brick and Michael Cusack is known to have played in it. The priests who left Blackrock in 1888 to found the Catholic High School, Pittsburgh (later to become the Duquesne University), brought the game with them and there were at one time no less than 10 ballcourts in the grounds of the school. The old ballcourt at Blackrock was demolished in 1869 but the game, far from being forgotten, continued to be played and two former pupils, Gus Weldon and John Clarke, went on to win All-Ireland senior titles. Weldon won his under IAHU rules while Clarke, having won Dublin championships under IAHU rules, won the All-Ireland title with his brother, Austin, under IAHA rules.

It would be very misleading to think that handball was never encouraged by the landlords and never enjoyed the patronage of the aristocracy. As far back as 1797, Lord Tyrawley gave a rent-free site for the erection of a ballcourt at Ballinrobe, County Mayo. The Duke of Leinster did the same for the town of Athy in county Kildare, supplying also materials for the building of the ballcourt, which was first leased to the Athy Urban District Council on 14 December 1856. The first Lord Morris and Killanin, who was Lord Chief Justice and the first Catholic to hold a legal post of importance after Catholic Emancipation in 1829, built the ballcourt at Spiddal, county Galway. Both the Earl of Cork and Orrery and Sir Josslyn Gore-Booth gave sites for ballcourts on their properties, the one at Charleville, county Cork, and the other at Lissadell, county Sligo, which was opened in 1925. But there was a dark side, too, to landlordism, and the ballcourt at Cloongullane beside the river Moy in county Mayo, has a plaque in the front wall with the inscription: 'Erected by the sons of the men who fought with Davitt of Straide to smash the tyranny of landlordism, December 1950.'

The interest of the Countess of Desart in the game deserves a separate paragraph. She was born Ellen Bischoffsheim, daughter of a wealthy Jewish financier. In 1881 she married the Earl of Desart and came to live in Kilkenny. After the death of her husband in 1898, she founded the Kilkenny Woollen Mills and went to live at the model village of Talbot's Inch. When the old city ballcourt at 'the Ring' fell into disrepair, Lady Desart offered a site for a new court at Talbot's Inch. She had the satisfaction of attending the opening by W. T. Cosgrave, President of the Executive Council, in 1928 and, up to the time of her death five years later, she was a regular visitor to the court. She is believed to be the first Jewess to have been given the Freedom of any city in the world, an honour bestowed on her by the Corporation of Kilkenny in 1910.

While the dimensions of a fives court can have had no effect on those of a handball court, the size of a racquet court may well have influenced the design of enclosed ballcourts. Most of those built before the end of the last century were longer than those of today and it was not until the second annual Convention of the GAA in 1886 that the length of the court was limited to 65 feet. Paddy Lyons, a noted player and a shrewd observer of the game, has left us the dimensions of 'the half-dozen best courts in the country': Cork (Grattan Street) 84 feet; Cork (Market Place) 78 feet; Kilkenny (City) 82 feet; Limerick 70 feet; Kanturk 66 feet; Ashtown 70 feet; Waterford 76 feet. All service was from the tossing-flag, a stone about 3 feet square set in the clay floor. Ace-line serving was an American innovation and was not generally accepted until 1910 or possibly later. Most courts had a tell-board of about 6 inches at the foot of the front wall.

Whatever the size and shape of the Irish ballcourt, there never was anything particularly distinctive about it. It may be that a rectangle consisting of four walls does not lend itself to imaginative design. A ballcourt could be and often was built by someone who never saw the game played. Certainly, when Jim Heeney, a stonemason, built the Fahy Cross court in county Offaly in 1950, all he had to guide him was the plan drawn from him on the inside of a cigarette packet! Where the imagination had some play was in the shaping of the gallery. In Virginia, county Cavan, the gallery was built so that standing room was provided beneath it for spectators to look over the back wall. A number of courts had short side galleries but this meant that the side walls tapered down too sharply from the front wall thus reducing the opportunity for the high 'scotch' service.

From all the evidence, it would appear that about the last thing that a handballer of a century ago could expect to find was two ballcourts alike. They varied in size and shape and even in substance, some being of brick, some of wood, some of cement. As late as 1915, the *Official Guide* of the GAA , in a reference to the rule for marking 'the short line' in ballcourts, stated that 'for alleys of courts with a clay floor the short line should be two-thirds of the length from the front wall, but for concrete, flagged or bricked floors the short line should be nearer the centre'. Quite clearly, the variety was considerable.

A little ballcourt at Roskeen Bridge, beside the Mallow-Killarney road, had a sanded floor and slatted timber sides. The entrance door was to be found in the front wall (Clogh), in the side-wall or, more usually, in the backwall. A stream flowing beside the ballcourt was a natural hazard in Donard, county Wicklow, great expanses of turf stretched away from the edge of the right-hand side of the two-wall court at Abbeylara, county Longford, and the faces of spectators looked down from the lancet windows in the front wall of the abbey ballcourt at Ullard in county Kilkenny!

If the courts conformed to no particular pattern, neither did the players. It was a game for the individual and it was as players with individual styles that they played it.

Lighted courts were unknown until the present century. A rudimentary form of lighting, consisting of bicycle lamps hung around the walls, made Tuamgraney, county Clare a popular venue for dancing as well as for handball when it was built in 1910. The first ballcourt to be lighted in Dublin was said to be that which formed part of the licensed premises owned by Edward Madigan at Cornmarket Street. Kilkenny, which has strong claims to be considered Ireland's greatest ballplaying county, had lights in its two covered courts, Talbot's Inch and Clogh, as far back as 1946.

Matches were often colourful affairs, with advance publicity in the hands of the town-crier and bands accompanying the players to and from the court.

When Barntown and Carrick-on-Bannow met in a series of matches in 1881, the Barntown Brass and Reed Band and the Wexford Workhouse Fife and Drum Band attended. Twelve years later when Wexford and Kilkenny met 'on the grounds of the Kilkenny Handball and Racquet Club', the Maudlin Street Brass Band greeted the visitors when they arrived in Kilkenny by special train. The teams on that August day in 1893, according to the programme, were: *Kilkenny* – Burke, Dunne, Dolan, Holland, Wall, Sweeney and Morrissey; *Wexford* – Hayes, Keegan, Simpson, W. & T. Doyle and E. & J. O'Leary. Two Portadown Club players, Tom Niblock and George McCourt, were greeted by McCalmont's True Blues' Flute Band when in 1902 they played an exhibition match in a three-wall court outside Larne, county Antrim.

Twenty years later in September 1913, on the occasion of the Cullenstown hardball final, the Carrig Fife and Drum Band was in attendance and the *Free Press* quotes a reporter's description of the scene: 'The players entered the alley to the strains of "Drowsy Molly" played on a fife by Andy Walsh, who was seated on the ledge of a bank, where he remained and played during the rubber, as he and the rest of the old school of handballers, including Jack Simpson, had a contempt for the softball game and they remained on the ditch waiting for the first sound of the alley cracker.' That was the day when two of Wexford's greatest players, Johnny Hayes and Phil Wade of Carrig, beat James and Pat Hayes of Wexford town.

On two occasions only did I see a band perform in honour of ballplayers. The first occasion was in Ballymore-Eustace, county Kildare, in 1933, when Tommy Leahy and Jack Byrne of the local club beat Morgan Pembroke and J. J. Kelly for the Irish title of that year. And, in 1950, when the President of the GAA, Michael Kehoe, opened the ballcourt at Fahy Cross, a Fife and Drum Band led the parade to the court.

For a game so simple in its requirements and so attractive to the onlooker, handball was almost unknown in some parts of the country. In large stretches of the north and midlands there were just no courts at all but there were 'pockets' where handball was always popular. Pomeroy, county Tyrone, was one of these, and Jimmy Quinn of the Diamond there remembered his grandfather's tale of going to play handball against a man named MacCracken at Toomebridge, county Antrim, sometime in the middle of the last century. That seemed a normal enough event until he added that he went on horseback and returned the same day. The game was always reasonably strong in parts of county Antrim where in 1914, a tournament at Ballymoney attracted entries from what was, and still is, hurling territory – Garvagh, Kilrea, Armoy, Bushmills, Rasharkin and Ballycastle. In the same county, the McBoal Cup, which was competed for annually at Ballymena Academy, attracted a large entry and the winner usually played the champion of the Rainey Endowed School at Magherafelt where there was a good three-wall court. Otherwise the game was played only in a few widely scattered villages of Ulster such as Pomeroy, Drumgath and Tullyvin.

The great ballplaying centres were Cork and Dublin. When the venue was

Making handballs. A ballmaker in the Basque country. The covering of a ball was a highly skilled task and in the 1880s, Matt Webb of Swords was recognised as the best 'coverer' of a ball in Ireland.

W. Aldridge, a maker of handballs, showing a sample of his work to All-Ireland Champion Bobby Grattan, Ballymore-Eustace.

Cork, Dublin supplied the marker and Cork the referee. The reverse was true when a Dublin court was the venue. A week before a big match, each player's manager would send six stamped handballs to the other player's manager to be weighed and tested. Only these could be used during the rubber.

The rules governing each half of the rubber, if it was a home-and-home rubber, were drawn up and signed by both the players and their managers. The stake money was usually lodged with the editor of *Sport* or with the editor of *the Cork Examiner*. Once a championship was decided, the winner had the right to defend it whenever he wished and on his own terms. This had as one result that a season might pass by without any title match being played if, for some reason, the reigning champion had no wish to risk his title in the ballcourt.

There were ballmakers in every village and town where there were players but many of these preferred to make their own. Forde of Lucan, county Dublin, Heffernan of Limerick, and Keegan and Sweeney of Kells, county Meath, were all noted ballmakers, while American players favoured what was known as 'the Donohue ball'. In recent years, Jack Begley of Ballyporeen, county Tipperary, made a good ball but the craft may be said to have died out with the passing of Jack Delaney and Bill Aldridge of Athy in 1960.

Hardballs were made of cowhair or wool in its raw state and, later, of woollen thread and elastic rolled round a 'heart' or core of wood, preferably from the root of a briar, though I have seen a champagne cork used (to make a lively ball) in place of wood. The Americans insisted that the best kind of thread was that used in sewing borders on carpets. Sheepskin, goatskin or foalskin were used for the cover, and Pádraig Óg Ó Conaire treasured a ball made from *fionnadh bó* or cowhide. The Basques have a preference for a ball covered in donkey-skin, perhaps because such skins are not difficult to obtain in the Pyreneen region. The weight of the ball often varied but the ruling of the 1886 GAA Convention that the weight of the ball was not less than 1¾ ounces or more than 2 ounces, seems to have been generally accepted. (This ruling was changed soon after the founding of the Irish Amateur Handball Association in 1924 so as to read 'not to be lighter than 1½ ounces or heavier than 1¾ ounces.')

The ball used in the USA did not differ greatly from that used in Ireland but there a greater degree of uniformity was insisted on. The ball used by members of the Brooklyn Handball Club was recognised as 'standard' and is likely to have been that used in most of the world-title matches by the USA champions. A description of it is given in a booklet on handball published at the beginning of this century:

The foundation is laid with a round bit of cork or solid rubber, upon the top of which is rolled yarn of the finest character. The covering is of horsehide, neatly stitched. A great deal depends on the strength of the wrapping whether the ball will be lively or just moderately so. Some players like plenty of life in the ball, some admire a hard, dead ball, while men like Casey, Dunne, Courtney and other leading experts prefer a

well-made ball above everything else, one neither too hard nor too soft, but with a true and fairly lively bound.*

* The ball used in *jai-ali*, a game popular in Mexico and Miami, is made from a layer of nylon and two outer coats of specially hardened goatskin.

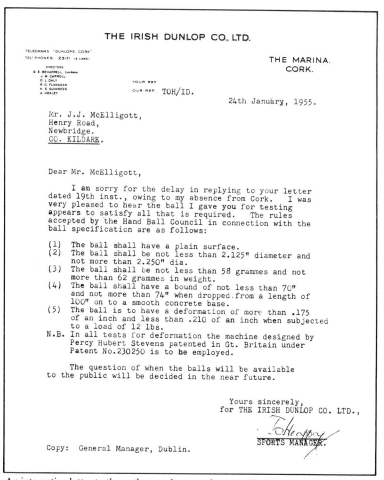

An interesting letter to the author on the manufacture of balls in Ireland in the 1950s.

Chapter 2

International Challenges 1881 – 1909

One hundred years ago there were no championships such as we know them today. Good players, rather like professional pugilists and wrestlers of the time, played for purses of varying amounts wherever they could find backers and opponents. William Baggs of Tipperary and Davy Browning of Limerick were two such players who, because of their unusual skill, caught the imagination of the public in the middle of the last century. Neither seems to have had any particular occupation but they were to be found at markets and fairs or wherever a convenient gable-end gave them an opportunity to demonstrate their talents as ballplayers. Baggs is the first player who is known to have limited each game to a certain number of aces, usually 15 or 21. The number of games still seemed to depend on the stamina of the players. Of the two, it is Browning who stands out more clearly as there are newspaper accounts of his achievements as athlete as well as ballplayer. He looked upon Kilkee, county Clare, as his home court but he played many of his matches at Tavern, county Louth, as well as in Dublin and Kilkenny.

Martin Butler of Kilkenny was a younger man than Browning but while they were playing at the same time, there is no record of their having met. In a doubles match in which he and his partner, Aidan McGlynn, defeated Lawlor and Brown of Dublin, he wore 'a championship belt' given to him after his defeat of James Stewart of Scotland. That was in 1881 and it is strange that Browning, never a man to let another claim to be better than him, does not appear to have challenged him.

Browning was himself challenged by the youthful Lawlor in 1884 when, for a stake of £10, Browning won by the odd game in 9 in a match played at what was then Kingstown. A year later, Lawlor had his revenge when, in a one-day rubber of 21 games each of 15 aces, he won by 11 games to 7. The match was in the timber-floored racquet court in Carlow and lasted four hours and a half.

After his defeat of Browning, John Lawlor issued a challenge to anyone to play him for the world title. A reply came, not altogether unexpectedly, from the USA. It was written from 263 Court Street, Brooklyn, and was published in *Sport* on 2 January 1886. It read as follows:

Sir – Some time ago I saw a challenge in your paper from a Mr Lawlor, of your city, to play any man in the world a series of games for £100 a side and the championship, half the number of games to be played in any court Mr Lawlor may select, and half in any court his opponent may select; his opponent must not weigh over 10st 7lbs.

Now, if Mr Lawlor means what he says, let him draw up articles of agreement and publish them in your journal, and deposit £50 in your hands. I will furnish a man to play him on the conditions he states for £100 or as much more as he desires to play for.

An early answer to this note will be thankfully received through the columns of your journal.

Yours very respectfully,
Philip Casey.

Lawlor replied in a letter to *Sport*, dated 6 January 1886, stating that he could not reply to Mr Casey 'until the matches are decided in Cork'. This was a reference to the Cork Tournament which each year attracted all the leading players, and the winner was generally recognised as Irish champion. In the summer of that year Alderman Dan Horgan, President of the Cork Handball Club and thrice Mayor of the city, put up a gold medal and a silver cup for a singles competition open to all Ireland. A list of those who took part included Davy Browning of Limerick, James Dunne of Brooklyn, Joe O'Leary of Fermoy, John O'Leary of Midleton, Redmond Tobin of Fermoy, John Lawlor of Dublin and Billie O'Herlihy of Cork. The matches were played at the Racquet Court, Duncan Street (a name which was later changed to Grattan Street). In the final Lawlor beat Tobin on the score of 21-0, 21-9, 21-5, 21-11, 21-0.

Lawlor's manager, Tom Waters of the Beaufort Club, Fleet Street, Dublin, was then in a position to bind the contract to play Casey, which he did. Alderman Dunne of Brooklyn, who had played in the Cork Tournament, on behalf of Casey, agreed to the conditions that the match should be £200 a side, that the rubber should be the best of 21 games of 21 aces each and that every alternate game was to be with American and Irish balls. The articles of agreement also stipulated that 'one minute be allowed after every game to get refreshments, which must be supplied in the court'. It will be noticed that there is no mention in the final draft of '10st 7lbs' and, in fact, Casey weighed well over 14 stone on the day of the match.

Sport published in its issue of 16 April 1887 a short statement to the effect that 'Lawlor, the Irish champion, called at the office yesterday and informed us that arrangements had been concluded for a match between himself and Phil Casey of New York, to play a rubber of 21 games for the single-handed championship of the world and £200 aside'. The articles were signed by the players and four witnesses – Bernard McQuade, Theo Bomeister, Thomas Waters and Michael Ryan.

The challenge did not pass unnoticed by Lawlor's old opponent, Davy Browning. Annoyed at what he must have considered a reflection on his own claim to be the best player in Ireland, he wrote to *Sport* on 16 April 1887 and asked, 'What on earth put it into Mr Lawlor's head that he was going to play for the World Championship?' He went on to challenge to play him in the court of his (Lawlor's) choice for a rubber of eleven 15-ace games. Lawlor ignored the challenge probably because he had by then deposited £50 to bind the contract for his match with Casey.

The meeting of the two best players on either side of the Atlantic had an interesting personal angle; Lawlor was born in Glendon, Pennsylvania, and Casey was born in Mountrath, county Laois. Casey's father died in 1856 when Phil was but fifteen and his mother decided to emigrate with her five children to the States. Young Casey had played ball in the three-wall court in Patrician College, Mountrath, and he soon became a familiar figure in the ballcourts of New York where he later built his own court at Hoyt. In 1868 he won the US title from Bernard McQuaide and for the next 25 years he is believed never to have lost any match played for money. And in those days stakes were high. In 1872, when James Everett and himself beat O'Brien and Foley of Chicago for the American doubles Championship, the side bets amounted to 1,000 dollars. Twenty-five years later, when Judge Dunne and himself won the same title against Keegan and Carney, the side bets were just double that amount. Little is known of Lawlor's early years beyond the fact that his parents returned to Ireland when he was two and after living for a time in Wicklow came to live at Patrick Street, Dublin.

Why Lawlor decided on Cork as the venue for the first leg of the rubber is difficult to understand. His home court was Kenny's court near which he lived in Dublin. He trained there and had won many matches there and we can only surmise that he was offered some financial inducement to select Cork. There was, of course, a large public for the game in Cork and, with seats in the gallery on the day of the match at a guinea each, this was a matter of importance.

Casey arrived in Ireland with an entourage consisting of trainer, manager and masseur on the Cunard liner *Servia*, which docked at Queenstown on 24 July 1887. The *Cork Constitution* described the scene:

On disembarking from the trans-Atlantic liner they (the Americans) were met by Mr John Lawlor, the Irish champion, when a warm greeting took place. The American champion, who is 45 years of age, weighs over 14 stone, and although he has been playing handball for the past 30 years, he does not look, so far as appearances go, a fit competitor for the Irish champion, who is light and most active, and weighs only 9st 12lbs, and from his recent performance with the ex-champion Browning appears to be in splendid form.

John Lawlor's American Medal 1891. Photo by Pat Maxwell.

The venue for the match was Dan Horgan's Court in Duncan Street, scene of Lawlor's triumph in the previous year. It was a huge ballcourt by modern standards: 84 feet by 49 feet at the front wall and 36 feet at the back wall. Nothing of it now remains, not even the high wall which long formed part of the forecourt of the Franciscan Church in Liberty Street. Of the officials in charge the referee was C. Conway of Kanturk, judges were P. O'Sullivan of Charleville for Casey and P. Barry of Midleton for Lawlor, markers were J. Dunne of New York and G. O'Herlihy of Cork.

Dick Anthony of Friar's Walk, Cork, who represented Cork first as a member of the Dáil and later as a Senator, was at the match. In a letter he wrote me in 1954, he recalls that memorable day, 4 August 1887: 'I was on the gallery with two old ballplayers and my father. One of these was, I believe, an old champion named Martin Butler, who used to make the hardballs or crackers, and the other was a man named John Edwards, a picture-frame maker, whose premises were opposite the ballcourt.'

The *Cork Examiner* described Casey as he entered the ballcourt as 'looking a giant beside Lawlor'. He was in fact over six feet in height and weighed more than 14 stone. Lawlor was about five foot nine and weighed nine stone twelve. What is more remarkable is that Casey was then 45 years old – almost 20 years older than his opponent. 'He was dressed all in white down to the ankles like an acrobat before he stripped off his vest, which showed him to be in anything but "condition". He was much bigger and stronger than Lawlor, so that the heavy two-inch balls gave him an advantage' (*Sport*, 6 August 1887). The court was crowded as Lawlor, in 'short blue satin breeches above the knee with a gold stripe down the sides and an open-web jersey', served the first ball.

Casey's heavy service in a court so wide meant that there was little open play which would have suited the faster Lawlor. Play was not, according to the report in *Sport*, 'the very best we have ever seen in Ireland'. With Lawlor leading by 5 games to 3, he appears either to have tired or become careless and, after leading Casey by 9 aces to 2 in the ninth game, Casey took the lead 11-9. The crowd, in no mood to see the money wagered on the first half of the rubber lost through Lawlor's carelessness, effectively stopped the match. *Sport's* reporter describes the scene: 'Then came a regular row all over the place amidst shouts of fire etc. People dropped out of the galleries into the court, a depth of some 25 feet, and all was in the utmost confusion when an adjournment was ordered till the next day. Tar barrels burning and other manifestations of joy were made outside Lawlor's lodgings in the evening'.

Each player won one game on the following day, the betting on the last game being 'half a sovereign to a bottle of stout' on Lawlor, with no takers.

The second half of the rubber was due to be played at Sweeney's Court at the junction of 35th Street and 3rd Avenue, New York, but as it became clear that it would not hold the expected crowd, the match was transferred to Casey's newly built court at 297 Degraw Street, Brooklyn. Lawlor travelled from Liverpool on the *Alaska*, which arrived in New York on 24 October 1887. This gave him a month in which to accustom himself to the American-style court with its wooden floor which made for faster service. Casey's Court, as it came to be called, was perhaps the first ballcourt in the design of which thought was given to the game as a spectacle. It was 65 feet long, 24 feet wide with a 35-foot high front wall which tapered down to 30 feet at the back wall. The front wall was of brick faced with marble and the side-walls of cement. With ace-line service insisted upon, the game as a spectacle was greatly improved.

Little need be said of the second half of the match in which, to quote the American press, 'Casey, with his kills, hops, screw ball, murderous toe shots, mixed with hard-driven passing shots, lashed Lawlor to the mast by winning seven straight games as well as Lawlor's crown'. In an interview with T. F. O'Sullivan, author of *The Story of the GAA*, Lawlor attributed his defeat to the boarded floor and the faster ball, adding, 'That is what knocked me out.'

Lawlor was back in the USA a year later when he challenged Casey to another home-and-home rubber for £200 which he lodged with the editor of the *New York Sun*. The challenge remained open to Casey or, failing him, to any other player, but was not accepted. Lawlor then claimed the championship of the world, a title which, however, he was never to win in any court. He did win a magnificent gold medal, inscribed with the words 'Championship of the World, 1891', in competition with the best players of the time whose names are in script on the reverse of the medal (now in the possession of the Weldon family of the Boot Inn, Ballymun). They were: William Courtney, Jim Dunne, Barney McQuaide, Michael Harney and J. McVoy.

Lawlor returned to Ireland in 1895 bringing with him one of the two horses which he was presented with before leaving the States. He set up his own cab business in Dublin and became a familiar figure at the old Broadstone Railway Station where he had his headquarters. He joined the Metropolitan Handball Club, founded some years previously, and presided at the meeting which discussed the attempt to alter the method of service. American players served from a centrally placed ace-line, whereas in Ireland the server stood close to the front wall. The meeting resolved to condemn 'the action of the American handball players in trying to introduce ace-line tossing and that as Irish handball players we unanimously agree to uphold the old style of serving'.

While Lawlor had been in the USA, one of the greatest of all players, Tom Jones (of whom more in the following pages), had come and gone and it was his fellow-townsman, James Fitzgerald, who challenged Lawlor for the Irish title. He had earned the right to do so by beating Tim Twohill of Liscarroll, county Cork, in 1891 by 8 games to 4 and Billie O'Herlihy of Cork City by 7 games to nil. A two-day match was arranged between them for the best of 21 games to be played in Cork on 16 August 1895. It was a match on which, because of the good record of each man, a good deal of money was laid and, to quote the *Cork Examiner*, 'the weight of money went from the commencement on Fitzgerald and his many supporters at the close of the day had no reason to feel disappointed' as he led by 8 games to 2. Four days later, the match was finished with Fitzgerald winning 3 games to Lawlor's 1.

The inhabitants of 'The Kingdom' did not leave the occasion pass unnoticed

Photograph dated 1898 of William O'Herlihy, one of the famous family of Cork ball players. His father Jeffrey O'Herlihy was a marker for the World Title Match between Casey and Lawlor at the Racquet Court in Grattan Street, Cork in 1897. William was the Irish titleholder in 1903 and again in 1905. His four sons played with Cork City Club until it was disbanded in 1960.

NO. 18.   DUBLIN, SATURDAY, MAY 2, 1896.   PRICE ONE

Masthead of Dublin's sporting press in 1896, the weekly *Sport*.

The first World Champion, 1889 - Phil Casey of Mountrath.

Father Tom Jones.

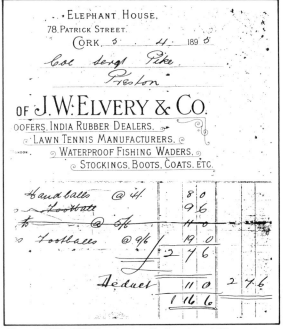

Elvery's bill in 1895 showing handballs at four shillings a dozen.

and the following resolution was passed unanimously by the Tralee Town Commissioners on 23 August 1895:

'We the Tralee Town Commissioners at this our fortnightly meeting assembled do hereby propose a vote of congratulations to Mr James Fitzgerald for the great victory he performed on last Tuesday in Cork by beating Mr Lawlor, Champion of the World, almost 4 to 1, winning 11 out of 14 games of ball, and we request our Clerk to convey this vote of congratulations to the highly respectable young man who is now Champion of the World.'

Even though Lawlor was an extremely fit player, he was 34 when he met Fitzgerald and probably somewhat past his best. He did offer to play Fitzgerald in the USA, where Fitzgerald had gone in 1897, but the challenge was never accepted. Such was the way of champions. Lawlor had, in similar fashion, avoided a meeting with Jones, despite the many efforts of promoters to match them.

It will be noticed that despite the great length of most rubbers, players such as Casey and Lawlor continued to play ball long after what might be considered 'retirement age'. When Casey was in his 55th year, he and his partner Alderman James Dunne won the American doubles championship and John Lawlor did not give up competitive singles until 1906 when, at the age of 45, he lost the Leinster title to Paddy Lyons at Baltinglass, county Wicklow. That he could still last a hard doubles match was shown when in 1912, he and John Clarke (father of two All-Ireland champions) took four games off George Robinson and Tom Aldridge of Athy in a 15-game rubber.

Few players of my generation, if I except the indestructible Mickey Walsh of Charlestown or Henry Haddock of Lurgan, have stayed in the game for quite so long. My own belief, after seeing Bill Aldridge, Jimmy Kelly and J. J. Bowles, is that the professional players developed their game to a point that enabled them to anticipate their opponent's placing of the ball and so they seemed to move effortlessly into position for the return. They did no unnecessary running and conserved every ounce of energy for the serious business of winning.

While sports' statisticians prefer to concentrate on records and record holders, no work on handball would be complete without reference to someone whose greatness as a player is not to be measured in terms of medals and titles. This was Father Tom Jones who, in the words of Monsignor Richard Collins of San Francisco who had seen two world champions play, 'would lick them all'. He never did 'lick them all' because, on his ordination to the Catholic priesthood in 1896, he gave up competitive handball. By then he had, however, done enough to convince Geoffrey O'Herlihy of Cork, an acknowledged expert on the game, that 'he was the greatest handballer who ever put foot inside a court'.

His career may be said to have begun in 1887 when he met Joe O'Leary of

Fermoy and defeated him without the loss of a game. For a youth of 19 that was an astonishing achievement as O'Leary was known, as one man put it, 'to beat anyone out of his way' who wagered money against him. They were to meet again two years later, when, with Jones leading by 4 games to 3, they quarrelled and Jones was awarded the match and title of Irish champion.

All those who saw him play agree that he played handball at a sensational pace, splitting a new ball with crashing kills off either hand, taking a ball low down behind his back and sending it dead level to the butt of the front wall or driving his opponent to the back of the court with raking shots along the side walls. During those eight years, 1887 to 1895, Jones never knew defeat. His only regret may well have been that he never met John Lawlor. In a letter dated 7 January 1949, he wrote to me saying, 'Perhaps you do not know that at long last a match was arranged between John Lawlor and myself to be played at Ballymun. A gold medal and a purse of sovereigns awaited the winner. The Ballymun court was crowded with spectators awaiting the match when Lawlor sent word that he could not play. He had a sore thumb. That was a disappointment.'

To resume the thread of our story, we must follow the fortunes of the Irish champion, James Fitzgerald, when he left Ireland in 1895 to seek his fortune in the USA. On his arrival he at once issued a challenge through the press to anyone willing to play him: 'I will play any man in the United States a match game of handball, the best of eleven games, *New York Sun* rules to govern, for five hundred dollars a side, and I hereby deposit one hundred dollars as a guarantee of good faith. Trusting someone will accept, I remain, Yours, James Fitzgerald, Champion of Ireland.'

There appear to have been few outstanding players at the time and his challenge went unanswered. He did, however, decisively defeat Carney of Chicago in the second of two matches, after having lost the first to him, and Phil Casey was sufficiently impressed to 'give' him the world title to defend. This was the title that was at stake when in 1902 he met Mike Egan at the Olympic Club in San Francisco. Once again it was the youthful challenger against the older champion and, in addition, the Fitzgerald who met Egan was already a sick man. Egan won by 8 games to nil and it proved to be Fitzgerald's last match. He died of tuberculosis at the age of 36.

Mike Egan was brought up in Jersey City where his uncle, John Egan, who was also Galway-born, had built a court at Mercer Street. He proved a worthy champion and only Oliver Drew of Cork ever succeeded in leading him in any rubber he played. Drew, even if his name does not appear in any 'official' list of world champions, was in the opinion of those who saw him play, the most stylish and skilful player ever to have come out of Ireland. He entered for the Fermoy Tournament, which was really the Munster championship of the time, when he was 17 and won the doubles in partnership with Billie O'Herlihy. In the same year, 1900, the same pair shared a purse of 20 sovereigns when they beat Lawlor and Corrigan of Dublin by 11 games to 7.

Stakes were higher when in 1902 he met Egan in Jersey City for 250 dollars and the world title. The Jersey City *Evening Journal* of 23 May summarised the first half of the match in one sentence: 'Michael Egan, America's handball champion, finished in second place in yesterday's match with Oliver Drew, the Irish champion, and no event has ever occurred in handball that created the surprise that followed the local champion's defeat.' The two players were different in almost every way: Egan so overwhelmingly powerful and Drew so slender and lithe; Egan serving in the American fashion from the ace-line and Drew serving close up to the front wall. Again, Drew favoured the lighter Irish ball while Egan used the two-ounce American ball.

We will never know what would have been the outcome had the match been finished from the point of stoppage, with Drew leading by 4 games to 3. As Egan's manager failed to hand over the first day's receipts, to which the Corkman was entitled under the terms of the agreement, Drew declined to continue. Everyone may not accept the testimony of Father Tom Jones, who referred to him in a letter he wrote me as 'that wonderful and unbeatable Oliver Drew', but it does seem close to the truth.

Drew did return to the States in 1904 after he had again been beaten in a non-title match. In 1905 he was matched with Francois Ordozgotti, the champion of France and Spain, whom he beat for what was called 'the International Championship' and a stake of 1,500 dollars at Tarrant's Court, New Jersey. A year later he took the American title, beating Dennis Sullivan of Chicago at Kennedy's Court by 6 games to 2. He stayed in the United States where he died in 1938.

Egan was challenged by the recognised Irish champion, Tim Twohill of Liscarroll, who had won his first Irish title from Billie O'Herlihy in 1898. Twohill's credentials were good as when he was no more than 19 he took four games off James Fitzgerald in a home-and-home rubber played in Tralee and Kanturk. He later won the Irish doubles championship with Dave Roche of Fermoy when they beat Lawlor and Devey of Dublin in 1899.

Egan accepted the challenge and a 15-game rubber for the world title and a purse of 300 sovereigns was arranged. Twohill travelled out with Dave Roche, Maurice Dineen of Ballingarry, county Limerick, and the two O'Herlihys, father and son. He was given training facilities at the Brooklyn Handball Club where, on the eve of the big match, Geoffrey O'Herlihy was presented with a gold watch and chain by Colonel Meehan on behalf of the club. The attendance at the match was a distinguished one and included the State Recorder, the Supreme Court Justice and the Under-Sheriff. Of the match little need be said, as Twohill found the American altogether too strong and fast. Egan won all 7 games at Jersey City on 23 July 1903, and a month later in Kanturk he won the one game necessary to complete the rubber. The stake-holder of the purse was J. A. Bradley of the *Cork Examiner*.

Twohill was a most popular player both on the football field with the Wolfe Tones and Cork as well as in the ballcourt. He was in the gallery when in 1933 his nephew, also Tim, beat Gus Moriarty of Mallow in a challenge match, but he died a year later. Egan died in 1954 aged 74.

J. J. Bowles.

When Egan retired as undefeated champion of the world in 1906, there was no obvious successor either in the USA or in Ireland. It was Casey's old partner, Alderman James Dunne, who on a visit to Ireland in 1908, arranged a match for the title between his son, James Jnr, and J. J. Bowles of Limerick. Bowles, who had earlier won fame as an oarsman with the Shannon Rowing Club, may be said to have begun his handball career when he won the Irish title in 1905. There was at the time an abundance of good players in Ireland and Bowles had beaten most of them at one time or another – O'Herlihy of Cork, Franklin of Cahir, Carver of Kanturk, Twohill of Liscarroll. He had, therefore, no difficulty in getting financial backing for the world title match which was for £200.

For professional reasons Dunne, who was a lawyer, was unable to play though this must have been known to his father when the match was arranged. In the event, the Americans nominated James Kelly, a New York policeman, in his place. Kelly, a native of Kiltimagh, county Mayo, where he had worked for the Great Southern and Western Railway Company before emigrating, was a left-handed player. Now, an unusual clause in the articles of agreement specified that all service was to be to the left side of the court. 'Obviously', as one sports commentator of the time put it, 'Bowles's mentors were not aware of the fire in Kelly's left hand.'

The first half of the rubber was played in the Rutland Street Court, Limerick, with Paddy Lyons as referee and Alderman James Dunne as marker. At the end of that day in July 1909, Kelly led by 5 games to 2 on scores of 15-21, 14-21, 21-18, 21-9, 21-8, 21-10, 21-6. Kelly picked up the necessary 3 games played in Brooklyn on 23 September, to become the recognised world champion. His exhibition in the second and third games, each of which he won by two aces, was said to have been the prettiest ever seen in the court. Still, it is difficult to say how the match would have gone but for that curious 'left-hand' clause in the contract.

This was the last professional match for the world handball championship.

AT KENNEDY'S COURT

808 Thirty-Seventh Street

Sunday, Dec. 2, 1906

HAND BALL MATCH

For the Championship of America and $100 a Side

OLIVER DREW of New York

vs.

DENNIS SULLIVAN of Chicago

Mr. Drew has Defeated all the Crack Eastern Players since the Retirement of Mike Egan from the Game. Mr. Sullivan is Classed as one of the Best Players in the Country, and good judges say that he will bring the Championship to Chicago.

Thomas Brice

Will play the winner of the match

For $100 and Gate Receipts

Advertisement poster from 1906.

'Smooth and square and dry the wall;
White, elastic, round, the ball;
Two on that side, two on this;
Two hands each to hit or miss.'

A. C. Ginger,
The Badminton Library (London 1891)

"Fives is entirely a game for amateurs. it has no professors who make their living and their renown as its teachers or exponents. It has no matches to be reported in newspapers with a minuteness of detail suitable to events of international importance. No fives player, as such, has ever had his portrait published in an illustrated journal, or has had the meanest article of dress in the hosiers' shops named after him."

A. C. Ginger, *The Badminton Library* (London 1891)

Photo taken in Kanturk in 1903. Dan O'Rourke, Tim Twohill, Mike Egan and Ald. James Dunne.

The playing field and handball court at St. Enda's College, Rathfarnham.

Chapter 3

Change and Controversy 1909 – 1921

During the years which our story has so far covered, the game changed but little. But change was coming. The gradual introduction of the rubber ball, which put an end to the traditional game of hardball known to our grandparents, made for uniformity in the weight, size and speed of the ball. Again, the insistence of service from between certain lines, by lessening the severity of the tossing, made for more play. And, an emphasis on skill rather than stamina was uppermost in the minds of those who recommended abandoning the excessively long rubbers and who, finally, brought about the introduction of the one-day rubber.

But, as frequently happens in life, uniformity in the application of rules and bye-laws imposes a pattern of behaviour and performance on the player and erodes individual eccentricities. No longer do players threaten referees and fight one another in the ballcourt, nor are stimulants let down by a string from the backwall to restore the strength of the tiring player; a ball unsuited to a player's style is seldom deliberately 'canted' (impossible, anyway, in the covered courts of today!), and hair-oil is no longer used to add speed to a slow ball. The big purses have gone, betting has gone, and some would say that much colour and excitement has gone, too.

After the victory of Kelly in the 1909 international match, 15 years were to pass before American players were again seen in Irish ballcourts. How to explain their absence? The abandonment of the annual Cork Tournament may have been one reason. Was the superiority of the Americans another? Few Irish players had the opportunities for training which the American courts, almost all of which were covered, afforded their rivals. Whatever was the cause, the 'Yanks' stayed at home and the Irish confined themselves to challenge matches within the country.

The prize money in these challenge matches varied from £5 a side, as when Franklin of Cahir beat Cole of Limerick for the 1910 junior title, to £50 a side which was usual when the more senior players, of whom Bowles and Coyne were the most prominent, met one another. These two men had strong personalities and there was more than a hint of aggression in their attitude towards one another when they met in the ballcourt. Bowles always liked to play the first half of a match at home and he regularly refused all challenges during the winter months. He favoured a slow ball and reckoned that a rubber of not more than 15 games was the best test of a player. Coyne liked a fast ball such as enabled him to take full advantage of the wooden floor in the Carlow racquet court. In fact, the ball he used when beating Bowles in Carlow in 1910 had a rebound of 3 feet 6 inches while that used by Bowles in Limerick had a rebound of 2 feet 3 inches. Bowles would appear to have been the master of Coyne in all the arts of the game except tossing and, even in this, Coyne needed a fast ball with which to exploit his strength.

Two other figures who appear in the ballcourts about this time were to become widely known to followers all over Ireland. Paddy Lyons of Clonakilty was one of these, Joe O'Leary of Fermoy the other. Lyons had taken up the game in 1904 when Mr Drew, a tailor in Princes Street, Cork, and father of the great Oliver, gave him a few hardballs to try out. He did so to such good effect he was considered unbeatable in the Ballymun court. He was a student of the game who measured his opponent's strengths with the same care as he measured the courts he played in with a view to using the walls to the best possible advantage. Joe O'Leary was a very different type of player, hard-hitting and durable. He played a number of rubbers against Tom Jones, always losing but always fighting to the last ace. He had few equals in the long reaches of his local court of which, as a present-day player said, 'if you could last 21 aces in Fermoy, you could play for a week in one of the modern 40 by 20 courts'.

The name 'O'Herlihy' has occurred already in these pages and three generations of the family are known to have played with the Cork City Club from the time of its foundation in 1885. The best-known was Billie, who took on all-comers over a period of years stretching from 1900 to 1915. He was at his best in the high, black-walled Old Market Place where he had victories over Drew, Bowles and Coyne. He was a rugged player who believed in keeping the ball on the wall, knowing that he could stay for ever and 'destroy' his opponent over a long rubber.

In the reports of the Inspectors of Intermediate (Secondary) Schools in Ireland for the year 1909-10, handball is the game most frequently mentioned under the heading 'Recreation'. At that time most of the grammar schools in Ulster had a ballcourt though very few of them were four-wall. The following schools listed handball among out-of-class activities: Lurgan College; Viscount Weymouth Grammar School, Carrickmacross; Classical School, Rathfriland; CBS, Armagh; St Macartan's, Monaghan; St Colman's, Newry; Royal Belfast Academical Institution; Intermediate School, Lisburn; Academical Institution, Banbridge; St Malachy's, Belfast; Rainey Endowed School, Magherafelt; Prior School, Lifford; Intermediate School, Ballyclare; Ballymena Academy.

War in Europe and rebellion in Ireland were to leave their mark on all sporting activities between the years 1910 and 1920. The Gaelic Athletic Association did, however, continue to grow in numbers and many hurling and football clubs began to hold handball competitions for their members. This interest on the part of a body which considered itself the 'parent' of such sports as hurling, football and handball was welcome, even if long overdue. As far back as March 1886, *Sport*, which was the only sports' journal of its time circulating in Ireland, had devoted an article to handball in the course of which it said:

> With the revival of ancient Irish pastimes those who still clung to the old games hoped for brighter days, more particularly as the founders of the Gaelic Association (sic), and particularly Archbishop Croke (under whose especial patronage it was placed), had made it one of the corner-stones of the new edifice. The result has been to some extent disappointing. Hurling and football seem to have completely monopolised the attention of the Association.

That, in the opinion of many, was the position. Even, when in November of the same year, the GAA at its annual meeting in Thurles did decide to promote a handball competition 'open to all qualified amateurs', nothing came of it.

By neglecting handball in those early years, the GAA turned its back on the one game that would have completed the circle of its activities. It had the supreme team game, hurling and a traditional pastime, football, but for the individual to whom team games had little appeal, it offered nothing. In fact, no attempt was made to control and develop handball until 1912 when, with John Lawlor in the chair, a meeting was convened to form an association 'for the purpose of governing the game of handball'. This was the Irish Handball Association which had as its chief aim 'to control *amateur and professional handball* [emphasis mine] and to frame definitions and rules for the game'. It must have been that the differences between 'amateurs' and 'professionals' were irreconcilable, because nothing further was done, and the *GAA Year Book* for 1915 comments: 'There are still some athletic exercises which, though nominally included in the GAA schedule are practically neglected. Principal among these are Handball and Wrestling, two typically Irish pastimes' (p. 22). It was almost 10 years later that an association confined to amateurs only was formed. This was the GAA-sponsored Irish Amateur Handball Association (IAHA), but by that time the Irish Amateur Handball Union (IAHU), with its less restrictive attitude towards those playing other games, was already established.

There were, of course, good reasons why the team games had first claim on the attention of the Association. Other team games such as rugby and association football posed a threat to hurling and football. No such threat endangered handball. Hurlers and footballers were never accused of professionalism;

handballers were. For an amateur body this was a serious charge but too much was, I feel, made of it. Players did play for sums of money, trifling for the most part. Some idea of the prize money to be won may be got from an advertisement which appeared in the *Western People* of 7 June 1924. It announced that a handball tournament would be held at Kilkelly, county Mayo, on 24 June for which a prize value £4 or cash would be awarded to the winner and a prize value £2 or cash to the runner-up. Only the very select few ever played for sums in excess of £5. The money did encourage players of ability to develop their skills, it did stimulate competition, it did help to attract the public. Dick Carroll, Sports Editor of the *Evening Herald* and one of the members of the Standing Committee of the IAHA, always maintained that the few shillings played for in the old days saved handball from extinction. Many years later, when *Gael-Linn* requested permission of the Irish Handball Council to base their 'Pools' on the results of handball matches, very similar arguments were advanced by Donall Ó Moráin and Roibeard Mac Ghabhráin in support of their request!

Even with limited support from the GAA, handball players were moving towards a point where championships would be organised similar to those for team games, i.e. on a provincial basis. This framework, which has proved so satisfactory for the team games, has not suited the 'individual' game of handball to anything like the same extent. Whereas it is easy to arouse parochial or even county enthusiasm for a team game, this is hardly true of handball. I have often felt that the one-day tournament, such as that at Delvin in county Westmeath or at Kilgobinet in county Waterford, was the real meeting-ground for ballplayers; places where they gathered, as players in earlier times had gathered at some crossroads ballcourt to match their skills with one another.

Some counties have played no part in 'provincial championships' simply because there was no worthwhile ballcourt within the county bounds. In other counties, 'pockets' of the game existed because of a good ballcourt or a good ballmaker. Athy, county Kildare, was one example: the ballcourt off Barrack Street was small and not even well-shaped but it produced a number of very clever players each of whom seemed to know instinctively how to serve and place and kill a ball. The Robinsons, Aldridges and Delaneys were all players of the very highest class. Even after his return from the First World War in which he lost his thumb and portion of the palm of his left hand, George Robinson could still beat such a good player as Terry O'Reilly by double scores. A writer of the time, Frank Doran of Athy, describes Robinson as 'a delightful player who could take a ball with either hand behind his back and, in close play, flick a ball into the opposite corner from that to which his puzzled opponent ran'. Forty years later, I watched another Athy player, George Aldridge, play similar strokes in his match against O'Donnell of Rathangan at Moone. Unfortunately, the court where they all learnt the game is now long demolished.

In those post-war years Bowles was still the great figure in the game; a man who did not disdain to stop on the roadside and have a 'dodge' with youngsters who, with a half-solid ball he found playing against a dead wall. When he was invited to play at the opening of the court in Bridgetown, county Wexford, in 1915, he was treated in a manner worthy of a champion and a special car was placed at his disposal by Mr J. J. Stafford of Wexford. Nor did he disappoint the crowd on that occasion, beating two different partnerships single-handed in each of three games.

Meanwhile, a young player from the St James's Gate Club in Dublin was beating all who stood between him and the senior title. This was Morgan Pembroke who took the junior title in 1914 by beating Tom Aldridge and, later, Jack Dynan of Limerick. Possessed of good hands, he trained seriously both at Clondalkin and Ballymun and, after beating Mick Dunne of Goresbridge, decided that he was ready to challenge Coyne. Of the 7 games played in Carlow, he won 3 and there was little money on Coyne for the second half in Ballymun. At the end of the second day, Pembroke had 8 games to his opponent's 5 and he was then ready for Bowles.

The champion, as we have seen, rarely played late in the year and it was 1920 before the two met in the rubber that was to crown Pembroke as Irish champion. It was for the best of 15 games, the first half in Limerick and the second half in Ballymun. Played at the height of the 'Black and Tan' war, Limerick was like a besieged city when Pembroke stepped off the train and with his supporters made his way down to Rutland Street. He must have been well satisfied to take 3 games off the champion and when, a fortnight later, Bowles came to Ballymun, Pembroke took all 5 games.

In 1921 in what was the last of the big professional matches, the little-known Mick O'Halloran of the Cork City Club was matched with Jimmy Kelly, the Irish junior champion, for a stake of £400. O'Halloran had won the State Championship in Adelaide while in Australia, but he was not expected to give Kelly a close game. How near he came to winning can be seen from his own account of the match in which he commends Morgan Pembroke as being 'a just, impartial and capable referee'. With the score in games standing at 5 games to 4 in Kelly's favour, I will let O'Halloran take up the story:

Kelly snapped the game after the interval which left play 6-4 in his favour. I won the next two leaving it 6-all. After which Kelly left the court for another interval and presumably a brandy and port. I vehemently protested to the referee [Billie O'Herlihy – Pembroke was the referee in Ballymun, O'Herlihy in Cork] and reminded him of the signed and counter-signed contract which specifically stated one interval after the 3rd game. The gallery was in an uproar and he (the referee) was babbling incoherently so I went in to serve and one of my followers commenced counting. Without undue haste, I tossed 12 aces before Kelly showed up. The referee disallowed them. Kelly was in great glee after his siesta and stimulant and set a cracking pace but I kept into him although the score-board said 13-4 until we eventually stood at 16-all. At this juncture I discarded my singlet and set for a do-or-die effort. I tossed a sneezer

Four Cork players in the Old Market Place, 1919. B. Buckley, J. Hunt, C. Guiney, T. Neville.

Morgan Pembroke, IAHA Champion.

Paddy Lyons - noted hurler and handballer.

down the right – 17th ace – which reared off Kelly's hand up the side-wall. The referee called 'No ball'. It was the first time in the rubber he declared 'No ball' of his own accord. Either Kelly or I would ask for judgement and abide by his decision without a murmur – but Kelly did not ask for judgement to my knowledge at the 17th ace. He played the ball, missed and that was that. I'd probably have finished it in my hand. Anyhow, I played on despite the bedlam in the gallery and when Kelly was 18 I threw the ball to the referee stating that, in my opinion, it was wet with body sweat. I may have been wrong, only Kelly knows the answer. If I'm wronging him, I'm sorry. Anyhow, he won 21-17.

First meeting of the Leinster Handball Council, 1922.
Front Row: Purcell; Carty; O'Toole; Breen; Lawlor; Harty; Carroll; O'Hanlon.
Standing: Shouldice; Daly; Kelly; McGrath; Clarke; Dunphy; O'Reilly; Bowles; Bourke.

First meeting of the Standing Committee of the IAHA, 1923.
Front Row: General O'Duffy, Andy Harty, Colonel Broy.
Back Row: Sean O'Hanlon, John McGrath, Terry O'Reilly, Jack Shouldice, J. Carroll.

Chapter 4

Struggle for Control 1922-1928

After the Treaty and the setting-up of the Irish Free State, the government was anxious to restore traditional links with the past and, to this end, it was decided to revive the Tailteann Games. The Tailteann Games of earlier centuries were held every four years in county Meath, not far from royal Tara. They had last been held in 1168 before the fall of the High Kings and the revival was intended to symbolise the partial restoration of Ireland's freedom. The programme for the Games included a wide range of athletic activities including handball. The committee charged with organising the handball competitions decided to hold trials for two places on an Irish handball team of three – thus acknowledging Pembroke as Ireland's No. I. J. J. Bowles, in a letter to the *Freeman's Journal* dated 4 August 1922, proposed that the trials should be held in neutral courts and not in Dublin only, or else on a home-and-home basis. When the committee rejected his suggestion, he refused to take part and, as a result of the trials, J. J. Kelly and Mick Dunne were given places on the Irish team with Pembroke.

The outbreak of the Civil War compelled the postponement of the Games until 1924, and in the intervening years the GAA took the first steps towards putting handball on the same footing as hurling and football. This was a matter of some urgency if confusion was to be avoided within the ranks of the GAA, as many prominent handballers were playing soccer in defiance of what was known as 'the foreign games rule', Rule 31 of the *Official Guide*. On 16 November 1922 the Leinster Council of the GAA sent a circular to all counties in the province with a view to setting up a provincial handball council. This was done at a meeting on 5 May 1923 when John Lawlor was elected Chairman, with Michael Davin of Kilkenny as Secretary and Eamonn Purcell, also of Kilkenny, as Treasurer. It was decided that the Chairman of the County Handball Committee should be a Vice-Chairman of the GAA County Board and that the Chairman of the GAA County Board should be a Vice-Chairman of the County Handball Committee.

At the same meeting, Mr P. D. Breen of Castlebridge, county Wexford, who was later to become President of the GAA, said, 'Handball has been neglected by the Association which has been wanting in its duty towards the game.' These words were echoed before the end of that year by Dr P. J. Cusack of Navan who, in the course of a letter to the *Irish Independent* (4 December 1923), said:

> Since the foundation of the GAA forty years ago, I find nothing to show that the Association did anything to encourage handball. The handball history of those years is one of sordid professionalism. One leading player challenged another for a stake of anything from £10 to £100. The loser was invariably dissatisfied, unpleasant incidents frequently arose, and an acrimonious and unsportsmanlike press controversy ensued.
>
> Twenty years ago Oliver Drew in an interview published in the *Daily News*, New York, complained that the GAA were doing nothing to help the game in Ireland, etc.

What the GAA did do when the four provincial councils had assumed control of handball, was to put softball and hardball on the same footing. To those unacquainted with handball, this may have seemed a perfectly reasonable decision. It 'legitimised' the form of the game played with the 'cock standard', but it also signalled the end of the game as it had been known in Ireland for generations. Oddly enough, in view of the GAA's decision, the strongest criticism of softball came from within the GAA. P. D. Breen condemned 'the softball pastime as alien to them, an innovation derived from English barrack-yards and lacking the splendid qualities of the Irish sport' (*Irish Independent*, 4 December 1923). We shall see that within a generation the 'alien pastime' was to replace the Irish sport with the tacit support of the GAA.

Few people interested in or involved in the organisation of the game today can quite understand how deep was the feeling of those who watched the infiltration of softball and the gradual decline of hardball. The word 'tradition' is incapable of precise definition but its meaning can be stretched to include nationality, and it was to this that P. D. Breen made his emotional appeal.

Various reasons have been advanced for the eagerness with which players took to the softball and one of them is that the rubber ball gave more immediate satisfaction to those who used it. The strength of the hitter was reflected in the manner in which the ball rebounded from the wall and so skill was eroded to be replaced by speed. The swing away from hardball was further hastened by the failure to realise that each ball had to be struck in an entirely different way.

The hardball player never *hit* the ball. He curved his hand and slung rather than struck the ball with the soft palm of the hand. In this way the ball never encountered any bone, no injury was done nor was any pain felt. A hardball player ran his hands under the hot tap after a long rubber and was prepared to play again in two or three days. Unfortunately there were then no coaches to advise young players on how to play the older game and so they turned to what they considered the less severe form of the game – softball.

While the administrative changes that were to alter the whole character of the game were slowly taking place, championship and challenge matches continued to attract the public. Morgan Pembroke retained his title of Irish champion by beating Paddy Lyons by 8 games to 4 in a two-day rubber at Ballymun, and the leading challenger for his title, J. J. Kelly, showed how good he was in the Tailteann trials. He beat Coyne, O'Reilly, Dunne, Collins and Lyons – *each in straight games.*

Once again the Cork Tournament was held at the Old Market Place, but it failed to attract the top players as in former years. The spirit of the game was, however, very much alive and at the end of the tournament a challenge was issued to 'James Kelly of New York, the present holder of the world title, for any sum up to £500, the rubber to be home-and-home. First half to be played in Cork'. It was a challenge that was never accepted though Kelly was playing ball as late as 1927, in which year he was defeated by Clifford Kauling for the US title.

1924 proved to be a year of great significance as it saw the foundation of the Irish Amateur Handball Association as well as the revival of the Tailteann Games. The inaugural meeting of what later became known as the IAHA and which represented all four provinces was held on 27 January 1924. John Lawlor became the first President and four Vice-Presidents elected were J. Kelly, Roscommon, B. Fay, Cavan, J. J. Bowles, Limerick, and M. Davin, Kilkenny. Those present at this 1st All-Ireland Congress of the IAHA were: John Lawlor (Dublin) presided. E. Purcell, M. Davin, Liam de Lasa (Kilkenny); J. Purcell, N. Kelly (Carlow); T. Deignam (Offaly); B. Fay (Cavan); P. Noonan (Clare); Sean MacCarthy, J. Donnelly (Cork); M. Batterberry, M. J. Barry (Waterford); J. J. Bowles, S. Gleeson (Limerick); M. Timmons, S. O'Brien (Wicklow); P. D. Breen, P. McCullagh (Wexford); P. J. Kenny, T. McGlovey (Meath); J. F. Shouldice, R. Carroll, A. Carty, B. J. Daly, J. Clarke, Sean O'Neill (Dublin); A. Harty (Tipperary).

In a discussion as to the procedure to be adopted with regard to the reinstatement of professionals, the chairman expressed the opinion that these players should first make application to their County Boards, who would in turn send on the application, with their observations, to the Central Council. Mr F. McGrath of Tipperary asked that a distinction be made between the professionals who were playing under an opposition association in Dublin and those in other parts of Ireland.

Paddy O'Keeffe, whose Secretaryship of the GAA spanned almost four decades, had a broad concept of the traditional games of the country. Petty disputes did not concern him and while Cork was a centre of hardball and so rather antagonistic to the GAA's attitude to the game, he had attended as Secretary of the Cork County Board the famous match in 1924 in which O'Shaughnessy and O'Mahony defeated the US pair, Heeney and O'Donnell. He had always sought to reconcile the conflicting interests of Union and Association and one of his first actions on becoming General Secretary was to have a ballcourt built beside Hill 16 so that Croke Park might be even more

In 1924 Cork beat America (represented by Heeney and O'Donnell) 4-3.
The Cork players were: *Back Row:* S. Connell, J. Creagh, T. Horgan.
Seated: D. O'Mahony, M. O'Mahony, J. Donnelly, M. O'Shaughnessy, Peter Healy.

Waterford City Handball Club, 1928.
Group includes the All-Ireland Senior and Junior Softball Champions.
Kneeling: W. Neary, J. Maguire, B. McCarthy, J. Murphy, M. Dowling.
Seated: Clr. Dawson, P. Kirwan, J. Flavin, W. Barry (Chairman), M. Batterberry,
M. Flannelly, P. Mordaunt. *Standing:* B. Murray, F. O'Gorman, L. Doolan, R. Curnam, T. Delaney,
W. Gallagher, D. O'Neill, M. Walsh, N.T., D. O'Brien, N.T., T. Batterberry,
D. Fitzgibbon, P. Campion, F. Coleman.

All-Ireland Senior Softball Finalists. *Players:* Joyce (Dublin), Brehony (Mayo), McNally (Mayo) and Ryan (Dublin).

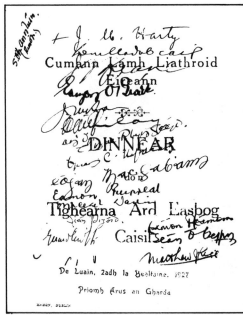

Autographed copy of the programme for a social occasion in 1927, in honour of Dr. Harty, Archbishop of Cashel.

Cover of programme for the Tailteann Games, 1928.

J. Flavin and M. Batterberry (seated), All-Ireland Senior Champions, 1928, with M. Flannery, All-Ireland Junior Champion 1928.

1929 Senior Softball Champions, Kilkenny. D. Brennan and J. Lucas.

matter - Articles of Agreement Subject - Handball

To It Whom It May Concern: -

This Day Aug 24, 192-- has been an agreement for a Handball Exhibition between M Heney of America and J J Kelly of Ireland Articles, t

(1) The said contest is strictly an exhibition only and it is understood that contest is to be played without any honors whatsoever or title to be involved

(2) That said contest is to be played under strict Amateur rules as jointly understood in America and in Ireland

(3) That said contest is to consist of 5 games of 21 points each and the winner of the majority of games (3) is to be declared victor

We, the undersigned in the interest of Handball Handball in Ireland, have agreed to this Handball Exhibition and to the above Articles.

The games to be played Sunday Aug 24, 1924 at 3 P.M at "the Book" Ballymun, Dublin, Ireland.

J J Healy
T H O'Rourke
Joseph M Heney
J J Kelly.

Example of a 1924 agreement to stage an exhibition written on the back of Jury's Hotel notepaper.

Portraits from the Wills Cigarettes cards series: T. Soye, P. Perry, M. O'Neill.

truly the headquarters of our native games. (That open court cost £1700 in 1933. It was covered in 1954. In 1970 a covered, glass-panelled court was built at Croke Park at a cost of £58,000. A further £120,000 was spent in 1980 to include, among other amenities, a 40 x 20 court.)

During its first 40 years the GAA was, as we have seen, intent on developing the great team games of hurling and football. Handballers were very much apart and of those who were most prominent in keeping the game alive, Lawlor and Bowles did not become members of the GAA until 1922. Even when the provincial handball councils had been set up and the IAHA established, many players preferred to be independent of GAA control and for the next 12 years there were two rival handball organisations in the country – the IAHA and the IAHU. The views of those who remained outside the GAA may be said to have been summarised by John Kavanagh, secretary of the Kildare Handball Board, in a letter to the secretary of the Baltinglass Club, dated 11 February 1924:

I would ask you to bring to your club's notice the fact that the GAA authorities who have failed miserably to do anything for the game in the past and are now seeking to gain support by representing to the public that the Leinster Handball Council are a professional body. I wish to state that such is not the case, and such of our champions as have played for money have been forced to do so by the action of those who now seek to cover up their transgressions by sheltering under the wing of the GAA. I refer to Mr J. J. Bowles who some years ago absolutely refused to play Pembroke for the championship unless the latter posted £100; since the day he beat Bowles, Pembroke has not earned one penny from the game, nor has he been challenged. Bowles did make an offer to play him last year and Pembroke accepted his challenge on the same conditions as laid down for their first meeting. This in my opinion was fair, but did not suit Mr Bowles – who then turned amateur. He along with Mr John Lawlor, a man who while he was able, never played unless as a professional, are now the stalwarts of the GAA and have been selected to preach the Gospel of Amateurism to handballers.

In addition to this inconsistency, the GAA Handball board, in spite of the 'Foreign Games' rule of the parent body, are openly playing men who no later than Saturday last took part in a game of Association Football for Ireland v Wales [A reference to J. 'Kruger' Fagan of Shamrock Rovers] and further they approached Mr J. J. Kelly, a well-known soccer player who plays under our auspices, and offered to overlook his football playing if he would only play with them; this offer is not being accepted.

Our Council may have, in common with all Councils, its own short-comings but we merit consideration from the fact that at least we are consistent in recognising merit, that is, we want players who play the game or any other game for the love of the game and we do not in any way

The views of those who remained outside the GAA. Letter of 11.2.1924 from John Kavanagh, Secretary of the Kildare Handball Club, to the Secretary of the Baltinglass Club.

OPENING OF THE
TALBOT'S INCH HANDBALL COURT, KILKENNY;
On SUNDAY, 1st JULY, 1928

PROGRAMME

1. HARD BALL SINGLE:—

T. SOYE
(DUBLIN). Winner Irish Amateur Championship and Dr. Harty Cup, 1926-27.

v.

DANNY BRENNAN
(KILKENNY). Winner Leinster Championship Tailteann Trials, 1924.

2. SOFT BALL SINGLE:—

TOM BEHAN
(URLINGFORD). All-Ireland Champion of Soft Ball and Holder of the Purcell Cup, 1927.

v.

MICHAEL BATTERBERRY
(WATERFORD) Present Holder Munster Soft Ball Championship

SOFT BALL DOUBLE:—

DICK BRENNAN
and
KIERAN WHITE
(TALBOT'S INCH). Junior Co. Championship Winners, 1927, and Lady Desart Challenge Shield.

v.

T. HARRINGTON
and
D. BRYAN
(URLINGFORD).

HARD BALL DOUBLE:—

DANNY BRENNAN
and
J. LUCAS
(KILKENNY CITY). Runners-up for All-Ireland Championship, 1926.

v.

T. J. O'REILLY
and
T. SOYE
(DUBLIN).

5. SOFT BALL DOUBLE:—

T. BEHAN
and
J. NORTON
(URLINGFORD).

v.

CHARLIE RYAN
and
M. JOYCE
(DUBLIN). Present Champions of Dublin in Soft Ball.

Judge
MR. SEAN O'HANLON (Dublin).

Marker
MR. P. LANIGAN (Kilkenny).

RUBBERS { SOFT BALL: Best 2 out of 3 Games.
{ HARD BALL: Best 3 out of 5 Games.

THE KILKENNY JOURNAL LTD.

Autographed copy of the Programme for 1 July 1928 on the opening of the Talbot's Inch Handball Court, Kilkenny.

interfere with or try to dictate to any man as to what game he should play. We are out to foster a love of the game and for that reason and solely that we are appealing to your club to throw in their lot with us.

Rivalries were, at least, temporarily forgotten with the arrival of the American team for the Tailteann Games early in August 1924. It consisted of Joe Heeney, Myles O'Donnell, Jack Driscoll and Tierney O'Rourke. Heeney was the first holder of the Senior National Four-Wall Hardball Championship of the USA and, in partnership with O'Donnell, he held the doubles title as well.

Heeney had some weeks in which to accustom himself to Irish conditions and he had a number of training sessions in Healy's Court at Clondalkin as well as at Weldon's in Ballymun. He is remembered by those who watched him as a superb player, possessing good hands, a severe service and, above all, the ability to dictate the pace of a game. On successive days, he beat Danny Brennan, Terry O'Reilly and Barney Daly without losing a game. Good judges reckoned that the Irish champion, Morgan Pembroke, would find him very difficult to beat. To the surprise of everyone, however, he was matched not with Pembroke but with J. J. Kelly. No really satisfactory explanation has ever been given for the refusal of the American to meet Pembroke. The American Handball President, Owen Brady, is said to have favoured a match between Heeney and Pembroke but all offers were rejected by O'Rourke, Heeney's manager. Pembroke offered to deposit any sum required to 'bind' his challenge but to no avail. And, as if to underline this determination to ignore the Irish title-holder, a purse of £1,000 for a double-handed world title match between Pembroke and Andy Durkin of Ireland and Heeney and O'Donnell was also turned down.

The contract for the Heeney versus Kelly match stipulated that it was to be 'under strict amateur rules as jointly understood in America and Ireland'. Despite the controversy which preceded the match, the great crowd at Ballymun on that August afternoon enjoyed an unforgettable display of handball. Heeney won by 4 aces in the 5th and final game, after 'all together' had been called six times in the course of the last game. So close, indeed, was the contest that after the 5 games had been played only 3 aces separated the players, Heeney scoring 87 and Kelly 84.

The other big event of the Tailteann handball programme was the victory of P. J. MacDonagh in the softball singles. MacDonagh, a native of Leitirmullen, county Galway, had won the first Junior National Softball Championship of the USA in 1920 and was recognised as senior champion when he came here in 1924. Unlike Heeney, he trained in an almost casual fashion, often cycling out from Galway to Barna where there was a three-wall court and then on to Spiddal – playing anyone who wanted a game. Paddy Perry, who had 'a knock-up' with him in the Depot, vouches for his ability and he was an easy winner of the Tailteann title.

One of the greatest upsets of the year was provided by the Cork pair,

O'Shaughnessy and O'Mahony, who beat the world police champions, O'Reilly and Daly, in the best of 15 games played at Clondalkin and Cork. The Dublin pair had claimed the police title after beating Heeney and O'Donnell.

The growing strength of the IAHA was shown when, in 1925, 16 counties entered for the championships which resulted in a triumph for Kilkenny players. They won the Senior H. B. Singles and the Senior S. B. Doubles, and it was a Kilkennyman, Martin Joyce of Urlingford, who also won the Senior S. B. Singles though playing in the colours of Dublin. On the other hand, Bill Aldridge of Athy joined the Clogh, county Kilkenny, Club and it was in the colours of that county that he won his senior title and with it the first Harty Cup. This was the cup presented by the Archbishop of Cashel who, in a letter to Michael Davin, had recorded his purpose in doing so:

> Dear Mr Davin,
>
> It gives me great pleasure to give my support to the revival of handball under GAA rules. I shall give a cup for competition open to all Ireland. I hope that success will crown your efforts to give handball its rightful place among Irish games.
>
> Yours very faithfully,
> J. M. Harty

The competition for the trophy proved worthy of its importance, In Leinster, Aldridge beat Delaney of Kildare, Dunne of Carlow and O'Reilly of Dublin. In Munster, Bowles beat Stephen Gleeson of Fedamore in the Limerick championship and then faced Gus Moriarty of Cork for the provincial title. On that occasion a special train brought the Limerick supporters to Cork where Moriarty won 4 of the 6 games played. The lead seemed substantial but Bowles reckoned that if he could keep Moriarty outside the short line, where the Corkman excelled, he could still win. The second half was at Kilfinnane, county Limerick, and there, before a 'gallery' of more than a thousand people, Bowles won by 5 games to 1 and earned the right to play for his first Irish title as an amateur. He was then in his 46th year and the handicap of age proved too much when he met Aldridge in the final. The score tells the tale: 7 games to Aldridge and 1 to Bowles.

The Harty Cup is matched by an equally splendid trophy for the softball singles. Purcell was the name of one of the oldest tobacco firms in the country whose premises in O'Connell Street were as well-known as that of Tom Clarke's to an earlier generation or that of Moss Twomey's to a more recent one. When the firm offered to provide a cup, it was decided to accept the offer and it was first competed for in 1925.

An important decision was taken by the 1925 GAA Congress with regard to the voting power of handball representatives. Mr Clifford (Limerick) moved an amendment to a motion before the Congress that handball delegates to the committees, councils and conventions of the Association be given power to vote. His amendment that power to vote be given only in relation to the

Central Council was carried. The decision was to be a source of much controversy for many years. It meant that decisions affecting handball were made by those whose interest lay in hurling and football rather than in handball and that no vote could be registered against such decisions except at meetings of the Central Council. Hurling and football are spectator sports, followers are numbered in thousands and not unnaturally, handball was often neglected.

The IAHU continued to promote the old form of the game and in Kelly and Pembroke it had what were acknowledged to be the two finest players in the country. Kelly beat Tom Soye in the 1925 championship but the closeness of the scores indicates the quality of Soye's play (Soye's scores first):- 11-21, 17-21, 21-16, 21-19, 21-10. Soye left the IAHU soon after that defeat and was reinstated by the GAA. A year later Kelly, who by his victory over Pembroke in 1925, was now undisputed champion, found himself 'on the fringe' of a dispute within the IAHA. In August 1925 a challenge match had been arranged between Kelly and Aldridge – the champions of their respective organisations. It was a home-and-home rubber of 15 games of which Kelly won 3 of the 7 games at Clogh and 5 of the 6 games at Ballymun. The IAHA acted promptly and at its September meeting, suspended Aldridge for ten years and ordered that the Harty Cup be returned to the Council and the 1925 title declared vacant.

The 1926 championships marked the last great triumph of J. J. Bowles when, in partnership with Stephen Gleeson, he won the All-Ireland doubles title. Tom Soye who, as we saw, had transferred his allegiance in the previous year, took the first of the six titles which he was to win under GAA rules in successive years. He also took part in an unusual tour of south-western ballcourts with T. J. O'Reilly as his partner. In nine days they played at ten venues, beating every pair matched against them in a series of hardball matches, with the exception of Ryan and Meehan who won 3-2 at Sixmilebridge, county Clare.

Hundreds of people came to see these matches and it made it all the more regrettable that the two handball organisations were so deeply divided. Rivalry which might have been of benefit to the game developed into enmity and for ten years the IAHU and the IAHA continued to award Irish championship titles to their respective winners. The origin of the differences which separated the two bodies may seem simple: the well-justified antipathy of members of an amateur organisation like the GAA to professionalism in sport and the unexpressed but latent fear that it might spread from handball to hurling and football. As we have seen, it was professionalism on a very small scale and many would in any case question its complete absence from any amateur sport. The divisions deepened when charges and counter-charges were made of players from one or other of the organisations breaking Rule 31 by playing 'foreign games'. The IAHU did not support the ban on such games but opportunities for actually breaking the rule were few as soccer, rugby, hockey and cricket were then largely confined to Dublin city. Most of the clubs affiliated to the IAHU were in counties Louth, Meath, Kildare and Wicklow –

areas where Gaelic football was and is widely played.

The following clubs were affiliated to the IAHU as on 1 January 1924: Tavern, Dunleer, Kilsarren, Ardee, Philipstown, Murray's Cross, Moone, Kildoon, Kildare, Ballymore-Eustace, Carlow, Prosperous, Rathangan, Curragh, Nobber, Kilmainham Wood, Crossakiel, Drumconrath, Kingscourt, Kells, Ballyjamesduff, Tankardstown, Drewstown, Oldcastle, Edengora (Baileboro), Ballymun, Clonliffe, Inchicore, Clondalkin.

Players tended to play where their talents would be best rewarded and it was clear almost from 1924 when the IAHA was founded that it would offer competition on a scale the IAHU could not match. This was because of the weight given to it by the parent body, the GAA, which was identified with the resurgence of the national spirit in the newly established Irish Free State. This, too, may account for the failure of the IAHU to attract any support in such Gaelic outposts as Cork, Kerry, Clare, Galway and Donegal.

The emphasis on sport at the time when the Irish nation, or that part of it that had achieved freedom, was slowly trying to heal the divisions of the past was important. The Free State Army and the Garda welcomed within their ranks young men who were often to provide the first sports' heroes of the new state. (I have heard it said that Pat MacDonagh, after his victory in the Tailteann Games of 1924, was invited by General Sean McKeon to accept the post of Athletic Trainer to the Free State Army but declined.) It was no accident that the cigarette cards of the time featured such handball stars as Paddy Perry and Tom Soye, each of whom had won the highest honours in the game. Tournaments were sponsored, ballcourts built and positive measures adopted to ensure that teams from the services entered for local and county championships.

The IAHA was always far stronger in softball – a game the IAHU rather disdained as being no more than a mongrel form of handball. I can myself recall the contempt with which Paddy Lyons spoke of the 'sponge-bag' as he called the softball. How to explain such contempt coming from a cultivated man such as Lyons? Tradition is never simple, and the old players of the old game never have put it into words but they may, nevertheless, have been aware that the game they played was part of a long-vanished past, and that they should keep faith with that past.

The IAHU must have felt that if only Rule 31 was rescinded, then the question of professionalism, by far the less difficult of the two issues seperating them from the IAHA, could be resolved. In January 1927 Dr Cusack and Mr J. J. Healy, President and Vice-President of the IAHU, interviewed General O'Duffy, then President of the IAHA, who promised that he would do what he could to have Rule 31 altered if not entirely removed from the *Official Guide*. Nothing was done and in the same year one of the foremost amateur clubs in the country, the Metropolitan Handball Club, withdrew from the IAHA and for the next eight years played under IAHU rules.

A newspaper controversy over the exclusion of IAHU players from the Tailteann Games only intensified the bitterness between the two associations.

While, as J. J. Kelly himself said, the only place to settle a dispute about the merits of players is in the ballcourt, it is difficult to believe that the Tailteann handball programme of 1928, confined as it was to IAHA players, was representative of Irish handball. In a letter to the *Irish Independent*, J. J. wrote:

I repeat that I beat Tom Soye and Mick Dunne. In 1922 I was competing in junior handball and made my debut in the senior ranks in the Tailteann trials of that year which I won, P. J. Lyons being the only man to take a game off me. It is true that Mick Dunne met with a mishap in his game with me. He was accidentally struck with the ball during a rally for the last ace of the game. Mick is a sport and I am sure that he will admit that I beat him on his merits. Since then I defeated Coyne, Pembroke, Lyons and Aldridge, all of whom beat Dunne. As regards Soye, I beat him in the Dublin Senior championship at Ballymun. I also defeated the late P. Fields and P. L. Purcell, who had victories over the GAA champion.

Within weeks of the publication of that letter, Pembroke regained the Dublin IAHU championship by defeating Kelly on scores 21-10, 21-12, 21-18, 21-6. But a young player from Ballymore-Eustace upset all the odds by beating Pembroke decisively for the Irish title. This was Tommy Leahy who, in the second half of the rubber before his home supporters, ran out the five games conceding only 30 aces to his opponent. He confirmed this form a year later when he beat Kelly for the same title and then, when his career was but beginning, he died tragically young in the year 1940. Pembroke, ever willing to acknowledge the qualities of those against whom he played, often said that he could not 'get under' Leahy's service which came at such speed both to left and right.

'A Green Street Reverie', R. H. Conn, *Dublin Opinion 1934*. Green Street Court is at the back of the Four Courts and remains unchanged today.

Chapter 5

Players and Partnerships 1927-1938

In most sports there are periods when it seems that the standard of play and sportsmanship is unusually high, years during which talented players display skills that set them apart. The end of the 'twenties and the early 'thirties was such a time. Two rival organisations were then promoting the game with an enthusiasm due in part to a growing awareness that only one would survive. So it was that players had a wide choice of tournaments apart altogether from championships. The country had also got over the effects of the Civil War and the crowds at sports fixtures generally pointed to a new confidence in the nation's future. Looking back on the outstanding performances of those years and choosing to recall some of the players, I am being selective in a way that is entirely personal.

The most remarkable performance of the year 1927 was undoubtedly that of two Ballingarry players, Tommy Forde and Danny Kelly, who met Soye and O'Reilly of Dublin in the senior hardball final. After losing 4 of the 6 games in Ballingarry, the Limerick pair then took the first 3 games off the Dublin pair in the Depot Court before eventually losing the rubber, 5 games to 7.

In 1928 the Tailteann Games were again held and while they did attract a few entries from Britain in the handball section, the absence of any American players was a great disappointment. Soye (Ireland) in singles and O'Reilly and Ormonde (Ireland) in doubles won the hardball and Brennan (Ireland) in singles and Ryan and Joyce (Ireland) in doubles won the softball.

Sport has never been without its heroes whose achievements do not find mention in official records. One of these was Mick Dunne of Carlow who figured in the memorable hardball final of 1927 postponed to 1928. He held Soye to level scores in aces and in games up to 18-all in the 13th and last game before losing by 3 aces. He then went on to reach the softball final where again he was beaten, this time by Joe McNally of Westport, county Mayo.

Two Munster partnerships of this time deserve mention. Batterberry and Flavin of the Waterford City Club were unbeatable in such long courts as the Spring Garden Alley in Waterford and that at Queen Street, Tramore. When they won out in 1928, many thought that they would retain the title for years but they retired early from the game. Flavin devoted himself to encouraging hurling with the Mount Sion club but Batterberry continued to play the occasional friendly game and I remember seeing him play good ball at Ballyanne, county Wexford, in 1938. The other partnership was that of Paddy Ormonde and Con Maloney of Ballyporeen, county Tipperary. I never saw Maloney playing but Ormonde was a frequent visitor to the Depot Court where his left-hand service is still spoken of by those who saw him play. It seemed effortless but once it touched the floor it seemed to spin away to 'die' before it reached the backwall. Maloney was, by all accounts, less heavy in service but a far better two-handed player than his partner.

Under IAHA rules, two brilliant performers from Kilkenny City came to the forefront. Danny Brennan had gained his first handball medals with the Army in the early 'twenties. By 1929 he was out of the Army and he then teamed up with Jim Lucas, a schoolboy friend. They went through to two All-Ireland finals, losing the hardball to Tipperary (Ormonde and Maloney) by the odd game in 13 and winning the softball from Waterford (Batterberry and Flavin) by the odd game in 13! Of the two, Brennan was the more stylish and in Kilkenny, whether in hurling or handball, style does count.

Good juniors were also coming up and the 1929 title in that grade was won amid great rejoicing by Tom O'Keeffe of Moycarkey, county Tipperary, and 'Shelly' McCarthy from the Horse and Jockey where that summer the new ballcourt was completed. Two Cork City Club players, Jerry and Danny O'Mahony, maintained the hardball tradition in an area where it was gradually dying.

The first important decision of the 1930 IAHA Handball Congress was to abolish the provincial councils which had been part of the framework of the association from the beginning. The control of the game passed to a small executive committee consisting of two representatives from each province. This, it was argued, would enable the Secretary to act more quickly when the need arose and also effect a saving in travelling expenses. (It is of interest to note that provincial councils were restored in 1950 as local clubs grew in number and strength).

Had the 1929 championships been completed before the end of the season, the name of Paddy Perry would have come before the public a year earlier. As it was, he actually won the Connacht senior title of 1930 before he won the junior title of 1929! Nor is it likely that any junior player will again have to play a rubber of 7 games, lasting two hours, as Perry did in beating Ned Hassett on scores of 21-7, 11-21, 21-11, 21-12, 12-21, 20-21, 21-12. Perry was then 19 years of age and for the next 10 years he was the player most spoken of wherever handball was discussed. His achievement in winning the junior at the age of 19 was, however, surpassed by that of Joe Hassett, a brother of the defeated 1929 finalist, who won the 1930 final at the age of 17.

In senior ranks, a new partnership brought an All-Ireland title for the first time to Wicklow. Martin O'Neill, one of a family of athletes from Ferns, county Wexford, was then living in Bray where he partnered Luke Sherry who had learnt the game in Maynooth. They began the season by losing the first round of the junior championship to Kildare but then went on to win the senior championship! Their partnership was in many ways an ideal one: Sherry had a superb service but was otherwise a rather unimpressive player; O'Neill was fast, clever and, what in those days was an advantage, had a good pair of feet. Their home court in the grounds of the Presentation College was, to say the least, somewhat eccentric in design, and I don't believe they ever lost a game there.

The hardball game was again dominated by the name of Soye who, in addition to winning the singles also won the doubles in partnership with Brown. In the final, when playing in the unfamiliar court at Ballyporeen, county Tipperary, he tossed from 15 in the 4th game to 21 in the 5th and last game of the match.

The success of the IAHA was marked by the number of young players coming into the game. This was especially so in 1931 when Paddy Murray of Birr, Paddy Delaney of Borris and Tommy Cherry of Kilkenny were all juniors in that year and each was to win a championship in that grade. Murray was easily the best three-wall player I ever saw. With powerful shoulders and a long reach, he could have made an outstanding player but there was then no four-wall court in his native Offaly and so he never had the chance to fulfil the promise he showed in 1931. When, 20 years later, Fahy Cross and Birr ballcourts were built, his career was almost at an end. It was a pity because there were few more sporting players than the tall, quiet-spoken Paddy Murray.

Delaney was another good junior who, largely because of lack of competition, never won what I believe he could have won – a senior title. Tom Cherry did win both junior and senior grades and even in a club like Talbot's Inch, where almost every member had at least one All-Ireland medal, he was considered to be one of the best. The record-book tells the score in the match he lost to Jerry O'Mahony in Tipperary Town but what it does not tell is the part played by O'Mahony's trainer, Mick O'Halloran, in that defeat.

After his great match with Ned Hassett, Perry joined the police force and was stationed in Dublin but availing of the 'non-resident' rule, he continued to play for Roscommon. His partner of the early days, Tommy Gaughran of Boyle, had gone to the USA and, in 1932, Alfie Mullaney of Ballinacurry came in as his partner on the right. Alfie was a very steady if unexciting player but I am inclined to think that he was the best partner Perry ever had. He understood Perry and, as he said himself, 'Perry was so anxious to hit *every* ball that in the early games of a doubles, he was simply blind to the fact that he had a partner'. Playing on the right-hand side is never easy but Mullaney proved that he knew what is required of the man placed there. First, he must be able to return service and, secondly, he must be prepared to leave two-thirds of the play to his partner. Mullaney did this and for two years himself and Perry defeated all opposition. As some indication of how level were standards in the softball game at that time, when Perry and Mullaney won the 1932 final on the 12th

Watching handball at the Garda Depot in the 1930s (Irish Press).

J. Dolan and M. Dowling (Kildare), J. J. Gilmartin and A. Cullen (Kilkenny) at the Garda Depot, Phoenix Park, 1937.

game in a home-and-home rubber, each side scored 192 aces.

There was no senior singles final in 1932 as Charlie Ryan, by decision of his club, the Dublin Metropolitan Garda, did not turn up for the final which was fixed for Terenure. He was subsequently suspended for twelve months and his club for six months.

The part played by players such as Perry and Ryan, Terry O'Reilly and Martin Joyce and, indeed, Garda players in general in arousing interest in the game is important. General Eoin O'Duffy, Chief Commissioner of the Garda, was a talented organiser who saw to it that good athletes were encouraged to join the newly formed police. In doing so, he aimed to raise the prestige of the force and associate the people more closely with them. In 1926 he was elected President of the IAHA and he immediately gave further impetus to the game by having a number of courts erected beside Garda barracks and facilitating Garda players who sought leave to play exhibition matches.

Many of the Garda players were so good that it is, perhaps, invidious to single out any one for special mention, but Soye, who won all his championships with Dublin, and Perry held records that may never be equalled. As I never saw Soye play, I can only say that in the opinion of good judges he possessed all the shots and all the skills of a first-class player. His record, from the date of his first All-Ireland triumph under GAA rules in 1926 until his forced retirement, owing to a knee injury, in 1931, was one of uninterrupted success. His command of the hardball was equalled by that of Perry with the softball. From the day in 1929 when Perry left his native town of Boyle, where he had been coached by Johnny Casey, he never knew defeat in singles competition until 1938. He was the complete player – clever, fast and strong, and ever courteous to referees and opponents.

The Garda championships of the 'thirties were miniature All-Irelands with so many champions taking part. Then, as the force grew old, players retired and the new recruits, enjoying a wider variety of sporting activity such as rowing, basketball and tennis, turned away from handball.

It may here be opportune to include mention of the game in the Army. When the Free State Army was formed, several trophies were presented for the various sports promoted in the various units. Sir Bryan Mahon, Major-General Gearóid O'Sullivan and Colonel Sean Quinn presented cups for the handball championships. The first winners of the Mahon Cup for hardball doubles were Volunteer Jack Delaney and Captain Whelan of the Curragh Command. Delaney, a native of Athy and a good ballmaker, was a nephew of the James Delaney who took part in the International Tournament in Casey's Court, New York, in 1891.

All-Army titles were hard won. Each September the Commands sent their selected players to a different centre where all the matches were played over a period of four days. One player may be said to have dominated handball in the Army from 1931 to 1938. This was Frank O'Reilly, a native of Kells, county Meath, stationed with the 4th Battalion in Cork. During those seven years O'Reilly won twenty All-Army titles, probably the most remarkable record of any Army athlete. At his best, O'Reilly was a magnificent player with two good hands and an incomparable style. He had the great advantage of coming from a town where in his youth hardball was the only form of the game played and also in having as partner Sergeant Joe Merriman from Delvin, county Westmeath, a player of endless endurance.

In the years following O'Reilly's resignation from the Army, the name 'Maher' appears again and again on all the Army trophies. There were, in fact, two of that name. Sergeant Dick Maher of Tullaroan, county Kilkenny, who was with the 1st Armoured Squadron at the Curragh Camp, and Corporal Tommy Maher of Rathnure, county Wexford, who was with the Southern Command in Cork. Tommy Maher was an extremely clever player who rarely failed to entertain the 'gallery' with an exhibition of step-dancing or a tune on the tin-whistle during any stoppage in the match. His namesake at the Curragh equalled O'Reilly in the number of titles won, but his victories extended over some 15 years, 1946 to 1961.

1932 could be said to be a turning-point in the fortunes of the game, as it was marked by the holding of the Tailteann Games and the resignation of Sean O'Hanlon who had as Secretary so ably guided the IAHA for almost ten years. O'Hanlon's organising ability was of the highest order and the fact that 28 counties were by then taking part in the championships under GAA rules, showed what he had accomplished during his years in office. He was replaced by Martin O'Neill.

The Tailteann Games were notable for the presence of a team of Spanish players who gave exhibitions of their native *pelota* and also played the Irish game with equal dexterity. Tailteann awards went to:

Stephen Ryan (Tipperary): hardball singles
Paddy Bell and Joe Doyle (Meath): hardball doubles
Paddy Perry (Roscommon): softball singles
Paddy Perry and Alfie Mullaney (Roscommon): softball doubles

By 1933 Paddy Bell had begun to make the name of his club, The Foresters, known throughout Ireland. He was a slight, delicately framed man who made aces by his sheer skill in placing a ball. His great friend and trainer, Jack Skelly, believed that he never played better than in 1933 when Doyle and he beat Ormonde and Maloney of Tipperary. The Meath pair were 3 games down and being led by 18 aces to 7 in the 4th game of a 7-game rubber when Bell got going. He served from 7 to 17 before losing his hand, and with Doyle's hand still in they won that game and reached 10 in the next before being put out. They went on to win the rubber by 4 games to 3.

Two most dramatic finals took place in 1934. One was a junior final in which Jasper Dunne of Kilkenny beat Sligo-born Jimmy O'Rourke, playing in the colours of Dublin. The other was the senior hardball singles final between Paddy Reid of Roscommon, playing in the colours of Carlow, and Jerry O'Mahony of Cork.

In the junior match, Dunne and O'Rourke had shared the first four games of their 5-game rubber and then exchanged ace for ace until '20 all' was called in the last game. Dunne had actually reached 20 when O'Rourke was but 14. Dunne was then put out for 0, O'Rourke got 2; Dunne 0, O'Rourke 0; Dunne 0, O'Rourke 1. Then with scores level at 20-all, each player again had a scoreless innings before Dunne got the winning ace.

In the senior final, the two players shared the first six games. Then in the last game of the 7-game rubber, a dispute arose on the question of introducing a new ball for the vital 7th game. The *Sports Mail* reporting on the match said of this incident, 'No fault was to be found with the ball in play, yet a replacement was permitted for the concluding game notwithstanding a protest by one of the players.' In fact, because it was a spectator and not the referee who changed the ball, O'Mahony refused to offer any of Reid's services and the score was recorded as 21-0. It was regrettable that the incident occurred because Reid, who had played in many counties in the course of his career, justly enjoyed the reputation of being one of the most courteous and sporting players the game has ever known. O'Mahony was less widely known but he was a dogged, resolute player, with a heavier service than anyone of his time, who never quarrelled with a referee's decision.

In 1935 Youth met Age when Stephen Tormay of Kells, aged 22, met the 42-year-old Bill Aldridge of Kildare in the senior final. It was the first final I ever saw in Dublin and I have a very clear memory of the scene when the referee, Martin O'Neill, introduced the two players. It was a Sunday morning and the Depot Court was crowded, especially as the footballers of Kildare and Meath were meeting that afternoon in Croke Park. Right through the match Aldridge played with what seemed to me deliberate casualness as, with deadly accurate strokes off left and right, he used the corners to keep Tormay constantly moving. He often used his service to tempt the Meath man out of position by tossing two 'shorts' to one side before driving a fast ball down the other. He slowed the game to a point that earned him a reprimand from the referee and must have been hard on the nerves of the youthful Tormay. However, the long rubber took toll of Aldridge in the end and it was Tormay who won by the odd game in seven.

Aldridge was never again to win the cup which he had won exactly 10 years before. A much younger player was waiting to come on court, and his name was one to remember. John Joe Gilmartin appears in the records for the first time in 1936 as winner of the junior hardball singles. There was nothing very special about his winning a title that others had won before him. But for the 12 years that followed, no one to equal him was seen in Irish ballcourts and there are many to tell you that there never will be. Before tracing his career, a word on the end of the IAHU.

Curiously enough, it was a cousin of Gilmartin's the great Joe McNally of Westport, who brought glory to the last years of the IAHU. While softball was never favoured by the Union, McNally, after proving himself the best softball player in Ireland under IAHA rules in 1928, changed his allegiance and proved

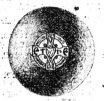
An advertisement from 1936 for Elvery's Elephant Handballs.

Handball collection. A permit, 1936.

Roscommon v Meath, Handball Championship at Talbot's Inch, Kilkenny, 1936.
J. Skelly (Co. Meath Sec.), J. Hassett (Tipp.), P. Perry (Rosc.), P. Reid (Rosc.), T. Tormay (Meath),
J. J. Gilmartin (Kilk.), P. Bell (Meath), J. Doyle (Meath), E. Purcell (Kilk. President, IAHA).

Women playing handball at Charles Fort, Kinsale, Co. Cork in 1938.

himself the best in Ireland under IAHU rules. He had the distinction of representing Ireland in soccer and playing handball for an Irish selection, which included Alec Finn of Dublin and Charlie Fitzsimons of Cavan, against Scotland in Virginia, county Cavan. The Union, however, could not, with its shrinking membership, continue to promote championships on a national scale and 1936 saw its end. The last winner of their senior title and the Weldon Cup, with its proud inscription 'Presented for the World Handball Championship', was Michael Dowling of the Ballymore-Eustace Club. Within the year his club and the Ballymun Club made application for admission to the IAHA, and the oldest of all handball clubs, the Metropolitan, was soon to follow.

What was the greatest game you ever saw? To answer that question is to roll back the film of memory and then try and recall the day and the circumstances that made it outstanding. In 1936 the two great partnerships in county Wexford were Willie Delaney and Mickey Fortune of Ballyanne and Frank Rossiter and Joe Sutherland of the Foresters, Wexford. They had met in the county final of that year when Ballyanne won and with it the right to represent Wexford against Mayo in the final of the All-Ireland which they lost. This caused great controversy as Rossiter and Sutherland had been the county's representatives in all the matches up to the final. Then in 1937 a big doubles tournament was organised by the Kilmannon Club and the same pairs reached the final.

Kilmannon is not marked prominently on any map and my first memory of it is on a cold April day when the furze was beginning to blaze on the bleak forbidding ridges of the Forth Mountain. It was a solidly built, four-wall court which seemed to be more than the regulation 30 feet in breadth but probably was not. It had been built in 1871 when before 600 spectators Andy Walsh and Martin Broaders of Carrig beat Jack Walsh and Nicky Devereux of Bridgetown.

Together with Ned and Patsy Murphy, Addy Culleton and Willie Kielthy of the Ballyanne Club, I set out on the morning of the match to cycle the 25 miles to the venue. I can remember that we stopped at Suttons of Ballinboola leaving Carrickbyrne on our left and arrived at Kilmannon as crowds were already gathering for the match. Jack Simpson of Cleariestown introduced the players and Bill Drumgoole was, I think, either referee or marker.

From the start the Wexford pair served and played to the right so as to keep the ball away from Delaney but Fortune when in form was well able to hold his corner. He had a deceptive stroke which, without much power behind it, cut the corners and was as effective as a direct 'kill'.

The 1st game went to Wexford on the score 21-13 and in the 2nd game Sutherland made a run of aces by serving low and hard to centre court so as to draw Delaney away from the left corner. Rossiter was then ready to drive any return along the lefthand wall out of Delaney's reach. This tactic seemed to upset Ballyanne and while Delaney's stamina was not in doubt it was clear that only by staying under the left wall could he give Fortune sufficient room for the latter's type of shot and at the same time defend his own left. So successful was this that after losing the 2nd game 2-11, they ran away with the 3rd on the score

21-2.

In the 4th game spectators saw some wonderful play from Delaney. He was a tremendous hitter and only by taking his service on the volley could Rossiter hope to deal with it. Once the service came off the wall it was almost unplayable. At this stage Rossiter changed places with Sutherland and tried a cross toss which ended up in Fortune's corner, forcing him to stay at the back of the court and cutting him off from the short-line game at which he excelled. Level scores were called at 19-all before two quick kills by Delaney gave Ballyanne the game by two aces.

I think that it was Rossiter who, by his tossing, really swung the match in Wexford's favour. He was a stylish player and in Sutherland he had the ideal partner, tenacious and reliable. They moved into an early lead and at one time led 9-2. Ballyanne then took up the running and it was ace for ace until 17-all was called. The end came when Rossiter's service cut the service line and spun away from Delaney's hand.

The last Senior All-Ireland IAHA Champion, 1934. M. Dowling (Kildare).

Right: J. J. Gilmartin and trophies.

Top Right: Gda. P. Reid and Gda. P. Perry, 1936.

CHAPTER 6

The Gilmartin Era 1937-1953

John Joe Gilmartin of Kilkenny fulfilled all the high hopes that his displays as a junior had aroused, and he won the first of his ten senior singles titles in Flood's ballcourt at Terenure. Gilmartin was an exciting player to watch: so fast to cover the court, so graceful in his movements, and yet so deliberate in his determination to win. When he was invited to appear in an exhibition match at Kanturk, the local followers, remembering the world title match once played in their court, wanted to have him sent to the States to win back the title. Had the Second World War not broken out, he would almost certainly have been given the opportunity of winning where so many Irish champions failed.

It was 1937 before he was matched with the then reigning softball champion, Paddy Perry. They met at Clogh, a small mining village in Kilkenny. Clogh is a splendid court, full-length and true, and the game between them matched the setting. How close the scores were in that 5-game rubber may be seen from the interval score: Gilmartin 2 games (55 aces), Perry 1 game (50 aces). The final score was: Perry 3 games (92 aces), Gilmartin 2 games (83 aces). The result does not really answer the question as to which was the better player. I have never altered my opinion that Gilmartin had no equal in hardball and that, at his best, Perry was the finest of all softball players.

The headlines of the handball columns in 1938 were to become familiar ones in the years that followed. Gilmartin took three of the four senior titles and only in softball doubles did he and his partner meet defeat. That was when the Hassett brothers from Nenagh won out. For the best part of five years, Ned and Joe played any pair who cared to take them on, whether in a standard four-wall court or at a gable-end, and beat them all. Their play was a joy to watch; as Joe moved in on the left, Ned moved out on the right and as Joe stooped to pick up a 'kill', Ned was there covering off the back wall. And they obviously enjoyed it all as did the followers who flocked to see them.

The past was to be recalled in that same year of 1938 by the victory of two Liscarroll players, one of whom, Tim Twohill was a nephew of the Tim who as Irish champion had played Egan for the world title. They proved themselves altogether too good for junior grade causing the Handball Council to reconsider the whole question of permitting senior county players to play as juniors in inter-county matches. After all, Twohill had gone 8 games with Soye for the 1926 senior title when he was but 23 years of age.

A curious feature of the 1939 season was the fact that all the defeated finalists were from Munster. Cork introduced a young player new to competitive handball, Don Keogh of Youghal. He looked slow and he was obviously inexperienced, but he was the player who took the eye of old followers because of his cool judgement of the ball to kill and his crisp, sharp service. One of those who admired his play was J. J. Kelly, who remarked that Keogh had the physique to last a long rubber and the hands to take the strain. He never trained seriously and, while he won two All-Ireland doubles, he had given up the game before he was 30. He was the one Cork player who, to my mind, might have won the hardball singles title – a title Cork has never won.

1940 was the first year in which the restrictions imposed by the Second World War began to be felt in Ireland. Softballs, manufactured in London, were not yet in short supply but travel was becoming difficult because of the petrol shortage. A young Galway soldier, named Michael Walsh, had shown in the previous year's junior final that he knew how to play ball. In that final he beat Jimmy O'Toole of Hospital, county Limerick, a fine two-handed player with endless stamina. Few, however, expected Walsh to make an immediate impression in senior ranks. The impression he made was little short of sensational. He beat Perry by 3 games to 1 in Perry's home court and then beat Joe Hassett with equal ease in the final.

Once again, Kilkenny turned out a ballplayer with all the traditional style and skill of his county. Paddy Molloy took the junior titles in hardball and softball and would certainly have won senior honours had he not emigrated. Cork put out an equally attractive young player, Willie Walsh of Midleton, who was to be a great favourite with handball followers for the next fifteen years. His first All-Ireland was won with Richie Ward of Mallow.

For all the brilliance of its players, Kilkenny rarely had a doubles pair to match the Hassetts. The county had many outstanding players, but to form an effective combination more than individual talents were needed. Perhaps the best was that of Dunne and Gilmartin in softball and Dalton and Gilmartin in hardball. Dalton may have been the easier to play with as he never played a lot of singles as had Dunne. Paddy Dalton, together with his father and brother, each named Michael, represented the best type of sportsman. Living almost under the shadow of St Canice's Church, they had only to cross the street or walk up a hundred yards to find the Delaneys, John McGrath, Paddy or Jack Phelan ready to get the togs and make up a game. Ballplaying and hurling were their games and they served the black and amber loyally in both codes. To them a game of ball 'abroad at the Inch' was far more important than any medal or trophy.

The 1942 season saw the departure of Gilmartin for England but not before he had taken another singles title, this time defeating Austin Clarke of

Dublin who was to figure in so many splendid matches in the following years. It also marked the only victory of his club, the Metropolitan, in the senior doubles. The winning pair, Austin and his brother John, illustrated what is needed in a good partnership. John usually played on the right but when his brother needed a 'rest' he moved into the left corner where he was equally effective and his heavy service took much of the sting out of the opposition.

The softball doubles was unusual in that two Tipperary brothers met two Sligo brothers in that final and, in addition, one of the Sligo pair was also playing in the Tipperary county championships. The Tipperary pair, Anthony and Con Collins from Ballina, were better balanced than Joe and Stephen Bergin, who lost by 3 games to 1. Con was later to win a number of Army titles when serving with the defence forces.

The full impact of the war was felt in 1943 and in the two following years when no softball championships were held. Hardball, however, continued to be played and a younger brother of J. J. Gilmartin, Jimmy, won both junior titles. Not very many followers outside Kilkenny saw him play but he had the same arm action as that of his better-known brother and the same speed around the court. Both he and Jimmy O'Connell, also of Talbot's Inch Club, had the distinction of winning All-Ireland handball honours and also playing in goal for their county in hurling. Jimmy Gilmartin's partner was Jimmy O'Brien who, as County and Provincial Chairman and later Central Council President, gave lifelong service to the IAHA.

It can be said that all the senior winners of 1943 were high-grade players. To Dowling of Ballymore-Eustace went the honour of winning titles under both the IAHU and the IAHA. He may have looked slow but that great swing of his held a deadly service and he did not hesitate to 'kill' any fair ball no matter how far from the front wall he found himself. Another title-holder of that year was Billy Walsh of Cork whose style was very different: he went for 'kills' at all angles, left and right, and always at full pace. That was what made his game so different: he flung himself at all manner of shots, returned impossible balls, and crushed players better than himself by his very aggressiveness. It may have been because we saw a lot of one another when growing up but I always enjoyed seeing him play, whether in victory or defeat.

The organisation of the game was rather haphazard in some counties, particularly in the larger ones where clubs might be almost 100 miles from one another. And, because of the difficulty in arranging fixtures, players were sometimes chosen to represent their county on reputation alone. In 1943 two rival partnerships arrived in Midleton, county Cork, to meet the Cork pair, Walsh and Ronayne in the Munster senior final: O'Gorman and Hassett of Nenagh and Gorman and Ormonde of Ballyporeen each claimed to represent Tipperary. No meeting could possibly be convened to decide the issue and there was nothing for it but to ask them to play the decider before playing Cork. This they did and after a 5-game rubber, O'Gorman and Hassett won through. Obviously, they were a tired pair when they faced the Corkmen, who ran out winners of the 7-game rubber.

So far I have scarcely mentioned Wexford, and yet there are probably more ballcourts to be found there than in any other county. In 1937 a great-hearted New Ross player, Willie Delaney, had won a junior All-Ireland when playing with the Ballyanne Club. Older players will remember the series of matches between himself and his partner, Mickey Fortune, against Joe Rossiter and Frank Sutherland in the Kilmannon Tournament. Delaney was killed at Anzio during the Second World War and it was a new generation from two old ballplaying families, the Murphys and the Lyngs, who revived the game in the 1950s. There was keen competition from the other end of the county where Charlie Drumgoole of Bridgetown, trained by his cousin Bill Drumgoole and by Aldridge, was beating all comers. While still young, Charlie gave up the game and a fine player was lost to handball.

By 1946, with the war at an end and restrictions on petrol being gradually lifted, the handball authorities resumed the softball championships. Two Dublin brothers, George and Larry Rowe, who learned the game in the open courts beside Green Street Courthouse, won their first senior title. Their play typified all that was best in doubles play; George was rock-steady under the heaviest pressure and Larry could put away most high balls with a short-arm cut to the right corner. They played their best ball in the court at the Depot, a court that is an excellent test of a player. Because of the sloping walls and short side-gallery, a player could not just belt the ball back to his opponent. He had to be able to finish it if he was to win.

At that time, few noticed the play of John Ryan who, with Aidan Power, had won a minor doubles for Wexford in 1946. Nor, indeed, did he attract much attention when he won a junior title a year later. But, for the next 12 years until a leg injury forced him to retire, he beat almost everyone whom he wanted to beat in tournament and championship. He was ever to remain the complete amateur who played a game of ball in his own way, at his own pace, never too concerned with titles or championships.

The hardball singles final of 1947 received extensive press coverage as it marked Gilmartin's tenth appearance in the final, his tenth victory and his last singles match. An extract from the *Irish Times* report (written by P. D. Mehigan, one of the best sports journalists of his time) will convey some idea of the stature of Gilmartin at that time:

Gilmartin, who has many championships behind him, trained assiduously for the final, and from the first service, he issued services of lightning pace, mostly low down into the left-hand corner or at the angle of the wall. When Gilmartin swung his tosses to the other side they were equally severe, and, of the four twenty-ones, three-quarter of the aces were from service. We had come to believe that the Kilkenny man was past his best, but his poise and balance, his perfect placing and deadly killing with either hand, even off the back wall, but, beyond all, his consistent lightning service, makes one who has seen many champions play, believe that he is, perhaps, the greatest all-round handball champion

Austin Clarke of Dublin in action.

The Clarke brothers, John and Austin (Dublin) 1942.

Army Handball Club, Curragh 1954.
Front Row: M. Redmond, M. Kelly, P. Dignam, J. Kehoe, J. Donovan.
Back Row: C. White, J. Parle, R. Maher, T. McElligott.

Left: C. J. Harwood, Joe Bergin, Larry Row and T. J. McElligott, 1951.

Right: IAHA, All-Ireland Handball Congress, 1944, showing the President, P. Murphy (Cork) seated 3rd left, and the Secretary, M. O'Neill (Wexford) seated 2nd left.

of all.

Gilmartin's career was all the more remarkable when it is recalled that he met with two serious accidents during his playing days. In 1938 he was working on the building of the new Savoy Cinema in Parliament Street, Kilkenny. He fell from the scaffolding breaking his collar-bone and damaging the muscles of his left shoulder. It was this accident which caused the deafness in his left ear and which explained why he would sometimes in the course of a match come up to the backwall to ask for the score. Spectators may have thought that he was questioning the accuracy of the marker but that was never Gilmartin's style. In any case, he was usually sufficiently far in front not to have to worry too much.

Some five years later, while working in England, the lorry he was driving collided with another while going over a hump-backed bridge on a night of dense fog. Both drivers were injured and Gilmartin suffered a broken neck and severe injuries to his spine. After several months in hospital he was discharged and returned to Ireland. Many more months were to elapse before he could even walk without discomfort. When he was able to walk he usually went out the Freshford Road to the 'Inch' and one day he was persuaded to go in to make up a four. He had always been a most intelligent judge of ballplaying and ballplayers, and he reckoned that he had lost much of his hitting power, and some of his speed but that judgement and reflexes were unimpaired.

Through the months of spring and summer in 1944, he continued to play with, however, little expectation of reaching match-play fitness. When Kilkenny selectors sat down to choose their representatives, he was chosen for the senior singles and doubles (there were no softball championships that year). And, when September came, the black and amber of Kilkenny was again triumphant and the name of Gilmartin reappeared in the records.

The last years of the forties were marked by the Rowe-Bergin rivalry. Three times in five years Larry Rowe won the singles and on the other two occasions Bergin was successful. Three times in five years Bergin and his partner (Jackie Sweeney in two finals and Jimmy O'Rourke in one) won the doubles and in the other two years the Rowes were successful.

Bergin was a master of doubles play and he was often heard to say that O'Rourke was the best partner he ever had. Galleries were packed whenever Rowe and Bergin clashed and their many meetings did much to popularise the game. Tournament secretaries matched them when it was possible and, despite all the rivalry of those years, the players remained fast friends.

The 'fifties opened with newcomers to the honours list in all grades. Maher and O'Brien from the Curragh Training Camp took three of four All-Army titles and then went on to win two All-Ireland junior titles. Mick O'Brien had begun playing with Stephen Ryan in the old ballcourt on the Bansha Road outside Tipperary Town, while Dick Maher had come in as a partner for Mick Desmond in the Kildare championships. In the same year (1950), a former Army officer, Gerry Moran from Mayo, won the senior title with Austin Clarke. Moran was naturally good at all games, with quick reflexes and tremendous confidence. He seemed always in command of the occasion, going for winning shots even when far behind. Clarke had few better partners.

Another newcomer to the highest honours was Bobbie Grattan who took the hardball singles. Like all the Ballymore players, Grattan relied a great deal on service. Indeed, it used be said of one of them, O'Rourke, that you could tell above in the village when he was serving, so tremendous was the impact of ball on wall. Grattan may not have been quite so severe but in the 1950 final he seemed to be well beaten by Walsh who led him 3 games to nil when he suddenly switched his service to the right. Within minutes the match had changed and Walsh, unable to stand up to the tossing, retired beaten.

Nothing showed more clearly Gilmartin's ability to assess a situation, whether in the ballcourt or outside, than his decision to retire in 1950. He had returned to Ireland during the previous winter and in the first match of the season showed much of his old form. He partnered Dunne to success in softball doubles, won an easy victory with Dalton over the 1949 champions, Grattan and Bolger, and then beat Ryan on scores: 21-10, 21-12, 21-8, 21-10. Then, when he seemed set for a further run of success, he notified the Kilkenny County Secretary who, as it happened, was his brother, that he was giving up all championship handball. As a full-time driver for an oil company, he found training difficult and he had no wish to be selected for his county on his reputation of other years.

Joe Hassett did something completely different. In 1951, after an absence of 13 years, he returned to the game to earn an even greater reputation. In the 'thirties he was known only as a softball player. Now, in the 'fifties, at an age when many players would have retired, he won honours in both softball and hardball. His partner was a young Tralee lad, Jimmy O'Brien, a player with all the courage and determination of his native county.

When, in the month of April 1952, the Ulster Handball Council met for the first time, the result of a 'census' of ballcourts in the province was presented to the meeting. There were about 30 ballcourts but some of these were on private property and at least one, at Drumaroad, county Down, was no more than 'the corner of a house'. The full list was Lurgan, Poyntzpass, Mobane, Derrynoose, Armagh, Pomeroy, Loughmacrory, Aughnacloy, Ballyshannon, Bundoran, Ballybofey, Glenties, Letterkenny, Killygordon, Loughanure, Gweedore, Magherafelt, Ballyronan, Derry, Moneymore, Derrylin, Garrison, Irvinestown, Enniskillen, Belfast, Bawn, Ashburton, Clones, Clara, Arva, Kingscourt, Kilnaleck, Rathfriland and Ballyconnell.

By 1979 this number had trebled and Belfast could boast of having the first publicly owned ballcourt in the country at the Leisure Centre in Andersonstown. Most of these new ballcourts were built with grants from the Sports Council for Northern Ireland and from local Community Associations.

The year 1952 marked the recognition of John Ryan as the player with the best claim to be considered as successor to Gilmartin. There were other players, outstanding in either hardball or softball, but none the equal of Ryan in both. He was never very given to training but he did have the natural swing of a great player and he effortlessly mastered all aspects of play for singles as well as doubles. He was fortunate that another Wexford club, Trinity, provided him with an ideal partner in John Doyle. How often, indeed, have I not heard it argued that it was Doyle and not Ryan who really brought about the defeat of Hassett and O'Brien in that tremendous final of 1952. Level scores were called six times in the 7th and final game before they reached 20-all. Wexford won by the odd ace and the scores in that memorable match are worth recording:

Wexford – 16, 21, 18, 21, 21, 20, 21.
Kerry –   21, 18, 21, 11, 9, 21, 20.

Those who believe that Doyle was the player of the day point to the fact that while Ryan took two-thirds of the play and 'killed' superbly, Doyle bore the full weight of service from both Hassett and O'Brien for the entire rubber.

1953 might, I think, be considered Cork's year of glory. Two players, Billie Walsh and Mick Griffin, playing together for the first time, won out in doubles and then Griffin went on to take the singles. Griffin was something of a mystery to handball followers as he lived from childhood in Tipperary, learned his ballplaying from Larry Rowe in Dublin and then declared for his native Cork. He played ball in a somewhat unorthodox manner, taking the ball very close to the body and cutting rather than swinging even when serving. Walsh, ever the most courageous of players, disdained all shots except the direct 'kill'. Even when far out the court, his shout of 'Leave it, Roney' or 'Leave it, Dinkie' (names for two of his earliest partners) meant that, given the chance, he was going to blaze for the butt of the wall.

Yet, good as they were, they were lucky to beat Ryan and Doyle in the final at the Horse and Jockey. It happened this way: the score was 2-1 in games in favour of Cork when, in the 4th game, Ryan serving at 19 was set to 'kill' when Griffin deliberately 'covered' the ball. Ryan made no effort to play it and looked at the referee (incidentally, a Wexford man) for judgement. To everyone's surprise, the referee gave 'hand-out' and Cork got home by two aces.

Two events which occurred during the 1953 season focused attention on minor competitions. While championships for the under-18s had been organised as far back as 1938, they had attracted only a limited entry and had even met with a certain amount of parental opposition. On the other hand, the colleges' competitions for the same age group had achieved a wide measure of popularity. These had originated in competitions promoted by the Students' Mission Crusade in which the diocesan colleges took part for trophies presented by Cardinal MacRory in Ulster, Archbishop Byrne in Leinster, Bishop Gilmartin in Connacht and Bishop Harty in Munster. However, no effort seems to have been made to match the provincial winners until the 'fifties when the All-Ireland colleges' championships were introduced.

Many young players who, because of parental choice, attended schools and colleges where hurling and football were not played, were debarred from these championships. The Handball Council decided to seek clarification of the position of boys anxious to play handball but who attended schools where rugby only was played. The matter was raised on the General Secretary's Report to the 1953 Congress of the GAA. The question of whether such boys could take part in the GAA-sponsored colleges' championships was discussed by the delegates and then referred to the incoming Central Council. At its first meeting after Congress, the matter was again discussed and the President, Vincent O'Donoghue, made a proposal to the effect that where any school or college had 15 bona fide GAA players, it is eligible to affiliate a club or take part in colleges' competitions. An amendment to refuse such affiliations except where the school played hurling and football as well, was defeated only on the casting vote of the President. It can, I think, be said that handball opened the door that led in 1971 to the deletion of the notorious 'foreign games' rule from the *Official Guide* of the GAA.

The other event worthy of mention was the first appearance, at the age of 11, of Joe Clery of Tinahely, county Wicklow, in the minor singles championship. He played in the doubles against Laois and, though on the losing side, he showed the promise that made him the best ever player in that grade where, in 1959, he won three All-Ireland titles in one season. Oddly enough, 10 years were to go by before he won a senior title. Two Wicklow officials, who had always accompanied him in the days of his boyhood triumphs, were again with him when he won the senior doubles with Paddy Lee of Arklow in 1966: they were Dick Arnold of Bray and Willie Pollard of Tinahely, two enthusiasts who organised the game in a county where courts are widely scattered.

The season of 1953 was to end on a nostalgic note when in November of that year four players entered the Talbot's Inch court to play in what was to be for each of them his last competitive game of ball. The occasion was the Silver Jubilee of the club and the four players had, between them, won almost 50 senior All-Ireland titles. Perry, Gilmartin, Rowe and Dunne were stylists in different ways and the match was made memorable by moments when each revealed some of the skills that had made their names known in every province in Ireland.

A SELECTION OF HANDBALL PROGRAMMES AND POSTERS APPEAR ON THE FOLLOWING PAGES

Comhairle Liathroid-laimhe na h-Eireann

PROGRAMME

FOR

August 27th, 1950,

At Talbot's Inch, Kilkenny,

ON THE OCCASION OF THE

ALL-IRELAND

SENIOR HARDBALL FINAL

FOR

PERPETUAL CHALLENGE CUP

2.45 p.m.—JUNIOR HARDBALL FINAL
CORK (J. O'HANLON) v. KILDARE (Sgt. M. OBRIEN)
Referee—P. DALTON, Kilkenny.
3.45 p.m.—SENIOR HARDBALL FINAL
CORK (W. WALSH) v. KILDARE (R. GRATTAN)
Referee—J.J. GILMARTIN, Kilkenny.

PROGRAMME,   -   :   ONE PENNY

Senior All-Ireland Doubles Final
CLOGH—SEPTEMBER 10th

THE PLAYERS

R. GRATTAN (Ballymore-Eustace). Aged 22. Comes from one of the great centres of the game. Came into prominence in 1946 when he won an All-Ireland Junior title and following up this victory with a Senior title in 1949. His trainers include the 1925 and 1943 All-Ireland winners—W. Aldridge and M. Dowling.

W. WALSH (Middleton). Aged 29. Played in the first Minor All-Ireland Championship in 1938 and won his first handball title—a junior one—just ten years ago. Came again with Dan Keogh to beat all-comers in 1943 and 1944.

M. O'BRIEN (Army). Aged 35. Born in Tipperary town and has played All-Ireland football as well as handball. Most popular player in the ball-courts of Kildare where he has won many All-Army titles.

J. OHANLON (Kilworth). Aged 27. Comes from the country which gave the Twohills, Dan Roche and Joe O'Leary to the game. Chairman of the Cork Handball Board.

Junior All-Ireland Doubles Final
DEPOT, SEPT. 3rd, 10.45 a.m.

Comhairle Liathroid-laimhe na h-Eireann

PROGRAMME

FOR

Sunday, October 1st, 1950,

AT

Depot Court, Phoenix Park,

ON THE OCCASION OF THE

ALL-IRELAND

SENIOR DOUBLES FINAL

2.30 p.m.—JUNIOR SINGLES FINAL
DUBLIN (M. GRIFFIN) v. CORK (T. MAHER)
3.30 p.m.—SENIOR DOUBLES FINAL
DUBLIN (L. & G. ROWE)
v.
TIPPERARY (J. BERGIN & J. SWEENEY)
Referee—Dr. C. J. HARWOOD.

PROGRAMME,   -   -   ONE PENNY

THE PLAYERS

L. ROWE (St. Michan's). Aged 36. Back in 1936 won the Dublin junior Single Title. In 1938 he won his first All-Ireland, a junior one, and since 1946 he has won an All-Ireland Senior Title each year and he means to maintain this record.

G. ROWE (St. Michan's). Aged 40. It was in the Dublin Hardball Championship of 1935 that George first won a senior title. In the years between he has won Dublin, Leinster and All-Ireland Softball Championships.

J. BERGIN (Nenagh). Aged 32. Made his debut in 1937 when he won Junior All-Ireland honours. Ten years later he won senior honours for Sligo. Is now trying to equal the record of D. Brennan, P. Perry, J. Dunne, and J. J. Gilmartin in winning both Singles and Doubles in one year.

J. SWEENEY (Nenagh). Aged 26. The only player to win All-Ireland Minor honours in successive years. Had experience of the game in America before teaming-up with Bergin to win the Senior Doubles of 1949.

M. GRIFFIN (Civil Service). Aged 23. This Tipperary-born player gained his early experience with the St. Mary's Club, Clonmel, and is expected to gain Dublin's second Junior Title.

T. MAHER (Army). Aged 29. Learned his handball at Ballyaune, New Ross, where Delaney, the junior Champion of 1937, was his first coach.

● COME TO RECEPTION AT FOUR COURTS HOTEL ●
AFTER MATCH (7/6)

ComAiᚱᒪe ᒪiAᚈᚱóiᴅ-ᒪáiᵯe
nA hÉiᚱeAnn

ᚈ-OscAiᒪᚈ nA Cúiᚱᚈe

i bᴘáiᚱc An CᚱócAiᵹ

ᴅiA ᴅoᵯnAiᵹ 2-5-'54.

Cᒪáᚱ An ᒪAé.

11.15 a.m. An oscAiᒪᚈ oiᚏiᵹiúiᒪ.

ᵯ. U. Ó ᴅonncAᴅA, UAcᚈAᚱán C.ᒪ.

11.30 a.m. cᒪuiᴄe beiᚱᚈe óᵹánAᴄ

S. Ó Cᒪéiᚱiᵹ (Ciᒪᒪ ᵯAnnᚈáin)

v.

ᚈ. ᴅe ᚏᚱéins (Áᚈ CᒪiAᚈ).

11.45 a.m. cᒪuiᴄe ceAᚈᚱAin sinnseAᚱ

S. Ó ᚱiAin (ᒪoᴄ ᵹCAᚱᵯAin) ⁊ U. Scoᚱᒪóᵹ (CAbán)

v.

S. Ó hAiᵯiᚱᵹin (ᚈ. ᚋᚱAnn) ⁊ ᒪ. Ó ᚱuAiᴅ (Áᚈ CᒪiAᚈ).

Comhairle Liathroid-laimhe na h-Eireann.

Cluichi Ceannais
ag an
Faithche i gContae Ui bhFhailghe

An 26adh la Lughnasa, 1951.

2.30 p.m.
Ciarrai v. Lughbhaidh
Cluiche Beirte (Mionur).

3.15 p.m.
Ciarrai v. Cill Choinnigh
Cluiche Aonair (Soisear).

4 p.m.
Ath Cliath v. Tiobraid Arann
Cluiche Aonair (Sinnsear).

CLAR - - - DHA PHINGHINN

T. COMMANE, of Tralee, has won three Munster titles, and feels that the time has come to move into senior ranks. Time will tell.

THE SENIORS.

L. ROWE, of Dublin, can make the game look very easy when the ball runs for him and he is in form. There are times when he is not in form. Hence the difficulty of forecasting the result of to-day's game.

J. BERGIN, of Tipperary, may make the task of the official " forecaster " easier if he is fit to last the strenuous rubber. He is anxious to win his fifth successive All-Ireland medal.

THE MEN OF FAHY.

The men of this "corner of a parish" have done what Ministers of State talk of yet never do. They have added to the wealth of the nation. A corner of rural Ireland is the richer for their work. And their work was done independently without State aid and therein lies its worth.

G. A. A.

HANDBALL

AT TALBOT'S INCH COVERED COURT

KILKENNY

On SUNDAY, 4th MAY. 1941

County Representation Finals

J. O'BRIEN & P. MURPHY

Intermediate County Champions---Doubles, 1940 and 1941

VERSUS

J. GILMARTIN & M. BREEN

Junior County Champions, 1941

TIME. 2.30 RUBBER. 3 GAMES OUT OF 5

T. McELLIGOTT

Intermediate Champion, 1941

VERSUS

DANNY BRENNAN

Junior County Champion, 1941. Former Holder of All-Ireland Titles.

TIME. 3.30. RUBBER. 3 GAMES OUT OF 5

ADMISSION - 6d.

KILKENNY PEOPLE LTD.

A poster from 1941.

FOCAL BROLLAIGH

CAD as don liathróid-láimhe? Cathain a tosuíodh ar í d'imirt annso in Éirinn? Ceisteanna iad siud nach bhfuil freagraí deimhne le fáil ortha, go bhfios don scríbhneoir ach go h-áirithe. Deirtear gur san t-sean-Ghreig Phagánaigh a h-imríodh liathróid i gcoinnibh falla aon chéad uair. Go dtí an la ata inniú ann ta Pelota, cluiche naisiúnta na Spáinne, beagnach ar aon dul leu ar liathróid-láimhe féin, ach amháin an liathróid a bheith níos mó toirt slótair inntí—agus níos truíme, agus gan ach trí fallaí a bheith san bpáimtir .i. ceann tosaigh, ceann ar cúl agus ceann ar an dtaoibh chlé. Bíonn an tarbh dhéas, mar a mbíonn an lucht feachana báilíche, ar oscailt.

Ta gach deallramh ann, mar sin, gurb' iad na ean Cheiltigh a thainíg a chur fútha in Éirinn on Spáinn, de réir lucht léinn, a thug an cluiche ársa seo leo. Pé scéal e, ta sé thar a bheith cinnte go bhfuil se ag cine Gaedheal mar chluiche leis na ceadta fada bliain. Ní go dtí tríocha éigin bliain o shoin, áfach, nuair a ghlac Cumann Lúith-Chleas Gaedheal fen a chúmiree e a d-imeadh éagruíocht ceart ar an gclúiche agus ar lucht a h-imeartha. Deineadh na rialacha do leagadh amach go h-oifigiúil agus comórtaisí séasmúlacha conndae agus idir-chonndae a bhunú.

O shoin i leith ta fás agus foirbeart iontach tagaidhe ar liathróid-láimhe. Ta súim an ghna-phobail inntí ag meadú in aghaidh na bliana agus pinntiúr nua 'a dtogail i gcuig airdibh na h-Éireann chun freastal ar éileamh na n-imritheoir. Buidheachas le Dia gur mar sin ata, mar níl a sharú le fáil mar chluiche shláint'úil, fhearúil. Ní haon dóchin e au fear a bhaineann an buadh amach do féin ins na Craobh-Chluíchí Naisiúnta, agus n.lair a léightfear amach annso i dtaobh na nguíomhartha gaile is gaisce ata deanta ag a mbuill caithfear a admháil go bhfuil fíor-chuis mhaoidhite ag muintir Chumann Talbot's Inch agus fíor-shuis áthais acu i gceiliúbhradh bunn an Chumainn fiche cúig bliain o sho'n.

WHEN in the early 1920's the Bramnigans, Davins, Daltons, Hogans and others began to play ball at a gable-end in Talbot's Inch little did they realise that almost on the same spot, within a few short years would rise a court that was destined to become Ireland's premier Handball Arena.

The "alley" had of course neither side or back walls, and its floor consisted of the public road, marked with chalk, with corners far enough away to enable the handballers to see the oncoming traffic or to dodge patrolling policemen who might be inclined to remember the laws against games on the highway.

Interest in the game gradually grew and eventually in 1923 players, spectators and friends to the original total of 21, agreed to subscribe a shilling a year each as a nucleus of a building fund. It was at this critical period in the club's development that the project gained the interest and patronage of the late Helen, Countess of Desart, great-hearted lady who, on the Kilkenny-Freshford road, at the edge of her Noreside Demesne, established the beautiful Model Village of Talbot's Inch, and created employment by starting a farm, a craft-shop, woodworks, Woollen Mills and other industries. She gave her workers and tenants the beautifully named hospital at Aut Even—Áit Aoibhinn—and tried to prevent sickness by encouraging plenty of open-air exercise.

Becoming aware of the efforts of her workers to build a suitable court for handball, she readily co-operated the infant, impoverished club members of which included farmers as well as tradesmen, boys as well as experts at the code. She gave them a lease of the site at a reasonable rent, and soon the tedious work of erection commenced. Workers, tradesmen, farmers, women and children, nurses and patients, rich and poor, handballers and those too old for such active sport—all in Talbot's Inch and the neighbourhood readily took some part in the building of the court.

Farm carts were given on loan to draw the sand and other materials, a building contractor gave expert advice and supervision free. Tools were borrowed. Scores of men on Summer evenings helped to put down the floor and erect the walls. The womenfolk organised dances and card drives to collect funds for the purchase of cement and wood, and eventually a three-walled structure arose, which was the original Talbot's Inch Court.

The game gained such ground in the few subsequent years that the supporters and committee decided to improve the existing court, and roof it if possible—a gigantic task. Ready help, however, was again forthcoming from their President, the Countess, who advanced a loan, interest free, of £900. She insisted on helping to supply electric light, club rooms, dressing pavilion, shower baths and other amenities, to make Talbot's Inch easily the best handball court in the country and one of the few covered against the elements.

It was a happy and glorious day for her, for the club officials and members who had pioneered the project, and indeed for all Gaels in Kilkenny when in 1928 the President of the Irish Free State Executive Government, Dail Deputy Liam Cosgrave, took time off from Government duties to travel from Dublin to declare the court officially opened. To-day Talbot's Inch remains the best equipped, the best known and boasts the finest record of any club in Ireland.

The club had to wait for years for its first success—although Kilkenny handballers from the famous City Club were then of course well-known throughout the country.

Jim Lucas had the honour of bringing the first of many titles to Talbot's Inch, when in 1932 he defeated Paddy Bell of Meath, in the Senior Handball Singles Final. The club never looked back, and for the next eleven years without a break, figured prominently in the lists of title winners.

The titles won by the club in the years 1932 to 1943 totalled 34, as follows:—1932, one; 1933, two; 1934, five; 1935, one; 1936, two; 1937, two; 1938, four; 1939, four; 1940, five; 1941, five; 1942, one; 1943, two.

The club drew a blank in 1944 but came back again with two titles in 1945, four in '46 and three in '47. With some of the stars reaching the veteran stage and with the retirement of some of the big names in the club Gilmartin, Cullen, Dunne, Dalton and Jordan, from competitive handball the club hit a lean patch, and the next, and last to date, successes were in 1951, when two titles were annexed.

With a total of 45 titles, 28 of them senior, over a 25 year period, Talbot's Inch has a record of which any club could be proud, a record that justifies in itself the celebrations in which you are taking part to-day.

An acknowledgment of the generous and unselfish help given by so many to the club in its 25 years of existence would fill a book of itself, but mention must be made of the Kilkenny Co. Board G.A.A., whose timely help in the 30's tided the club over a major financial crisis, and whose continued interest and co-operation has been magnificent over the years in many ways. Of the multitude of players, officials, members and supporters who have never failed us, and of the present committee who this year saw a great ambition realised, the re-installation of floodlighting in the court.

With such a tradition and with such a court, it is certain that the future of handball is safe in the Marble City.

From the Talbot's Inch handball Club Silver Jubilee programme.

HANDBALL CHALLENGE

BRIDGETOWN v. BALLYANNE

Under the G.A.A. Rules,

AT BALLYANNE,

On Sunday June 6th, 1937,

F. O'Neill & Partner, Bridgetown   V.   Culleton & Fitzgerald, Ballyanne

Best 3 out of 5 Games, 21 aces.   Soft Ball.

W. Drumgoold & Partner, Bridgetown, v.

W. Delaney and Fortune, Ballyanne,

Best 3 out of 5 games, 21 aces.   Soft Ball.

C. Drumgoold and D. Gott, Bridgetown, v.

McElligot and Murphy, Ballyanne.

Best 3 out of 5 games, 31 aces.   Soft ball.

FIRST GAME STARTS SHARP AT 2.30, new time.

Admission   -   6d.

CULLEN AND SONS. Printers, New Ross.

A selection of posters from the 1930s-1960.

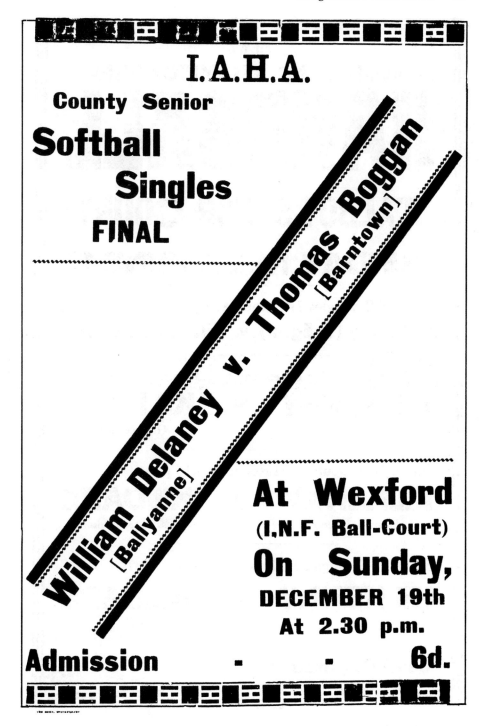

I.A.H.A.

County Senior

Softball

Singles

FINAL

William Delaney
[Ballyanne]

v.

Thomas Boggan
[Barntown]

At Wexford

(I.N.F. Ball-Court)

On Sunday,

DECEMBER 19th

At 2.30 p.m.

Admission - - 6d.

C. L. C. G.

ALL-IRELAND CHAMPIONSHIPS

HANDBALL

AT

TALBOT'S INCH COURT

ON

SUNDAY NEXT, JUNE 12

Minor S.B. Singles 1st Round at 2 p.m. S.T.

Kilkenny (L. Egan) v. Kildare (S. Boyle)

Juuior S.B. Singles 1st Round at 2.30 p.m.

KILKENNY   v.   KILDARE

(C. Delaney)   (T. J. McElligott)

Junior H.B. Doubles 1st Round at 3.15 p.m.

KILKENNY   v.   KILDARE

(Doherty and Breen)   (Maher and O'Brien)

Senior H.B. Singles 1st Round at 4 p.m.

KILKENNY   v.   KILDARE

(Garda J. McGrath)   (G. Grattan)

Cead Dul Isteach   :   1s.

Kilkenny Journal Ltd.

BIG
HANDBALL
CHALLENGE
BALLYANNE v. BRIDGETOWN

Under the G.A.A. Rules, to be played

AT BRIDGETOWN
ON THURSDAY, MAY 27

McElligott & Murphy, Ballyanne, v.

C. Drumgoold & D. Goff, Bridgetown

Best 2 out of 3 games, 21 aces. Soft ball

W. Delaney & Fortune, Ballyanne, v.

W. Drumgoold & Partner, Bridgetown

Best 3 out of 5 games, 21 aces. Soft ball

Culleton and Fitzgerald, Ballyanne v.

F. O'Neill and Partner, Bridgetown

Best 2 out of 3 games, 21 aces. Soft ball

First game starts sharp at 1-30 p.m., old time

ADMISSION   SIXPENCE

DEVEREUX & CO. PRINTERS, WEXFORD.

Irish Amateur Handball Association

ALL-IRELAND HANDBALL
CHAMPIONSHIPS
AT
BROADFORD
ON
SUNDAY, 16th JUNE, 1940

Junior Hardball Singles
CORK v. LIMERICK

Junior Hardball Doubles
CORK v. LIMERICK

Minor Softball Doubles
CORK v. LIMERICK

Great Softball Singles Challenge

J. KEARY (Limerick Champion) v. T. McELLIGOTT (Cork Champion)

Gala Day Assured.   First Match at 2 p.m. (s.t.)

ADMISSION - - 1/-

SUPPORT A WORTHY CAUSE !

COMHAIRLE LIATHROID-LAIMHE LAIGHEAN

LEINSTER HANDBALL

CHAMPIONSHIPS

AT

DEREEN

CO. LAOIS

SUNDAY, 1ST MAY, 1955

E. Flanagan, Laois v. J. Curran, Kildare

T. Dollard & A. O'Neill, Laois v. J. Curran & J. Byrne, Kildare

S. Rhatigan, Laois v. S. Parle, Kildare

S. Rhatigan & M. Frayne, Laois v. C. White & T. McElligott, Kildare

☞ FIRST MATCH AT 2 P.M. 🎺

ADMISSION   :   :   :   1|-

BRADLEY, PRINTER, NEWBRIDGE   PHONE 126.

BALLYPOREEN HANDBALL CLUB

HANDBALL

AT BALLYPOREEN
ON
SUNDAY, SEPT. 18
1960

ARMY (SELECTED)
V.
BALLYPOREEN (SELECTED)

The Army Team will include: Austin Clarke [Dublin], Christy Delaney [Kilkenny], Sgt. Maher, Sgt. Geary, Cpl. M. Hore, T. McElligott.

First Match at 2.15 (S.T.)

ADMISSION   -   -   -   -   2/-

DANCE in Parochial Hall Same Night

Music by JOE FARRELL & HIS BAND

Dancing 9 to 1 (S.T.)   ADMISSION, 3/6

E. M. Casey, Printer, Clonmel

SAINT JOSEPH'S RECTORY
1415 HOWARD STREET
SAN FRANCISCO, CALIFORNIA

March 5, 1950

Dear Mr. Mc Elligott:

Thanks for your interesting and very well composed letter. It was generous for Father Tom Jones to give me a mention under the famous hand-ball players of past years. I knew Father Jones in his peerless prime when I went to school in Tralee where Father Tom Jones and Jim Fitzgerald and many other famous players were born and trained and played, and conquered all others. May I say here at first that in my opinion and experience. Father Tom Jones had no equal in hard hand-ball. Jim Fitzgerald was in the opinion of some, his "ex sequo". It is true I never met or saw Casey, who in his day supposedly had no equal. He was fading as Father Jones and Jim Fitzgerald were coming in the spotlight of their prime. If my memory serves me accurate, Casey and Jim Dunn of Brooklyn, N.Y. played Jones and "Fitz", in the City of Cork, an exhibition game which Jones and Fitz won easily. However, it was the case of two very good old champions against two very good young champions, and age will be served. Jim Fitzgerald, as I presume you know, became the champion of the world, having defeated every good man in Ireland, and then came to America.

At that time there were not many really great players in this country. However, a match was made between Fitz and Lawlor and played in Chicago (as I think) and Fitzgerald was defeated. It was, however, in the midst of summer and Fitz got completely overcome by the heat. Mr. James Dunn, who at the time of the match was away from Brooklyn, and on his return immediately challenged Lawlor for a return match which was arranged. Fitzgerald just crushed Lawlor. There was no one left to play Fitzgerald and after many years without a contest came to San Francisco, where we had magnificent courts and pretty good players. I was here then and was not the good player Fitzgerald became in a few years. However, I was proud to show off Jim Fitzgerald. I challenged the two champion players we had to meet him. They were very good, but dear Jim easily defeated them and yet I could see he was not the strong and powerful player I once knew in the old court in Gas Terrace, Tralee.

At this time Mike Egan, a powerful man, six feet tall, weighing about two hundred pounds, was attracting the notice of the experts in Brooklyn. Mr. Dunn, ever eager to keep the great Irish hard handball game alive, asked Egan for the championship of the world against his friend Jim Fitzgerald. He brought Egan to San Francisco. The match was played in the Olympic Club and Egan won easily. I worked with Jim Fitzgerald for weeks before

(2)

the match and could not understand how slow he had become and how weak and how weary. He would turn to me and say "Father, you are stronger than I am". I knew it and I felt sick, however, in the actual match with Egan he acted like a champion. He ran Egan off his feet but had not any strength. Egan was, as I said, a powerful man. Dear Jimmy (at this time weighed about 140 pounds) was quite pale and sick looking. After the match, which was fifteen games (seven the first Sunday afternoon, and eight the next Sunday) it was apparent Fitz was in very poor condition.

Here, I regret to register that the consequences of this last championship game of hard handball were painful in the extreme. Egan had a hemorrhage in a few days. We staged a charity game to raise money and take him to a tubercular hospital near New York, where he remained a broken man. More bitterly and sorrowfully still is the fact that in ten weeks or so I buried Jim Fitzgerald from a sudden and deadly attack of tuberculosis, galloping consumption. It then became evident to us all that Jim Fitzgerald was a victim of tuberculosis in the advanced stage when he played Egan for the world's championship. His remains now rest in the warm hillsides of sunny California, at the foot of Mt. Tamalpias, nestling by the Bay of the marvelous Golden Gate.

I wish to go on record that that last match between these two great champions of Irish hard handball saw the actual 'finis' of Irish handball championship of the world. Not another exponent has arisen, not another place, and I include Ireland, presents or encourages the great old game of Irish handball. There is in the United States at present, and has been since that last famous handball championship (mostly in private athletic clubs and among real athletes) much handball, but the ball used is a small rather hard rubber ball which compares with real Irish handball called "the alley cracker" as a dog-skin football compares to a modern rugby or gaelic football. Do try to revive the old hard-ball game. It belongs to Ireland. You can get samples of the ball and have them made. I regret I gave away only recently, some I had, the exact ones that Egan and Fitz used in their match.

You speak of Oliver Drew. Oliver had a great reputation. His friends who knew him and think like you, told me that he was an unconquerable champion. I have since learned he was an expert exponent of the game; the poetry of motion in the court; ambidexterous in a most expressive way. However, I think it ended there. I asked Mike Egan, who knew him

SAINT JOSEPH'S RECTORY
1415 HOWARD STREET
SAN FRANCISCO, CALIFORNIA

(3)

well, and played him regularly, what he thought of him. Egan praised him highly but remarked he was "more stuck on his appearance than the will to win". Egan tried hard to get Drew to play him in an open challenge but could never induce him to enter a court for a real fight. In my opinion, Egan would have crushed him, as would Jim Fitzgerald, even in his fading hours. And my dear friend, Tom Jones would lick them all.

I am deeply grateful in the evening of my life that you have given me the honor of urging me to dream again of the glorious days gone forever.

Very sincerely yours,

Richard Collins

P.S.: Please convey to Father Tom Jones my everlasting admiration and affection. - R.C.

As to Bowles & Kelly &c all good men second class as was I and that's that.

Thanks

A letter from Mgr. Richard Collins of San Fransisco in 1950 reflecting the spirit and enthusiasm that surrounded the game and its players.

Chapter 7

The Modern Game 1954-1970

In most seasons some new player is seen whose play gives promise of greatness – a promise not always fulfilled. Kilkenny had long considered Christy 'Scotcher' Delaney to be such a player and in 1954 he justified the hopes of his county. Partnering him in the doubles was Jasper Dunne who, 20 years before, had won his first All-Ireland title. Each had a very distinctive style: Delaney served high to the left and seemed to push rather than hit the return on the volley to the left-hand corner; Dunne had a deceptively slow but stylish stroke and was by far the most graceful player I have ever seen.

During that summer, hundreds of voluntary workers turned up at the Horse and Jockey in Tipperary each evening to help rebuild the ballcourt – then fifty years old. In 1904 Dick O'Keeffe had given the field on which to build it and it was his two sons, John Joe and Bill, who were now drawing gravel to the site. Dick O'Dwyer had played in the first game ever played at the 'Jockey' and it was his namesake, Father Michael O'Dwyer, who performed the re-opening ceremony. The club became the first in Ireland to have a glass backwall installed – the panels being made in the nearby factory at Templemore.

As a commentary on the Ireland of the time, it is of interest that following Paddy Molloy who went to England, three of the four winners of titles in 1955 emigrated to Canada. Jimmy Lyng was from Wexford (Ballyanne) as were Redmond and Parle, but as the last-named were stationed on the Curragh, it was in the white singlet of Kildare that they won their titles.

The junior doubles in softball went to a tiny club called Ullard situated in the hills above Graiguenamanagh. Two farmers living near the ballcourt, Tim Ryan and Syl Lennon, had played together since their schooldays and, in 1955, they represented Kilkenny in the All-Ireland final. Michael Doherty was the hope of the Mayo pair who opposed them, and I will always rate him the best player who never won the title. He trained in the Foxford court which overlooks the river Moy and had the advantage of playing with Paddy Clarke and Robin Foy of Cong who were the Connacht senior champions for the best part of 10 years. He played beautiful shots, shots that few seniors would attempt, and he usually brought them off. Ryan and Lennon were, however, the better balanced pair and they won an exciting final.

Ever since the softball, manufactured by the firm of William Warne of London, was introduced into this country some time before the First World War, they were marketed by the firm of Elvery and Co. At that time the price of a hardball at Elvery's shop in O'Connell Street, Dublin, was one shilling, and the best softball cost two shillings and threepence. The 'cock standard' was the first softball and then came what was called the 'Congress medal' ball. Oddly enough, the firm of Slazenger who make handballs for the Australian market never seem to have considered 'breaking in' on the Irish market. In 1955 the Irish Dunlop Company was approached with a view to making handballs and after many months of negotiations, the firm decided to undertake the manufacture of an Irish softball. The General Manager, Mr R. C. Flanagan, proved to be extremely helpful and an extract from a letter of his reveals the extent of the debt that handballers owe the firm: 'We have gone into the manufacture of handballs more as a gesture to the national game than commercially; the business will undoubtedly be unprofitable' (letter to author dated 7 February 1955).

When the exhaustive tests that preceded the actual manufacture of the balls were completed, the specifications of the new ball were then laid down as follows:

(1) The ball shall have a plain surface.
(2) The ball shall be not less than 2.125" diameter and not more than 2.250" diameter.
(3) The ball shall be not less than 58 grammes and not more than 62 grammes in weight.
(4) The ball shall have a bound of not less than 70" and not more than 74" when dropped a length of 100" on to a smooth concrete base.
(5) The ball is to have a deformation of not more than .175 of an inch and less than .210 of an inch when subjected to a load of 12lb.
(6) In all tests for deformation the machine designed by Percy Hubert Stevens patented in Great Britain under Patent No. 230250 is to be employed.

The great difference between it and previous softballs was that the new ball consisted of two halves rather than four quarters and that it was inflated by a pellet of gas enclosed within the two shells. This method was expected to prolong the life of a ball and ensure more uniformity.

One of the courts in which the new ball was tested was The Horse and Jockey where, as we have seen, a glass backwall had been fitted. The glass proved almost entirely satisfactory for the softball but, not altogether unexpectedly, the hardball did not rebound off the glass as well as off the usual stone or concrete backwall. Champions from the four provinces were brought to the Tipperary court to test both the wall and the ball. The ball passed all its tests and the wall was 'passed' for all softball matches, and for hardball when both sides agreed to it.

No one interested in the efforts made to preserve hardball should forget the generosity of Bart O'Brien when he was chairman of Milford (county Carlow) Tanneries. Back in 1953 he was approached by the Handball Council and made aware of the difficulties in procuring skin for the making of the hardball. He had set aside six pony skins which after having them specially stretched and tanned he presented to the Council.

The handballs in use at the moment with their place of manufacture are of three types: the Vulli (France), the Spalding (US) and the Merco-Seamco (Australia). The Vulli retails at £1 and is largely used by juveniles in 60 x 30 courts. The Spalding is generally sold in a container of two which costs £5. It is used in the 40 x 20 courts. The Merco-Seamco, better known as 'the family ball', costs 80p and is used extensively in 40 x 20 courts by juveniles and women.

A new name came into the handball headlines in 1956 when Joe Maher of the St Mary's Club, Drogheda, won his first of many Irish titles – the junior singles in hardball and softball. Five years were to pass before he again won an All-Ireland and then it was in senior hardball. He owed much of his success to his strength and seeming endless reserves of stamina to which, with experience, he added a high degree of skill and subtlety in play. He was popular in the ballcourts because he played it fair and hard at all times. A match of his against Des Dillon, then representing Dublin, will indicate his staying power. They were meeting in the Leinster final of 1957 and they entered the court at 2 o'clock. Dillon quickly won the first three games and reached 5-0 in the 4th game of the 7-game rubber when Maher came at him. He beat him to an astonishing 6 in that game, won the next two and took the last on the score of 21-7. By that time it was 4.40 pm.

Two young Kerry players, Paddy Downey and Jimmy O'Brien, were then beginning to win a new reputation for Tralee, the birthplace of Tom Jones and James Fitzgerald. They were the most unspectacular of players but they could and did fight every ace of every game. They had learned a lot from Joe Hassett who was then living in Tralee and I like to think that from him, too, they learned how to enjoy a game of ball no matter what the result. They were successful in six All-Ireland finals and their displays won many friends for them far outside their native Kerry. I always felt that even in retirement they would give any pair a close game because, above all else, when they walked into a ballcourt they were in there to win.

All the minor honours of 1956 went, for the first time ever, to one county. Johnny Murray and Waterford-born Mick Sullivan were partners in the doubles while Murray took the singles – all in the colours of Kilkenny. I think that Murray could have come from no county other than Kilkenny. His style was that of many of the great players, particularly Gilmartin, whom he resembled in many ways. In Mick Sullivan he had the earnest, whole-hearted partner his play demanded, unselfish but reliable.

The achievements of the minors in 1956 were equalled by that of two seniors in 1957. It was the high point in the career of two great players, Ryan and Doyle, who were on their day unbeatable. I saw them lose as well as win but I hold to the opinion that when in determined mood, no pair could withstand their combination of power and accuracy. Ryan went to the States on invitation in the autumn of 1957 but, as his visit was unofficial, no record was kept of his games though he did meet such well-known players as Ginty and Hyde at the New York Athletic Club court.

Limerick had long been out of the handball limelight but when the county did come back, it did so in style. McGarry and Mullins won minor, junior and senior honours all within two years – which when you read it again more closely means that they had the very unusual distinction of taking All-Ireland honours at two levels in one year! McGarry was also a hurler of quality, and his talent for sport led him to play first-class soccer and rugby in later years. He never developed a fluent style which meant that he had to work hard for his scores but, such was his energy, that he could play a full 5-game rubber of handball and line out in a hurling match later on the same day.

Unlike Limerick, Tipperary had never been long out of the handball limelight, and in 1958 the county was represented by three newcomers to the All-Ireland scene. John Ryan of the Turnpike and Tom Doheny and Mick Shanahan of 'the Commons' won the junior hardball titles. 'The Commons' was made famous by the great hardball player, Boggan Healy, who on one occasion after beating Franklin in his own court cycled to Laffan's Bridge and there beat Neary of Waterford.

Handball has always had its characters. Fintan Confrey of Drogheda was one. He was so good that if you watched him on one of his good days you were unlikely ever to forget him. His backwall play was even better than that of John Ryan and he had an amazing variety of strokes both overhead and underhand. I saw him playing in the Delvin Tournament and in no two matches was he the same. That was his weakness: he was utterly unpredictable, utterly uncertain, but to those who saw him in his triumphs as a senior, he will be remembered as good enough to rank with the greatest of softball players. Anyone who could beat John Ryan, as he did, on his way to the All-Ireland final of 1959, deserves a place in any record of the game. They were level at 19 for three hands each in the last game before Confrey won by two aces. He then beat Downey in the final and retained the title the following year. He emigrated to Canada and some years later was drowned when swimming in the Bahamas.

In 1959 John Ryan met with a very serious accident when working on the farm of Frank Drumgoole in Bridgetown. An overall he wore while harvesting became entangled in the power drive of a tractor and he was thrown to the ground. The accident ended the career of the great Wexfordman. Never again did he play championship handball.

In all sport, there are years when a certain calm settles over a particular game and its players: colour fades, excitement dies. 1960 was one of these years. The championships ran their course, titles changed hands but nothing very dramatic happened. Yet the strangest scores of any final were those recorded in the senior hardball when Tipperary's John Ryan and Mick Shanahan beat Bobbie Grattan and Robin Winder of Kildare. It did not appear to have been a particularly close final, as Tipperary won by 4 games to 1, but, when you add the scores, you find that each pair scored precisely the same number of aces:

Ryan and Shanahan: 9, 21, 21, 21, 21.

Grattan and Winder: 21, 20, 13, 20, 19.

The Delaneys of Kilkenny were the surprise winners of 1961 as they were considered better at softball than hardball, yet it was the latter title they won. Without belittling their achievement, it must be said that hardball was not attracting new players and, consequently, standards were falling. There was, however, a style and finish about their play that made them attractive to watch.

Of the junior winners of 1962, four of the five went on to win senior championships in the following years. They were McCabe (Monaghan), McGee and Walsh (Mayo), and Hickey (Tipperary). Yet it was the fifth player, Tommy Breedy of Clogheen, county Tipperary, who was the cleverest of them all, especially inside the short line. Long before Clogheen had a ballcourt, Tommy Breedy was cycling the six miles to play in the Ballyporeen court. There in the company of Dermot Wall and John Donohue, he played hardball and softball. A local harness-maker named Begley used to make a beautiful hardball, and though he told me one time that he rarely measured them for weight or size, they were always almost exactly within the specifications.

The year 1963 was a sad one for all who had watched handball over the previous 20 years. Austin Clarke, six times holder of the highest honour in the game, the senior hardball singles, died at the age of 46. He had won fifty Leinster and Dublin senior championships and was, in turn, secretary, treasurer, and chairman of his club (Metropolitan) and his county. His father had partnered the great John Lawlor and as well as his brother, John, with whom he won the 1942 All-Ireland, his brothers Frank and Jim had played the game at the highest level. His action was perfect and he would, I think, have preferred to miss a shot rather than play one lacking in style. And he had style. He might occasionally hit the floor or a side wall when serving but he did it with such elegance and grace that even were you his partner, you would forgive him.

When he was playing all was action, all was movement. He seemed incapable of rest and even when waiting his turn to serve, he was constantly moving, panther-like, backwards and forwards. But he could, as they say, put away a ball off right hand or left and few players could equal the crashing power of his service. He had some great duels with Grattan of Kildare and Ryan of Wexford; Grattan he could usually master but Ryan was too well armoured at all points and Clarke never faced him with confidence. Still, it is worth noting that of the ten titles that were decided in the years following Gilmartin's retirement, Clarke won five, Ryan four and Grattan one.

The senior championship of 1963 did no more than emphasise the superiority of Maher in singles and Downey and O'Brien in doubles. However, in junior ranks, two brothers from Kingscourt, county Cavan, Louis and Joe Gilmore, took that county's first doubles title. Cavan had only once before

From an autographed copy of the Souvenir Programme (price 6d.) for the Talbot's Inch Handball Club Silver Jubilee Commemoration tournament, 13 December 1953, Talbot's Inch, County Kilkenny.

P. J. Kennedy, P. Downey, Canon W. J. Carroll, J. O'Brien and Jack Killackey. The 1955 and 1956 Senior Softball Double Champions - Kerry.

From left: J. Dunne, P. Perry, C. Delaney, J. Ryan, L. Rowe and J. J. Gilmartin on the occasion of the Talbot's Inch Commemoration Tournament, 1953 (See Tournament Programme also illustrated here).

won any All-Ireland handball title and that was when Victor Sherlock took the 1949 singles. He beat a very good player, Mick Fahy, one of the Larry Rowe type of ballplayers, in the final. Sherlock was a fine athlete whose achievements on the football field made him better known in the team game than in handball.

Handball seems to differ from most other sports in that for long periods there may be no interest in it in a particular place. Then, with the coming of even one good player, all is changed. Sligo had its great players in Hunt, O'Rourke, the McTernans and the Bergins, but, for some 20 years, there seemed to be no one to replace them. It was in 1963 that followers began to notice the play of Marcus Henry of Sligo who won a minor title and repeated the performance a year later. He then went up to the junior grade where he won out. Then when he was beginning to win local tournaments open to senior players, he gave up the game. Sligo-born US champion, Tom Ginty, thought him the equal of Henry Hyde who had won the New York pennant in the same year.

As in Sligo, so, too, in Wexford many years went by before the Ballyanne Club produced a player to win the title first won by Willie Delaney in 1936. Then came Jimmy Lyng who won out in Ireland before going to win a Canadian title. His brother, Richie, became the first player ever to win minor, junior and senior All-Irelands. The Murphys, near neighbours of the Lyngs, shared the glory of their triumphs and it was the older members of that family – Paddy and Ned and Nick and Phil – who had helped to build the first court at Ballyanne on the edge of the three counties of Wexford, Kilkenny and Carlow.

No other player has ever achieved quite the same distinction as Paddy Bolingbroke of Castlebar, who in 1964 won his way to two All-Ireland finals in the course of one evening.

He had been losing heavily to Pat Sheerin of Birr, county Offaly, when the hardball semi-final at Ballymote was stopped owing to rain. The unfinished match went on at Croke Park a week later and there, already with a lead of two games, Sheerin ran up a lead of 16-0 in the third game. Then Bolingbroke got going. He caught Sheerin at 16-16 and, never losing his nerve, won that vital game 21-20 and easily won the last two games.

After an interval, the same two players took the court for the softball semi-final. Here again Bolingbroke showed great courage when Sheerin reached 'game-ball' to his 17 in the first game. He put Sheerin out, scored the necessary four aces and went on to win in straight games. Six games of ball without defeat in one evening!

A player came into prominence in 1966 at an age when many players might well have considered retiring from the game. Had Mickey Walsh of Charlestown in county Mayo been born earlier or later, had there been no Second World War and no emigration, then he might have won more titles than anyone ever did. He was playing in what was then a three-wall court when he was 12, he was out of the country for close on 10 years and yet, in 1966, he was the All-Ireland doubles champion with Peadar McGee of Newport. Perhaps the best description of his play is that given by his friend, John Healy of the *Irish Times*: 'He could mark a circle of six inches on the alley floor and then toss a round-the-houses ball to touch all four walls and hop at the end in the circle.' The only other player to do anything like that was Jackie Sweeney of Nenagh who belted any ball that came near him so hard that you did well to follow its flight let alone return it. But he had nothing like Mickey Walsh's skill and accuracy.

The changing pattern of handball was clearly marked in 1967 when the dominance of Leinster and Munster seemed at an end. Of the eight junior and senior titles, four crossed the Shannon and one went north. The senior champion, Seamus McCabe, came from Clones, Monaghan, where he learnt a lot from Gerry Moran who was then a customs and excise officer on the 'border'. He was a natural left-hander who never really mastered right-hand play. In his first All-Ireland final he had the unnerving experience of being a game down and hearing 'Look sharp' called in the 2nd game of a 3-game rubber, but he made up the aces from 12 to 19 and then went on to win 9-21, 21-19, 21-10.

Much more astonishing was the junior final. Mark O'Gara of Roscommon won an All-Ireland in his one and only championship match of the season! The Roscommon selectors, dissatisfied with the player who had won the Connacht championship and the All-Ireland semi-final for the county, chose O'Gara for the final. His opponent, Tom Geoghegan of Kildare, had played four matches to get to the final. The final itself was a dramatic one with O'Gara serving 'Game ball' six times in the 2nd game before winning out. Scores were: O'Gara 9, 21, 21; Geoghegan 21, 20, 18.

In any record of handball, the contribution of one family must not be ignored. When the ballcourt at Tuamgraney, county Clare, was built in 1911 with the help of the MacLysaghts of Raheen Manor, there were Kirbys living in the village. Much later, five Kirby brothers won All-Ireland medals in different grades. Of the five, Pat was outstanding. Irish champion, USA champion, world champion – he won matches in the 40 x 20 courts with the same ease as he won in the 60 x 30 courts. He had the qualities that we have noticed in all the champions. He studied his opponent, he was two-handed, he hit hard, and as he saw no advantage in being a popular loser, he became and remained a popular winner.

Pat Kirby was the only player to have won Irish, American, Canadian and world titles. He has won trophies in distant Vancouver and Toronto, in New York and San Diego, but it is possible that he prizes more than all else the statuette sculpted from Tynagh silver by Edward Delaney and presented to him by the people of Clare.

Of him it may be said that he was above all else a player 'of his time'. Brought up to play in the traditional 60 x 30 court, he adapted his game to suit American conditions. He learnt new shots, practised long hours to correct weaknesses, studied how to exploit any lapse of concentration in his opponent, and taught himself to use even a slender lead to the best psychological advantage.

All a world removed from the punishing 21-game rubbers of an earlier age when men of immense endurance sought to overcome their opponents by the sheer strength and power of their service. Tireless in the court, constantly keeping the pressure on his opponents, often by standing up near the front, confident that he could cut off shots early, he was the complete player. As good as 'Gil'? As good as Perry? My answer is 'Good enough to be compared to them.'

Pat Kirby has seen a great deal of life and has done much for the game both here and abroad, and when he looks back on a quarter of a century of triumphs he may well recall as his happiest moment the night in 1970 when the road was lighted with sods of burning turf to welcome back the world title holder to his home in Tuamgraney.

U.S. Players on visit here, 1957. Charles J. O'Connell, New York, Chairman National Handball Committee, U.S.A. Tom Ginty (Sligo born), Senior Singles Handball Champion USA in 1953. Henry Hyde (Cork born), Junior Singles and Doubles Champion, U.S.A. in 1956. Canon W. J. Carroll.

Pat McGarry and Martin Mullins. All-Ireland Senior Softball Champions 1958 and 1959 - Limerick.

The World Champion - Pat Kirby of Tuam-graney, Co. Clare. The sweetest striker in the game to-day, he is a player who has studied the game and mastered the skills, taking American, Canadian, Irish and World titles. Endlessly resourceful, he has power and precision in shots off either hand.

Chapter 8

The Seventies, and Beyond

As the game continued to spread, the need for new competitions was felt and in 1965 the National League was introduced. This gave counties an opportunity of drawing on their handball strength regardless of age and grade. Wexford county was the first to win a League title with a team made up of the brothers Lyng from Ballyanne, King of Wexford and Dempsey of Barntown.

In addition to increasing the number and variety of competitions, it was about this time also that the range of ballcourts was altered and extended. For the first time an alternative to the traditional 60 x 30 court was made available and players were quick to see the advantages of the new 40 x 20 court. It was attractive to the beginner who saw in it a smaller area in which to practise his skills and it was equally attractive to the older and more experienced players who found themselves able to control the play without having to run too much. Evidence of this came in 1982 when Mick Hore, after playing with his native Wexford and Dublin for well over 30 years, won the over-50 singles title – his first All-Ireland ever! These courts became immediately popular and it is possible that in the years to come the 60 x 30 courts will be looked on as are the round towers today.

The smaller court also helped to make the game popular among women. Women's handball may be said to have begun in 1959 when John Clarke organised a one-day event played with a small sponge ball at the Beggar's Bush Alley. The winner was Rosemary Brady of Broadstone and from that humble beginning the game developed until today there are three provincial councils to promote the game among women. Mavis O'Toole, who learned the game in Green Street, was the outstanding player throughout the 'seventies and held the Irish Ladies title from 1970 to 1981.

The most striking feature of Ladies' Handball is the speed with which the game has developed. As recently as 1974 there were few competitors and fewer competitions for those who wished to challenge the right of men to monopolise the ballcourts. Yet by 1982 so widespread was the interest that Provincial Councils were set up and the game has since been on the same basis

Mavis O'Toole in action. January 1983.

Susan Carey in action. January 1983.

as that for men.

The game owes much to the style and skill of Mavis O'Toole, mentioned above, whose displays encouraged many girls to follow her example. No man has ever gone near equalling her record of twelve senior titles in succession. And, as if this was not enough, she also won eight doubles titles in partnership with Elizabeth Nichol.

International competitions for men, which brought players from many countries to Ireland, prompted the women to enter teams for the United States championships. A team of five players (Mavis O'Toole, Mary Twomey, Elizabeth Nichol, Bridín Ní Mhaolagáin and Anne Barnes) travelled to Tucson, Arizona, in 1980 and since then Irish women have played in all the major venues in the States.

A significant feature of Ladies' Handball is that it is confined to no county or province but is spread throughout the country. The four Mythen sisters from the Coolgreaney Club in Wexford have their counterpart in clubs all over Ireland and there are minor players like Nora Brooks of Roscommon to challenge the distinction of Elizabeth Hall of Oldtown who was playing senior handball when still under 18!

All in all, the game is popular, the players enthusiastic and the future bright for the women who in increasing numbers are thronging to the ballcourts.

In 1968 the Tailteann championship were begun and these ranged from a competition for the under-14s to one for the over-40s. (There are some who deplore the use of the word 'Tailteann' for what is a commercially sponsored championship and believe that the historic title should be reserved for the Games traditionally held at intervals of four years.) The Tailteann handball matches became immediately popular and enabled many young players to come to the forefront.

An inter-club championships was added in 1969 and Sligo had the distinction of taking the first trophies with a team from Ballymote (M. Henry, D. Walsh, J. Mattimoe, E. Hannon.)

The growing strength of the game in Ulster was reflected in the winning of the 1970 senior doubles by Seamus and Louis Gilmore of Monaghan and of the junior singles by Mick Conway of Tyrone. The Handball Council showed itself ready to adapt to changing conditions when it was decided to run the National League on regional rather than provincial lines and to introduce a Second Division.

While all these developments were going on, the building of 40 x 20 courts outstripped that of the older 60 x 30 courts. This involved the Handball Council in a further extension of its championships and in 1972 the Shannon Club made history when it won the Team-of-Four title for courts of each dimension. The team was Pat, John and Tom Kirby together with Michael Hogan.

In the same year Richie Lyng of Wexford, who for almost ten years had few equals in the country, was replaced as softball champion by his fellow-countyman, Pat Murphy from Taghmon. Peadar McGee of Mayo took the

M. Walsh in action against U.S.A. in 40 x 20 Doubles.

At the first national Coaching Course, Gormanstown, August 1975.

Pat Fanning, G.A.A. President, speaking at the official opening of the World Championships in 1970.

At the opening night of the World Championships, 1970, were:
President Eamon De Valera, An Taoiseach Jack Lynch and the Australian Ambassador, Mr. Honnor
(Front Row, 2nd, 3rd and 5th).

Contestants for the first Top Ace (RTE) Championship 1973.
Front Row: M. McEllistrim, P. Kirby, S. Buggy, P. Clarke.
Back Row: R. Lyng, P. Murphy, J. Maher, P. McGee, S. McCabe.

Jubilee dinner of the Irish Handball Council 1974.

senior hardball title to the west with a display which marked him as a very strong, two-handed player. He was to hold it until 1978 during which time he represented his country with distinction both here and in the States.

With handball attracting more and more young people, it was inevitable that the television cameras would focus on a game that is ideally suited to the medium. The playing area is small, the flight of the ball easily followed and the movements of the players stand out clearly against the walls of the court. Pat Murphy confirmed his top ranking by winning the first-ever television tournament in 1973. As the network of competitions continued to spread, the universities and other third-level colleges were now involved in special leagues and championships.

A significant change, and one which I think did much to add variety to the championship, was the introduction of the Open Draw system. This came about in 1974 and it did give a greater number of players more chance of getting through to the later stages of the senior championship. Under the old system some excellent players never wore the county colours because the way was barred by the county champion, while many county champions never qualified for the All-Ireland series since only provincial champions were eligible. The example of the handballers may encourage hurlers and footballers to give the Open Draw a trial!

All in all, the 'seventies was an exciting decade and while there have been many gains there has been some loss. The gains are in the increasing number of clubs, the increasing number of courts and the increasing number of competitions – in all the areas where a new generation of players is coming to play the old game in a new way. To control this flood of entrants to the courts, and to hold their interest in the game, is the task of one man. Joe Lynch has been in charge of this nation-wide Handball Council for 30 years. He has never waited for changes to be forced upon him, rather, has he made the changes and in doing so moved handball into the forefront of individual sports.

Of the many achievements to his credit, none is greater than that of securing the affiliation of all 32 counties and by promoting the building of courts spreading the game to areas where it was unknown. All statistics date rapidly and the following list of courts in each county is that compiled in 1982:

Antrim 30	Galway 43	Monaghan 28
Armagh 8	Kerry 16	Offaly 10
Carlow 15	Kildare 17	Roscommon 16
Cavan 17	Kilkenny 28	Sligo 11
Clare 22	Laois -	Tipperary 35
Cork 40	Leitrim 2	Tyrone 10
Derry 8	Limerick 18	Waterford 4
Donegal 15	Longford 4	Westmeath 15
Down 7	Louth 7	Wexford 24
Dublin 39	Mayo 37	Wicklow 8
Fermanagh 6	Meath 19	

Since his own playing days with the St James's Gate Club, Lynch has known all the great figures of the game. He has seen the shift of influence from city to country, from a game for the few to a pastime for the many. He has watched the game come in out of the cold to be played more extensively today in indoor courts than in open courts. Can he now preserve something of the rural background with at least one open court in each county, where on the high walls of a 60 x 30 court the shouts of 'Look sharp', 'Game ball' and 'Game' will long continue to be heard?

There are, today, rewards for the successful ballplayer which were never dreamed of by players of earlier years. A trip to the US and/or nomination as 'Handballer of the Year' (with a special B & I award) are but two of the prizes awaiting title holders. The distinction of being chosen Handballer of the Year was first won by Pat Kirby in 1975. He also won it in the two following years. Then in 1978 Dick Lyng of a well-known Ballyanne family was chosen for the award. Pat McGarry (1979), Liam Bourke of Kilkenny (1980) and Tony Ryan of Tipperary (1981) all won it before Dick Lyng was again adjudged the winner in 1982. A sports scholarship has also been awarded to a handballer, John Duggan of Clare, who will study at University College, Galway, where he will be coached by Frank Mullen of the National Coaching Council.

The present-day game has certain very definite merits. The introduction of the 40 x 20 American-type court, by placing less emphasis on stamina, has increased the need for players to develop new skills. It also allows players to continue playing at an age when, formerly, they would have retired. Above all, it has given the sport an international dimension, enabling Irish players to compete with those from other countries in matches under the same rules and in very similar conditions. 'New skills' means that the coaching of players has come to assume an importance it never had enjoyed and an excellent booklet has been produced by Frank Mullen for the Handball Council. The international coach, Pete Tyson, has also come to Ireland on invitation and has conducted a number of courses throughout the country.

Having brought the game so far and so fast, there may now be need for a period in which to take stock of what has been done before planning a further advance. Is the financial umbrella that the GAA provides still necessary? Can the game develop more freely without such powerful partners as hurling and football? The triple alliance worked only because handballers accepted the subordinate role allotted them and loyally abided by rules laid down by what is called 'the parent body'.

The attitude of the GAA has always been one of goodwill marked by a certain condescension. Such goodwill is not a constant quality: it may fluctuate both with the Presidency and with the composition of the Central Council. Only a Handball Council independent of all outside influence can establish links with other sporting organisations and promote the game at a truly international level.

Immediate benefits would follow: freedom for handballers to regulate their affairs without reference to County Committees and Provincial Councils

ob Wilson of Canada playing during the World Championship 1970.

action during the 1970 World Championship. V. Yanar of Mexico and B. Leach of Canada.

which, for the most part, have little interest in the game; freedom to establish links with other organisations, such as Squash Ireland Ltd, for the interchange of facilities and to organise a new range of competitions and attract new players. The GAA has always suffered from a certain paralysing fear of significant changes and this has not been without its effect on handball. The game should be given an injection of 'excitement' by basing the World Series on the home court of the champion – whether he comes from Ballydehob or Boston.

A game intended for individuals can never exist happily within the framework of an organisation established to legislate for and promote team games. Handball is a game that has made progress under the GAA but it is now at a crossroads when, with international competition attracting increasing attention, young players may be drawn to sports having their own controlling body. The GAA is a great but complex organisation in which handball seems at times to be much less important than hurling and football. This will always be so and the question to be answered is whether handball can develop into a world game while remaining in the shadow of the present controlling body.

Freedom to develop the game, its rules and governing structure, without reference to the body controlling hurling and football is necessary. Separation is not hostile to the spirit of the GAA. Rather is it to be considered as an inevitable step in the advance of the non-team game and, at the same time, a measure of the great strength of the parent body. It will give liberty to the Handball Council to negotiate an entirely new set of relationships with other sporting organisations, not least of which is the International Olympic Committee.

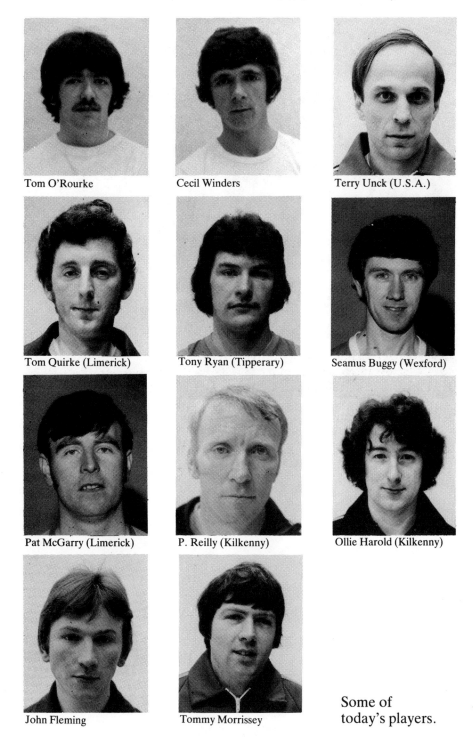

Tom O'Rourke

Cecil Winders

Terry Unck (U.S.A.)

Tom Quirke (Limerick)

Tony Ryan (Tipperary)

Seamus Buggy (Wexford)

Pat McGarry (Limerick)

P. Reilly (Kilkenny)

Ollie Harold (Kilkenny)

John Fleming

Tommy Morrissey

Some of
today's players.

Cyril Kemp, Sports Sales Manager, Irish Dunlop, chatting to leading Irish handballers Joe Maher (2nd left) and Murty McEllistrim (right) and RTE Sports Director Michael O'Carroll about the newly coloured red handballs specially developed for RTE's Top Ace Handball Series. January 1973.

Chapter 9

Envoi

We never seem to regret the immediate past as we do that which is more remote. So it is with me when, on looking back, I recall the players and the matches of well over 50 years ago.

Yet the present is far more exciting, more dynamic for anyone now taking up the game. The horizons certainly are wider, the fame to be won far greater and, for all I know, the simple pleasure of having a ball and someone to play with no less real.

We may become misty-eyed when remembering, as I can, the winter's day when we burned newspapers on the floor of what was then an open court at Ballyanne to melt the frost so that we could play. We may regret that no longer does someone present a sheep as first prize in a handball tournament as John Clarke tells me once happened, forgetting that the first prize may now be a return ticket to distant Los Angeles or San Francisco. We may regret the passing of Sastre, the Spaniard, who could strike ball after ball to a ringed circle 3 inches in diameter at the foot of the front wall, forgetting that handball has, in the Mexican Alvarado, a marvellous ballplayer equal in skill to any whom I have seen.

In sheer statistical terms, handball is today light years ahead of the game which in 1924 was divided and torn by dissension. There are now thousands of players where there were hundreds, hundreds of ballcourts where there were scores, and a range of competitions for all ages and for both sexes. Where money for the building of ballcourts often depended on grants for the relief of unemployment (and quite a few were built with such grants), the Handball Council is currently spending £70,000 on the erection of ballcourts. The Annual Report for 1982 mentions that during the past ten years over 110 new courts have been built at a cost in the region of £3 million.

With new ballcourts and more players, there was need for more guidance if the skills of the past were not to be altogether lost, and coaching courses are now a normal feature of the handball year. My one and only 'coaching' lesson was from old 'Ducker' O'Reilly in Cork, who reproved me for brushing out the ballcourt while holding the brush in the right hand when, in order to develop both hands, I should occasionally transfer the brush to the left! For much of the present attention to this aspect of the game, credit may, I think, not unfairly be given to Frank Mullen and Pat Kirby.

In their work they had the full support of the officers of the Handball Council who also encouraged the youth to take up the game. From having no competition other than the minor singles and doubles, a juvenile programme has been developed and hundreds of players from all four provinces now take part in the various under-age championships. In 1951 M. Walsh of Kilkenny became the first Irish juvenile to win a United States handball title. To do so at the age of 14 is no small tribute to the player's skill and the excellence of the coaching he received.

Nor has publicity, without which so little can nowadays be achieved, been ignored. Films of matches are replayed for the benefit of players anxious to correct faults, and television has introduced the game to homes in many of which oral traditions of the game in earlier times still survive.

Another measure for gauging the importance attached to the game is the fact that the Annual Congress is now a two-day affair. Nor is the Annual Report written in long-hand, as it was as late as 1926, when it was read, not circulated, to the delegates present. Even as late as the 'forties the Congress was usually held in Barry's Hotel and the entire business transacted on a Saturday evening between 8 pm and 9.30 pm.

The game has benefited considerably from the regular fixtures between Irish players and the best of those playing with the United States Handball Associations. Travel is now very different from what it was when Lawlor and Casey each spent a week on the sea voyage before completing their home-and-home rubber. The USA players are still supreme in the 40 x 20 courts and even in the 60 x 30 game they have shown that they can defeat the home players.

It may seem strange that in this account of handball, I have made no great effort to establish when first a man hit a ball against a wall. I am not convinced that it would be a useful exercise to do so. Where rubber is most easily obtainable the climate does not favour violent exercise. Without some substance such as rubber, it is not easy to imagine how material of any sort can be got to bounce. There is evidence that by the eighteenth century rubber had been brought to Europe and it was then but a question of time before it would be made use of for some form of relaxation. In its pure form rubber is too heavy and too resistant to be struck by the hand, so small portions came to be used to lend elasticity to various materials that covered it (see Chapter 1).

Given a ball that was small enough and light enough to be thrown or struck, it was inevitable that man would seek some surface against which to throw it. A windowless wall, the gable-end of a house (*pinniúr*, the old Gaelic word for handball, makes clear its origins, i.e. a game played against a gable-end), a conveniently large door, all proved opportunities. The 1782 painting in Monaghan County Museum illustrates what must have been fairly typical of what 'handball' meant for anyone living in the Ireland of 200 years ago. Castles were not, however, to be found everywhere and even when they were, access to them was not exactly open to everyone. So it was that rudimentary ballcourts, with or without side-walls, came to be built in which players matched their skill against one another.

For a people by nature gregarious and sociable, the gable-end of an ale-house proved an opportunity both for sport and good fellowship. As the game developed, lines were drawn to enclose the playing area and as the wing or side-walls were raised, spectators tended to stand at the back of what was called the end-line. Here they had an uninterrupted view of the game and this is the memory that older people will carry with them, of matches played in open courts on summer days by players with shirts tucked inside their trousers and, not infrequently, in bare feet.

For those with a sentimental attachment to old customs and old ways of life, there was a certain patterned tranquillity about a game played in a three-walled court with a line of onlookers to comment on the play and the players. It was a game that prospered in the countryside but seemed to wilt in the air of cities. It may be that it fitted more easily into rural life where the work of field and farm was lightened by the evening game of ball or, as on fair days, after the serious business of buying and selling was at an end, a group would go to the ballcourt there to play endless rubbers for 'sixpence a corner'. And rarely would young lads coming from school pass by the alley without piling their schoolbags by the wall and 'having a dodge' while dinners grew cold as the afternoon shadows lengthened.

Just as it seems more easy to recall the summer days and sunshine, so is it easier to recall the great players who graced the ballcourts in distant days. And, if I appear to make a sharp distinction between the players of the past and those of the present, it is because I believe that such a distinction does indeed exist. No player of the present plays the same gentle, unhurried strokes of Jimmy Kelly or Bill Aldridge. No player of the present glides into position and strikes a ball with the swift deadly precision of J. J. Bowles.

It is said of them, as though it were an offence, that they played for money. They did. They worked during the week when work usually meant a six-day, 48-hour week. They could be said to have supplemented their wages by the small amounts which their skill as ballplayers earned them. They were sometimes scorned for doing so and yet, today, the amateur handballers of Ireland and the professional handballers of the USA participate in the same championships and this is seen to be perfectly reasonble.

It is easy to say that standards in the game have gone down. To my mind, it is not so much the actual standard of play that has declined but the game itself that has changed. The neglect of the hardball game, which dates almost from the foundation of the IAHA, and the support given to softball, has led to the development of what is a very different game. The closed fist, the hand muffled in a glove, the rubber ball, all have combined to present spectators with a game that bears little resemblance to hardball. The accent in present-day sport is on speed; the softball, made of rubber, bounds around the court at a great pace, gives satisfaction to the striker and provides more play. In favouring the big hitter, it has reduced the degree of skill necessary for the placing of a ball and taken from the game as a spectacle.

The truth is that the past rarely yields to the present when standards of performance are called into question. So it is with handball. I was brought up to believe that the only form of handball worth playing was hardball, that the only exponents of hardball worth watching were Corkmen, and that all the Cork players worth watching were dead! Yet I still believe that handball, when well played, is a splendid spectacle; the speed and graceful movements of the players setting it above all other games played with the hand.

Appendix A

The Game Abroad

Despite the fact that the game of handball is played in not dissimilar fashion in a number of countries, it has not been easy to form an international body to promote international matches. The first efforts were made in 1926. The IAHA became a member of the International Amateur Athletic Federation in that year and the Irish Secretary, Sean O'Hanlon, was elected President of the Court Handball Commission. It was decided that as Ireland and America were foremost in playing what was referred to as 'court handball' (to distinguish it from 'field handball'), the IAHA and the American Amateur Union should be asked to come to a decision on one set of rules.

When the Second Congress of the IAAF was held in Berlin in 1930, it was proposed to hold the first official world handball championships at the Los Angeles Olympics of 1932. This was rejected as it was pointed out that the events for the Games of 1932 had been decided in 1928. O'Hanlon, who seems to have been acting almost entirely on his own initiative, resigned from his position as Secretary of the IAHA early in 1932. He also resigned from the IAAF and nothing further was heard of handball as an Olympic event. Even though no international body was formed to govern the game, it has at the same time continued to be widely played.

United States of America

There is little doubt that American handball was born when the Irish began to pour into that country after the famine of 1847. The emigrants settled in Brooklyn, Boston, Jersey City, seldom venturing far into the interior, and so we find that most of the ballcourts were built along the eastern seaboard. They joined the police, the fire service and the river patrols, but they seldom tried to buy land or farms. The story of Michael Cunningham from Roxborough, Ballinrobe, county Mayo, is very typical. He emigrated in 1905 and joined the St Louis Fire Department. He won prizes for his skill in driving the 'six-in-hand' fire engine through the city streets and was made deputy-chief. He played all over the States and as late as 1927 was one of five Irishmen who qualified for the quarter-finals of the National AAU singles championship.

Barney McQuaide from Castleblayney, county Monaghan, Phil Casey from Mountrath, county Laois, and John Egan from Galway – owned ballcourts that they built or had built to their design. McQuaide's ballcourt, which was completed about 1850, stood at the corner of Madison Square and Grand Street, New York. Phil Casey's Court, generally known as '297', was at that number in Degraw Street, Brooklyn. The finest was, perhaps, that of John Egan, a boss plasterer, built by himself at 223 Mercer Street, Jersey City.

The dimensions of Egan's Court show that only in the materials used did it differ greatly from a typical Irish court of that time. It was 60 feet long, 25 feet wide and 30 feet high at the front wall. The front wall was of brick and cement, over 18 inches in thickness. The side walls were of hard wood while the back was also of brick and cement. The floor boards were made of narrow strips of maple.

Irish names predominate in those early days, but gradually native-born Americans began to beat the Irish at their own game. Casey's first matches after he went to the States were against James O'Brien and William O'Byrne of Chicago and, later, against Burke and McGrannagan of Philadelphia. When Lawlor returned to the States in 1888, he was matched with, and defeated, such Irish-born players as Grady and Courtney of Brooklyn and Sullivan of Jersey City. Best-known of all these emigrant handballers was Athy-born James Dunne, who was the great handball promoter of his time. He travelled extensively and visited Ireland regularly to take part in the Cork tournaments of those days. He was the promoter of the Casey – Lawlor match and, twenty-one years later, he promoted the Kelly – Bowles match. Franklin of Cahir was his guest when, in 1913, Dunne matched him with Owen Brady at Kennedy's Court, New York.

It is not difficult to believe that no 'recognised' championships were held in the States until well into the present century. Most courts were either on the east or west coasts and travel between the two was not easy. Owen Brady, for example, though rated No. 1 by Brooklyn YMCA and recognised as the New York champion from 1916 to 1920, is not listed as having ever won the Amateur Athletic Union Hardball championship. These championships, though begun in 1897, failed to attract a nation-wide entry until some twenty years later. The winner of the first of these championships was Mike Egan and, in later years, Joe Heeney (1924), Michael Fitzgibbon (1934) and Tom Ginty (1954) had their names inscribed on the roll of champions.

With the falling off in emigration and the rising popularity of the game among Americans, the Irish influence declined. During the last 50 years all the leading players have been American-born, often, it is true, of European parents. Again, the game has moved away from the saloons of the cities and it is today a popular pastime at universities, YMCA clubs and Sports Centres. With coaches for handball now attached to many of these, the standard of play is rising and it may yet be recognised as an Olympic event. A style of play has developed very different from that of the Irish and the new American-type ballcourt has served to emphasise the difference. In 1950 handball in the USA became a 'television sport' when Bob Kendler built the first glass-walled court, and a year later he founded the United States Handball Association. It gained immensely as a result of his flair for publicity and soon the champions became nationally known figures.

While players from the USA, mostly of Irish parentage, had come here from time to time on holidays, no effort was made to organise matches between the two countries until the middle 'fifties. Harry Hyde, his brother Robert and Tom Ginty, all members of the New York Athletic Club, came in 1957 with Charles O'Connell as their manager. While they did not claim to represent the States in an official capacity their visit was, nevertheless, recognised by the Irish Handball Council which organised all the matches. Each of the visitors had high credentials; Ginty being the American senior champion in 1953 and Henry Hyde a former American junior champion.

The touring players, by choosing to play only with the rubber ball, USA and Irish types, may be said to have ended any hopes that were held of a revival of the old international matches with the hardball. As will be seen from this table of results, the tour brought them to all four provinces.

At Fermoy: J. O'Brien (Kerry) beat T. Ginty (USA) 2-1.
H. Hyde (USA) beat W. Walsh (Cork) 2-1.
R. Hyde and T. Ginty (USA) beat J. O'Brien and W. Walsh 2-1.

At Newport, co. Mayo: E. Connolly and R. Foy (Mayo) beat H. Hyde and T. Ginty 2-0.

At Ballingarry, co. Limerick: H. and R. Hyde (USA) beat E. and L. Hogan (Limerick) 2-0.
H. and R. Hyde (USA) beat M. Mullins and T. McGarry (Limerick) 2-0.

At Croke Park: H. Hyde (USA) beat R. Grattan (Kildare) 2-0.
D. Dillon (Dublin) beat T. Ginty (USA) 2-1.
D. Dillon and R. Grattan and R. Hyde and T. Ginty drew 1-1.

At Wexford: H. Hyde (USA) beat J. Ryan (Wexford) 3-0.
J. Doyle (Wexford) beat T. Ginty (USA) 2-1.
H. and R. Hyde (USA) beat J. Ryan and J. Doyle (Wexford) 2-1.

At Talbot's Inch, Kilkenny: J. Ryan (Wexford) beat H. Hyde (USA) 2-0.
J. Delaney (Kilkenny) beat T. Ginty (USA) 2-0.

At Kingscourt, co. Cavan: J. Maher (Louth) beat R. Hyde (USA) 2-0.
V. Sherlock (Cavan) beat T. Ginty (USA) 2-0.

H. Hyde and T. Ginty (USA) beat V. Sherlock and
F. Confrey (Louth) 2-1.

At Clogh, co. Kilkenny: H. Hyde (USA) beat A. Clarke (Dublin) 2-0.
M. Sullivan (Kilkenny) beat T. Ginty (USA) 2-0.
H. and R. Hyde (USA) beat C. and J. Delaney
(Kilkenny) 2-0.

Before returning they discussed with Irish officials the possibility of an
international competition. This took place in 1964 at the New York Athletic
Club and five countries, including Ireland, participated. The competition took
the form of a round-robin tournament in which each team played the other in
singles and doubles, and the championship was decided by the number of
matches won in singles and doubles. The Irish team of Joe Maher and Des
Dillon never adapted to the conditions and won only one singles and one
doubles. The final result was: 1st United States; 2nd Canada; 3rd Mexico; 4th
Ireland; 5th Australia.

Of the Irish players, a great deal is known of Maher and little of Dillon.
Yet Dillon was, in many ways, the complete athlete who had style and skill and
who, above all, understood the psychology of sport. Anyone who saw him play
the US champion Ginty in 1957 will understand what I mean. In that match he
was faced by a determined opponent who was in the ballcourt to win. As the
match progressed and the exchanges became somewhat ruthless, Dillon showed
how he could gain control of a game by aggressive, attacking methods. He
never revealed anything like his best form in the USA and it is possible that he
was already feeling the effects of the illness from which he died soon after his
return. He played with Clare, Offaly and Dublin, represented Leinster in
hurling and, in his day, had few equals as a midfielder in that game.

Many of those who saw Maher play in the international matches saw in him
a future champion. He had much to learn but he was prepared to listen to
advice and then put that advice into practice. He altered his swing and
adjusted his game to the requirements of the indoor game with its overhand
strokes and 'roof shots'. He went to Canada in 1965 with his eyes on Toronto
and the 1967 championships. He trained hard, won the Canadian title in 1966
and was chosen to represent Canada in the international championships of
1967.

On this occasion Ireland sent a team of three consisting of Liam Molloy
and Des McGovern from Kells, county Meath and Seamus MacCabe from
Clones, county Monaghan. Once again the opposition proved too strong,
Canada (Maher) winning the singles and the USA winning the doubles. All
the matches were played at the West End YMCA court in Toronto.

The USA and Ireland are now very closely linked and in recent years some
of the finest displays of handball have been those given in Ireland by John Sabo
of New Jersey and Naty Alvarado of Mexico who is now playing most of his
handball in the States where he holds the USHA title. There is great confidence

that the young players now reaching maturity here will soon challenge the world's best, and Irish victories in the 1982 USA Junior championships point to the quality of our players.

USA under-15 singles Winner: Eamonn O'Neill (Limerick).
USA under-17 singles Winner: Michael Walsh (Kilkenny).
USA under-19 singles Runner-up: Gerard Coughlan (Clare).

If I were to hazard a guess as to future trends in international competition, I would say that inter-club and inter-city games will become increasingly important. Some ten years ago an Irish team of five met the Olympic Club of San Francisco in a series of matches. The Olympic Club, the oldest in the United States and able to boast of champions back to the time of Mike Egan, won narrowly by six matches to four. It would be a wonderful way of commemorating the 1887 world championship if a Laois club were to play the Brooklyn Handball Club in a home-and-home rubber in 1987.

United Kingdom

The game seems to have been popular in Scotland for close on two hundred years and the *Statistical Account of Scotland*, published in 1789, lists 'Curling, Table the Duck and Handball' among the pastimes of the people.

A three-wall ballcourt built in the late 'twenties stood where the present Miners' Rehabilitation Centre of Uddington, Glasgow, now stands. The two players, Ferguson and Canavan, who played for Scotland in the 1928 Tailteann Games were from Paisley but played their handball mostly in Glasgow. Ferguson returned to Ireland in 1930 with his usual partner, Lachlan McEwan, and they gave Tom O'Keeffe and Ned Fitzgerald a hard match at the Horse and Jockey, losing only on the 6th game.

When Paddy Perry and Martin O'Neill played at Bootle, outside Liverpool in 1935, one of their opponents was Michael Garvey who had also played in Glasgow. Bootle was a one-wall court with lines, as in tennis, marking the area of play. It has since been demolished.

Wales has at least one ballcourt – a most unusual one. In the mining town of Nelson not far north of Cardiff there is a small, three-wall ballcourt. It is believed to have been built by miners, some of them Irish, about 1900. This ballcourt is 'protected' by a local bye-law which states that no vehicles may be parked in or near it. The site was originally given as a Deed of Gift to the townspeople by the Marquis of Mackintosh, once the ground landlord, and it is now maintained by the local Urban Council. Malcolm Jones, who organises the annual tournament, had to arrange referees and markers for an entry of over 80 in 1982. He has no worries about the quality of the handballs to be used as the competitors do not disdain to play with old tennis balls.

John Phillips of Toronto, the 1982 Canadian National Handball Champion.

R. Lyng in action in International Doubles in U.S.A.

This was the scene at Central Park, New York, where exactly thirty years ago
Sheila Maroshick of Brooklyn (wearing white blouse) defeated Florence Abadinsky
in the final of the Greater New York handball championship.

Natividad Alvarado of Mexico, the top handball player in the world.
He holds the U.S.A. singles and doubles titles for both three-wall and four-wall courts (Sports file).

Handball in Spain.

Spain: Spaniards from the Basque provinces play the same game with a similar ball made from sheep or goat skin, woollen thread and elastic. The French have adopted the Spanish form of the game and new courts have recently been built at *Le Quai du Point de Jour in Paris.*

A handball tournament in the three-wall court at Nelson, the mining town in South Wales.

A game in progress at the Fives Court at Kaduna, Northern Nigeria, 1960.

Spain

Ballcourts in Ireland and *pelota* courts in Spain were often built at gable-ends, with this difference, that in the one they were at the gable-end of a public house and in the other at the gable-end of a church. Most Irish seminarians have played handball either at Maynooth or at the many diocesan colleges and so the Irish priest and his Spanish colleague share an interest in the sport. In fact, the last official Spanish handball team to visit Ireland was led by a priest, Father Ramon Laborda. That was in 1932 when their displays at the Depot Court attracted crowds during the Tailteann Games of that year. The names of that group of brilliant Basque ballplayers are well worthy of recall: Manuel Urcelay, José Aramendi, Teodoro Hernandorena, Father Laborda, Dr. Irigaray.

No mention of *pelota* would be complete without mention of Peter Sastre, a native of Santander, who came to Ireland in 1899. He played in Kenny's Court, Dublin, before going to Cork where he stayed in Dominick Street with the O'Herlihy family. He was something of an artist with the ball, capable of playing a variety of trick shots while, at the same time, able to take games off such noted players as Tim Twohill and Billie O'Herlihy. He had with him some Spanish hardballs, all of them of thread covered with sheepskin but differing slightly from the Irish ball in having a heart made of cork. The French novelist Pierre Loti describes such a ball in *Ramuntcho* (1897); *'une petite balle de corde serrée et recouverte en peau de mouton'*.

A pelota player plays a prominent part in *Destiny Bay*, a novel by Donn Byrne published in 1928 in which most of the action takes place in Donegal. An incident in the story tells how the player, Don Frasco by name, came to discover handball and later cause a near riot in the village.

> One of the reasons for the little man's happiness was the discovery of our national game of handball. He strolled over to the Irish village and discovered the court back of the Inniskillen Dragoons, that most notable of rural pubs. He was tremendously excited, and getting some gypsy to translate for him, challenged the local champion for the stake of a barrel of porter. He made the local champion look like a carthorse in the Grand National. When it was told to me I couldn't believe it. Ann Dolly explained to me that the great game of the Basque country was *pelota*.
> 'But don't they play pelota with a basket?'
> 'Real *pelota* is *à mains nues*, "with the hands naked." '
> 'You mean Irish handball,' I told her.

Don Frasco won many matches in the local court before being challenged by Mike Tierney, a Portrush jarvey and jockey.

> The match was billed for the championship of Ulster, and Don Frasco was put down on the card, to explain his lack of English, as Danny Frask the Glenties miracle, the Glenties being a district of Donegal where Erse is the native speech. The match was poor, the Portrush jarvey, after the

first game, standing watching the ball hiss past him with his eyes on his cheek bones. All Donegal seemed to have turned out for the fray. When the contest was over, a big Glenties man pushed his way towards the jockey.

'Dublin and London and New York are prime cities,' he chanted, 'but Glenties is truly magnificent. *Kir do lauv anshin a railt na hooee,* Put your hand there, Star of the North.'''

'No entiendo, senor,' said Don Frasco. And with that the fight began (pp. 279-80).

Africa

Northern Nigeria would appear to be the only part of North Africa where handball is at all widely played. English education officials introduced the game of 'fives' in the 1920s but the Nigerians abandoned that game in favour of a form of handball in which they used tennis balls. They built a number of three-wall courts with, in some of them, projecting pillars presumably to make the game more difficult! A team of four players visited England in 1961 where, in addition to playing Eton College at fives, they played their own game of handball. One of the most enthusiastic players was the then Prime Minister, Sir Ahmadu Bello.

Australia

Irish settlers also brought the game to Australia. The *Chronicles of early Melbourne*, written by 'Garryowen', recorded that Michael Lynch, owner of the Rising Sun Hotel, (burnt down 25 June 1982), Little Bourke Street, built a court opposite the hotel. 'It had walls of brick and flagging with flagged floor and was covered with network. Even at that time the game apparently was a matter of Governmental Regulation. An 1838 Act of the New South Wales Legislative Council (which was then controlled by Melbourne) provided that no publican "have in or about his house ... any ballcourt". So Lynch built his court opposite the hotel.' He cannot have been the only one to see the advantage to an hotelier or publican of having a ballcourt close to his premises, a hotel at Sunbury is called 'The Ball Court Hotel'.

In those early days most courts were either privately or publicly owned but gradually such Catholic teaching orders as the Christian Brothers and the Marist Brothers built courts at their schools until today almost all ballcourts are owned by these religious orders. Most of them are three-wall courts with a playing area of 60 x 38 feet, a 30-foot front wall and side walls at least 12 feet high.

Interstate games were played between Victoria and South Australia half a century ago and some time later New South Wales entered to make it a three-cornered contest. The championships are usually held on a number of days at one central venue. Rules of play are similar to those governing the game in Ireland except that all service is alternately to right and left. The O'Connor Cup and the Foley Cup are competed for at the annual Carnival of

Handball, and there is also a Masters Title open to players of 40 years and over.

Before concluding this short account of Australian handball, there is one name inscribed on its roll of honour which we came across in the early history of the game in Ireland. Back in the early 'twenties Jimmy Kelly and Mick O'Halloran met in their memorable 13-game rubber. In 1927 the same Mick O'Halloran and his partner Willie Brown won the Australian doubles title at Adelaide. The emigrant ships must have brought many an Irish player to Australia and, in successive years, the winners of the singles title bore the not unfamiliar names of McCarthy, Drew, Leahy and O'Hara!

Handball in Australia in the 1930s. The caption was *"Handball for Olympics is Australian Hope:* Enthusiastic handballers are keeping the standard of this indigenous Irish game flying in far-off Australia where it was introduced and fostered over the years mainly by Catholic teaching orders. Most of the handball courts are in the Catholic secondary schools and monasteries and these courts are the venue for pennant, State and National Championship competitions. Young handballers in Australia are today developing a virile, fast and hard-hitting game which makes terrific demands on the fitness and stamina of the players." St. Kilda's, Melbourne. *Australian News Bureau* photo by Neil Murray.

Appendix B

Great Players of the Past

BILL ALDRIDGE   1893 – 1959

I have a feeling that we will never know just how good a player Bill Aldridge was. The difficulty of summing him up lies in his way of life. Handball to him was as much a medium for a gamble as a sport and in the small village courts of Nurney, Moone and Kildoon he took on anyone with a shilling or a sovereign to wager on the game.

He grew up beside the ballcourt in Barrack Street, Athy, and apart from the years spent in the British Army he was playing first-class ball for 20 years. 1925 was, perhaps, his greatest year. He was then in his 'thirties but as his game was never dependent on speed, he beat much younger players without being extended. He beat the great J. J. Bowles in a two-day rubber played in Limerick and Clogh, county Kilkenny, to take his only Irish title and the first Harty Cup. Ten years later I saw him in his last All-Ireland final when at the age of 42 he held Stephen Tormay of Kells to level scores at 3 games all before losing the last game.

He played handball in a way that changed all my ideas of the game. He never seemed to hit hard but rather did he place every ball with deliberate care. He never seemed to make a hurried move but he was seldom out of place for a service or return. Admittedly, he did nothing to make the game easy for his opponent. He was in there to win and the first his opponent often saw of the service was when he swayed his body slightly to let the ball go past him, and by then it was too late!

JOHN J. BOWLES   1879 – 1949

No first-class player ever dominated the scene in quite the same way as Johnny Bowles of Thomondgate, Limerick. He was playing for the Irish title in 1897 and he was still there 30 years later when he won what was to be his last championship, with Stephen Gleeson of Fedamore.

He was old when I met him in 1944 walking across the meadows by the Shannon but he could still pull a boat up the river where he had also known many successes in the colours of Shannon Boat Club.

His first 'ballcourt' was the walls of Walker's Distillery and, later, Frank Quilty's four-wall court in Patrick Street. Good players were plentiful and he had won some local fame as a player before he sent his entry for the Cork Tournament of 1902. This tournament was looked upon as the Irish championship and the Lord Mayor's gold medal with which the winner was presented the equivalent of an All-Ireland trophy. He won the final from Billie O'Herlihy by 6 games to 2 but, within a year, O'Herlihy had his revenge winning a hard rubber by the odd game in nine. He was back again as champion in 1905 when he beat both Twohill and O'Brien and, from then until 1920, Coyne was the only one in Ireland to give him a game.

The defeat that he must have felt most keenly was that by the American champion, Jimmie Kelly, in 1909. Why his backers allowed a contract to be drawn up containing the unusual clause that all services should be to the left-hand side is difficult to see. It may be that the clause was agreed to when it was believed that Dunne (Jnr) would represent the States. The score of 5 games to 2 in Kelly's favour in the first leg of the rubber at Limerick must have been very different if Bowles could have varied his service. As it was, it gave him no chance in New York where Kelly won 3 games and rubber.

The end of his career could scarcely have been more dramatic. In Limerick in September 1920, while armoured cars patrolled the streets outside, Bowles defended for the last time the crown that had been his for so long. He was in the lead at the end of the day, having won 4 games to Morgan Pembroke's 3. But, a fortnight later, the Ballymun Club in North County Dublin hailed its first champion when Pembroke took 5 games in a row.

PHIL CASEY   1841 – 1904

Phil Casey of Shannon Street, Mountrath, must for many reasons be in line for the title of the greatest figure in the game. He was born in 1841, the son of Patrick and Brigid Casey who had four other children. When his father died in 1856 the widow and family emigrated to the USA.

As a boy he had played ball in a three-wall court attached to the Patrician College, Mountrath, where he went to school. Handball was almost unknown in the States and it was some time before he had enough money to build a small court in Douglas Street near Hoyt, New York. In 1875 he moved to Degraw Street, Brooklyn, where he built what later became known as 'Casey's Court'.

Records of the time are imperfect but it is clear that from the day he won the US title from Barney McQuaide (who was born in Swinford) in 1876, he was never defeated in singles competition. More remarkable still, partnered by Judge James Dunne, he won the American two-handed title from O'Brien and Farron in 1871 and, 26 years later, they again won the same title as well as a side bet of 2000 dollars.

Casey filled many positions in the public life of the city and for over a quarter of a century he was an Alderman, on the Independent Democratic ticket, of Brooklyn Council. He was also a member of the Consolidated Stock Exchange of Manhattan from 1890 until the time of his death in 1904. His friend Judge Dunne paid a splendid final tribute to him: 'He was one of the best all-round men that I knew, both personally and as an athlete. He never smoked or chewed and was always exceedingly temperate in his drinking. He began the training of John L. Sullivan for his fight with Corbett and if John had followed his advice he would not have been beaten.'

AUSTIN CLARKE   1918 - 1963

Six times in ten years Austin Clarke received the Harty Cup that marked him as the best player in Ireland. He came from a family where handball was very much part of life. His father was playing ball with the great figures of the game before the close of the last century and he would have taken pride in the glorious shots that his son could play - shots that had style and power and precision.

He was never at his best with the rubber ball. He needed the swift flight of the 'alley-cracker' to match the speed and grace of his own movements where, as in a fast court like Talbot's Inch, he was a delight to watch. He was all restless energy reminding one of John Mackey on the hurling field.

He was first and above all else a Dubliner, in his tendency to regard any match fixed for a venue beyond the edge of Dublin as a day in the jungle and his love of a gargle in the company of his supporters after a match. Training never had much attraction for him and he contended himself with tying the togs to the crossbar of his bicycle after his day's work at Brown, Thomas & Co. and going up to the Depot or across to the Castle to play a few games. He often told me that John Bray and Francie Mulligan were the two who taught him anything he knew of the game. They were all part of the handball fraternity which, together with Paddy Monroe and Mick Fahy, wore the blue of Dublin to many a famous victory.

PADDY COYNE   1886 – 1966

Coyne was one of the last of the professionals to have known tossing from a flagstone near the front wall. He was also one of the last to have made his own hardballs, unusually fast and unusually hard if we are to believe reports of them.

He was a rugged player who relied on his strength and endless endurance to wear down better-equipped opponents. In October 1910 he played Johnny Bowles in Patrick Street, Limerick. At the end of the day he had lost 8 of the 10 games played. A fortnight later, he faced him in the second leg of the rubber at Carlow and won the 9 games he required for the loss of 1. That was for the Irish title which, two years later, he lost to Bowles who won all the 11 games.

He had probably the most splendid collection of championship cups that I ever saw, and among them were the Governey Cup which he won in 1917, the Murphy Cup won in 1912 and the Bergin Cup won in 1919. He believed that a good trainer and a good manager were worth many aces to a player and he was well served by Tom Lawlor of Thomas Street, Carlow, and by M. J. Doyle of the same town. He liked to play the first half of a match in his opponent's court and then, with the money on, come from behind to win. This he did with Paddy Lyons, with Terry O'Reilly, with George Robinson and, once, with J. J. Bowles.

Choice of ball meant a lot to Coyne and in that long rubber with Bowles, the ball used by Coyne is said to have had a rebound of 3'6" on the wooden floor in Carlow, while in Limerick the rebound was no more than 2'3"! One result of this was that the 10 games in Limerick lasted in all for 176 minutes while those in Carlow, where 10 games were also played, lasted no more than 95 minutes.

MICHAEL DOWLING   1914 – 1980

The powerful shoulders and square stance of Dowling indicate a slow-moving player with a heavy service; and his service was heavy though he was deceptively quick in moving to the ball. As a member of his club, Ballymore-Eustace, I saw him play scores of games and no player ever played a 'kill' so perfectly even at a range of over 50 feet from the front wall.

I never saw him strike a softball and, indeed, he may never have done so, but he was playing hardball as a schoolboy against Carlow in 1929. Each afternoon he was down at the ballcourt with his friend, Jimmy Dolan, and it was with Jimmy that he won the Slater Cup and the All-Ireland doubles title of 1937. They played a game rather like that of Bell and Doyle of Kells; the man who took the service staying out while his partner moved up to the short line. They understood one another's play so well that rarely was there need to call.

It was, however, in singles that Dowling showed his real strength. He took the Irish title under Handball Union rules in 1935 after leading Grimes of Meath in an unfinished rubber and beating J. J. Kelly in the final. That was the last year that the Weldon Cup was competed for and it is, I think, fitting that it should rest with Ballymore-Eustace – a club that had such close links with the Weldon family and with Ballymun. Eight years later he won the Irish title again, this time under the rules of the IAHA, beating Austin Clarke in the final.

Dowling holds a record that no one can equal – to have won the senior Irish championship under the two unions – and no player is more worthy of the distinction.

OLIVER DREW   1883 – 1938

Of the two Corkmen who challenged for the world handball title, there is little doubt but that Drew must be considered the greatest. He was still a schoolboy at Presentation College, Cork, when he won the Fermoy Tournament with Billie O'Herlihy in 1900. In the same year they won a purse of sovereigns in a contest with John Lawlor and John Corrigan of Dublin, losing 3 – 7 in Dublin but winning 8 – 0 in Cork. His brothers were tailors in Prince's Street and the family home was at Drew's Ville at the top of Nicholas Hill, Evergreen.

Perhaps he was too young when he came on the handball scene, astonishing older players with his speed and skill. Before he was quite 20 he had sailed on a spring day in 1902 to play Mike Egan for the title of world handball champion. He trained at Tarrant's Court, New Jersey, and the newspaper accounts of his form make strange reading at an interval of almost 70 years: 'The Cork player is no counterfeit. He certainly has all the ability that has been claimed for him, and his playing in yesterday's series was of a sensational character.'

Egan and Drew met on 22 May 1902 for a purse of 250 dollars. The match was something of an anti-climax as Drew won the first leg of the 15-game rubber by 4 games to 3 but refused to finish the match when Egan would not meet his expenses. Reports of the match all praised Drew's play, the Jersey City *Evening Journal* stating that the Irishman treated the spectators to an exhibition of handball such as had never before been seen on American soil.

The two were never again to meet though Drew returned to the States and won the 'International Championship' from Francois Ordozgoili, champion of France and Spain in 1905 and the Championship of America from Dennis Sullivan of Chicago at Kennedy's Court, New York, in 1906.

His handball career leaves several questions unanswered. Was he a great player who never fulfilled his boyhood promise? We will leave the answer to Father Tom Jones, who in a letter written in 1949 spoke of him as 'that wonderful and unbeatable Oliver Drew who was slowing down a little as a handballer when I met him at Casey's Court, Brooklyn, with Fr Devane in June 1905.'

MICK DUNNE   1890 – 1969

Mick Dunne of Goresbridge, County Kilkenny, was one of those players who could keep putting the ball back on the wall for the length of a summer's day. His first representative match was at the age of 23 when he played with Mick Dalton of the Kilkenny City Club against Delaney and Aldridge of Athy.

From that day until 1930, when I saw him in one of his last matches at Timmons's ballcourt in Naas, he played all the great players of his time. He struck me as wonderfully fit for a man of 40 years of age and wonderfully courteous in giving his young opponent, Paddy Reid, every encouragement apart from allowing him win!

Two years earlier, in 1928, he beat five players on successive days during the Tailteann Games. He beat Glynn of Athenry, Hassett (M) of Nenagh, Gleeson of Fedamore, Ormonde of Ballyporeen and Cullotty of Mallow. In doing so, he totalled 20 games for the loss of 1 – a record that takes beating.

Most of his big matches were played in Borris and Goresbridge, but Father Prendergast of St Mullins told me that Dunne was at his best when playing against students in the three-wall court at Knockbeg College. He would play them two at a time, using alternately only his left or right hand.

MICHAEL EGAN   1880 – 1954

Mike Egan was born in Galway but was brought up in Pittsburg, USA. When he was 16 his parents moved to Jersey City where he had an opportunity of playing handball and also doing some boxing. He is said to have trained in the camps of the great heavyweights of the time – Jim Corbett, James J. Jeffries and Bob Fitzsimons.

How good he was as a ballplayer is somewhat difficult to say as the sports writers all speak of his strength rather than his skill. Commissioner John Condon who watched his match with Jim FitzGerald at the Olympic Club, San Francisco, is quoted in ACE as saying, 'Egan simply drove the ball about three feet high on the front wall and every time an opponent got his hands on the ball, it would almost burn his arm off'.

When in 1902 he met the youthful Corkman, Oliver Drew, he seemed to have been unable to counter the clever play of the latter and was being led by the odd game in seven when the match ended. Yet those who saw him when a year later he disposed so easily of Twohill considered him the equal of Lawlor at his best.

In later years he came back more than once to Ireland and Pat MacDonagh met him when he was making up a four for a friendly game at Barna in 1924.

JAMES FITZGERALD   1870 – 1909

James Fitzgerald grew up in Tralee, a town where handball standards had been set by Tom Jones. They were high standards and James Fitzgerald measured up to them so well that the same Tom Jones could say of him 'he was the only one to ever give me a game'.

He was recognised as Irish champion in 1890 (Jones was then a student for the priesthood at Maynooth) but it was not until 1893 that he showed his true greatness. On September 17 of that year he played Billie O'Herlihy of Cork in Kilkenny in a one-day rubber of 13 games of 21 aces for the Irish title. The stake money was £50 and both Cork and Kerry supporters laid substantial bets. He won seven games without reply and retained the title against Nolan the following year at Carlow. In 1895 he added to his growing reputation by defeating John Lawlor and winning the Cork Tournament.

He worked at his trade of coach-builder in Tralee until 1897 when he emigrated to the USA. Phil Casey, after watching him playing in his Brooklyn Court, looked upon him as his successor, and it was for the world title that he was challenged by Michael Egan in 1904.

The match was played at the Olympic Club and Egan won easily. Monsignor Collins, also of Tralee, tells the story of his defeat: 'I worked with Jim Fitzgerald for weeks before the match and could not understand how slow he had become and how weak and how weary. He would turn to me and say, "Father, you are stronger than I am". I knew it and I felt sick.' Fitzgerald retired after the match and died of tuberculosis in June 1909.

JOHN JOE GILMARTIN   1916 - 1980

'The most perfect player since the days of Oliver Drew.' That was the judgement of Paddy 'Carbery' Mehigan, who had seen close on 60 years of first-class handball. It gives you some idea of the player who won every senior title and trophy in the country during his 10 years as champion.

An uncle of his, Joe McNally of Westport, had won the softball title in 1928 and exactly 10 years later Gilmartin won the same title. Even then, at the outset of his career, he looked the complete player, and I never in all the years that followed saw any weakness in his play. Many players had almost equally good hands, many others were as fast in their movements, but none had anything like the same relentless will to win.

From that September day in 1936 when he beat Paddy Bell at Flood's ballcourt in Terenure, he never lost a hardball singles match. He met with two accidents – one in Kilkenny and one in England – that might well have ended his career. He was forced to be a spectator for almost all the season 1943. Yet on the occasion of his last final, in 1947, the *Irish Times* reporter could say of him, 'We had come to believe that the Kilkenny man was past his best, but his poise and balance, his deadly killing with either hand, even off the back wall but, beyond all, his consistent lightning service, makes one who has seen many champions play, believe that he is, perhaps, the greatest all-round handball champion of all.'

One indication of his supremacy may be seen from his record in doubles competition. In five successive years he won the All-Ireland senior title with a different partner each year! Alfie Cullen, Tommy Jordan, Tom Cherry, Paddy Dalton and Jasper Dunne were his partners in those five finals. Each was a ballplayer in the sense that the word is used in Kilkenny by all who frequent Talbot's Inch. Each contributed to the final victory, but 'Gil' it was who organised his rivals' defeat.

He appeared somewhat less formidable in softball but then that game lacks some of the fire and fervour of hardball. His talents were less obvious in the slower game; his lightning reflexes less in evidence. But of one thing I am certain; never again will I sense the excitement that his appearance aroused as he would walk slowly into the court and drive the first ball given him to the butt of the wall.

JIM HUNT   1891 - 1968

Of all the figures who came on the handball stage during a period of 100 years,

Jim Hunt of Moygara, Gurteen, county Sligo, was one of the most interesting. To have played handball when in the RIC (1913) and, later, when in the Free State Army (1923) is at least unusual. But, in addition, he played both as a professional and under GAA rules, won tournaments as far apart as Ballaghadereen and Brooklyn, and was the champion of Connacht in softball and of Munster in hardball in the same year!

There is so much to say of a man which bare statistics will never reveal. His photograph shows him as a strongly built man of above-average height, and his cousin, Paddy Reid, speaks of his long reach and ability to get down to low balls. It is, however, his stamina which make present-day players wonder if he would even have bothered to put on togs to play a 2 out of 3 rubber. In a one-day match at Drumacoo he beat John Deane of Frenchpark by 9 games to 6!

Small wonder that he was in no way distressed when in the IAHU softball final of 1924, Paddy Reid and himself lost the first three games to Moynihan and Brady of Meath before going on to win the next four.

His career ended on a high note when in 1928, to mark the 50th year of Casey's Court in Brooklyn, Peter Bourke and Hunt played two former world champions, Joe Heeney and Jim Kelly.

JOE HEENEY   1897 – 1965

When writing of Joe Heeney all those still living who saw him play at Ballymun just 60 years ago agree that they saw a world-class ballplayer. Yet there are a few in the thinning ranks of those spectators who would wish that he had been matched with the Irish champion of the time, Morgan Pembroke.

Heeney's parents came from Nenagh but he was born in New York where he lived all his life. He joined the New York Athletic Club and while still in his teens won a junior club title. He won his first US title by beating Dublin-born Owen Brady in the 1924 final and was then selected to visit Ireland and take part in the Tailteann Games.

His great friend, Myles O'Donnell from Kilmeena, county Mayo, accompanied him and played with him in the doubles. Heeney quickly adapted himself to the Irish courts and Danny Brennan, T. J. O'Reilly, Aidan Carty and Barney Daly were all beaten by the visitor. In the last match of his visit he was matched with J. J. Kelly of Ballymun. Kelly was a tough, uncompromising opponent with a left hand which drove his returns with a piston-like movement along the left-hand side-wall, drawing his opponent across the court and enabling him to exploit all the centre and right-hand side. Even 15 years later when I saw him playing at Ballymun, he could still play that shot.

That Heeney beat him in a match played at the end of an exhausting tour was no small tribute to the US champion. Scores were close in the last game and I have heard it said that Heeney only extended himself when a voice from the gallery urged him to finish it. Certain conclusions may be drawn from that remark but the only certainty is that on that August day in the North County

Dublin court followers saw a superb match between two superb players.

TOM JONES 1868 – 1951

It is hard to do justice to the memory of Father Tom Jones. He seemed to have been fitted for greatness in so many ways. In his short career as a player, eight years in all, he never tasted defeat. Yet when he retired at the age of 25 he was only beginning to realise his powers.

Paddy Mehigan, who wrote as 'Carbery' for the *Cork Examiner*, says that he could go into a ballcourt with a new ball and, such was the strength of his hitting, split the ball before one hand had put out the other! Monsignor Richard Collins wrote me from San Francisco in 1950 and, after recalling matches he had seen with Fitzgerald, Egan, Lawlor and Drew, ended his letter ' . . . and, my dear friend Tom Jones would lick them all'.

Tralee where he was born is no more than 80 miles from Cork – then the centre of ballplaying in Ireland. When he had beaten everyone in Tralee he took on a Corkman, Joe O'Leary from Fermoy, and 'trimmed' him by 8 games to nil. Now Joe O'Leary wasn't used to being beaten and he was a rough, rugged player. He challenged Jones and when they met again he took 3 of the 7 games played before a dispute caused the match to be left unfinished.

But nothing could stop Tom Jones. The championship of Ireland was his before his 20th birthday – Delaney of Athy and O'Shea of Carrick-on-Suir had lost to him for sums of £200 and £400 respectively. Had the priesthood not claimed him, he would have, as John B. Keane might say, 'beaten the world'.

He was gone out of handball before he was 22 and, after his ordination in 1896, he was out of the country for 10 years on missionary work in Australia. He made one brief, brilliant appearance at Casey's Court on his way back to Ireland, and then for 56 years ministered throughout 'the Kingdom'.

J. J. KELLY 1900 – 1960

J. J. Kelly played all his handball with the Ballymun Club but in football he played with Artillery, Shamrock Rovers and Shelbourne. It is for his handball he is best remembered, and particularly for his great match with the American, Heeney, in 1924.

Kelly grew up with good players and it is the opinion of good judges that he had the most perfect pair of hands of any player of his time. In three of his greatest matches, his opponent switched service to the right after failing to score on his left – yet he was a right-handed player. O'Halloran did it in 1920, Heeney did it in 1924 and Reid did it in 1938. And what is quite remarkable about the last two matches is that in each case Kelly led by 2 games to nil, reached 16 aces in the 3rd vital game and then lost!

His career really began in 1920 when he took the Leinster junior title after beating Bill Aldridge and then the Irish title when he beat O'Halloran. He won the Tailteann trials in 1922 but when 1924 came and the Games were held, he was outside the ranks of the GAA. The Boot Club continued to play with the IAHU until the 1936-37 season, in which year, as a fitting climax to two wonderful careers, Morgan Pembroke and himself won the Dublin senior doubles title.

Kelly and Pembroke made the crowds flock to Ballymun in the 'twenties. Pembroke had held the Irish title for the five years, 1920 to 1924, and Kelly who beat him in 1925 held it until 1929. Side by side with the IAHU championships were the championships run by the GAA-supported IAHA. But the great hardball players were to be found in such strongholds of the game as Ballymore-Eustace and Ballymun, and these clubs were in the IAHU.

JOHN LAWLOR   1860 – 1929

Pennsylvania is separated from Wicklow by some 3000 miles. John Lawlor made that long journey before he was three years of age and grew up near Baltinglass, county Wicklow. The family moved to Dublin in 1870 and soon afterwards he began playing ball at Kenny's Court in Patrick Street.

In 1885 he was matched with Dave Browning of Limerick for the Irish title and he defeated him at Carlow by 11 games to 7. His victory came as a surprise to country followers but, within a year, he had successfully defended it in the Cork Tournament. Then came the match with Casey which, for the first time, brought the USA champion and the Irish champion into opposition. Casey won both title and purse of 400 sovereigns and began a run of successes for the USA which ended only with Joe Maher in 1967.

Lawlor himself went back to the States in 1887 and stayed there for eight years. He challenged and beat all comers and, while he failed to get Casey into the court, he won a most unusual medal which bears the words 'Handball Championship of the World'. This medal is now to be seen at Matt Weldon's Boot Inn, Ballymun.

His departure from the States was marked by the presentation to him of a magnificent pair of bay horses, a most suitable present for the man who later had his own fleet of cabs plying for hire to and from Broadstone Railway Station.

He continued to play ball, chiefly doubles and, when he became a member of the Dublin Corporation, mindful of the game he loved, he moved that £3000 be made available for the erection of a ballcourt. A final honour was accorded him when, in 1923, he was elected first President of the Irish Amateur Handball Association.

TOMMY LEAHY   1910 – 1940

They always maintain in Ballymore-Eustace that when Leahy or O'Rourke were playing, a person above in the Square could hear the sound of a 'kill'. Leahy was said to have had the hardest service of any player of his time, an opinion confirmed by Pembroke when talking of his own rubber against Leahy in 1928.

After taking a county novice title in 1924, he was matched with Coyne of Carlow in 1927. Coyne was then in his 42nd year, just twice the age of Leahy. Still, Coyne gave him a lesson on the timber floor of the racquet court and led him 5 games to 1 at the end of the day's play. But in the 2nd half at Ballymore-Eustace, Leahy took the 6 games necessary and won his first big match, 7-5.

His next match was against Pembroke whom he beat in a home-and-home rubber (of 15 x 21) in 1928. By the following year he was ready for a tilt at Kelly's Irish title. The 15-game rubber was begun in Ballymun where Kelly had to concede him 2 games and in his home court he took 6 games of the 8 played to win his first Irish title.

He won it again in 1930 when he was also presented with the Weldon (World Championship) Cup given by Mrs T. Weldon of the Boot Inn, Ballymun, in memory of her husband. Illness prevented him from playing in 1931 and the vacant title was claimed by Kelly. In a letter to the press, Leahy rejected his claim saying, 'I have never been defeated either in singles or doubles competition. I did not take part in this year's championship owing to an injury to my hand sustained three days prior to my defeat of J. J. Kelly the second time. I congratulate him upon his winning the Irish title this year, but I dispute his right to claim the world's title. If the Irish Amateur Handball Union grants permission I will play J. J. Kelly on any date he desires.'

He did meet Kelly in competition in 1933 when, in partnership with Jack Byrne, they defeated Pembroke and Kelly by 8 games to 4 in a match for the 1932 title. In the same year, in partnership with Jimmy Dolan, he won the 1933 title, beating Kelly and Weldon by 8 games to 3. But the hand injury to which he referred was to prove more serious than anyone realised. When in 1936 Jack O'Rourke and himself lost the Kildare title to Aldridge and Foley of Athy, he was already a very sick man. Four years later he died in London at the early age of 30.

P. J. MacDONAGH   1892 – 1961

P. J. MacDonagh was born in Leitirmullen in Connemara where his mother was a schoolteacher. After attending the local National school he was sent to Blackrock College. In 1900 he went to the USA where he had relatives and joined the New York Athletic Club. Playing in the colours of that club he won the national senior softball championship of the US in 1924.

He came back to Ireland in February of the same year and was invited to enter for the Tailteann Games. He trained in the University College ballcourt with Pádraig Óg Ó Conaire and a teacher from Spiddal named Dolan. His style was quite unusual, as he served and volleyed with an overhand stroke. Padraig Óg described him to me in a letter: *'Duine gleoite, spoirtiúil é, ar an lúthaire is deá-cumtha dá bhfaca ariamh'*. This estimate of him as an athlete is borne out in another letter from the late Professor Conor O'Malley of Galway. He speaks of him as a racing cyclist and also as a man who 'could throw a very good long jump'!

When he came to the Ballymun court for the Tailteann Games, he won all his matches without being unduly extended, beating MacDermott of Roscommon, Dowdall of Dublin and Leech of Ballaghadereen. Little is known of him after his return to the States where he was surprisingly beaten by a one-armed player, named George Quam, in the 2nd round of the 1926 national AAU singles championship of 1926.

He returned to Ireland in the late 'thirties where he lived for a while near Spiddal. He played Paddy Perry in the Depot court in a 'ball-and-ball-about rubber', i.e. alternate games with the Irish and American ball, which Perry only won by the odd game in five. He later went to live in England and died in London where he is buried.

MORGAN PEMBROKE   1891 – 1978

In the memory of old handball followers one name constantly recurs, that of Morgan Pembroke. Morgan Pembroke of the old St Catherine's Club is remembered by the hundreds who, 50 years ago, took a Glasnevin tram on a Sunday afternoon and then walked from Washerwoman's Hill to the Boot Inn, Ballymun. Yet the idol of the Dublin fans was from Wicklow where he was born of Welsh parents in 1891.

They had reason to be proud of him for he had won many a good match. They had seen him beat Aldridge (3–3 in Athy and 4–1 in Ballymun); Coyne (4–3 in Carlow and 4–0 in Ballymun); Dunne (4–2 in Carlow and 3–0 in Ballymun); Bowles (4–3 in Limerick and 5–0 in Ballymun); Lyons (4–3 and 4–1, both in Ballymun). Even in defeat, when he met the youthful challenger, Tommy Leahy, he led him 4 games to 3 in Ballymun before losing 0–5 in Ballymore-Eustace.

Perhaps he was never better than in those years from 1920 to 1925 when he held the Irish senior title. Yet, when the Americans came to play in Ireland during the Tailteann Games of 1924, they ignored Pembroke and chose instead to play J. J. Kelly. The motive behind this refusal to meet the Irish title-holder has never been made clear but Pembroke's challenge, on the basis of a home-and-home rubber, was refused by O'Rourke, the Americans' manager. (A purse of £1,000 was offered by A. Durkin for a double-handed match between Pembroke and Durkin and Heeney and O'Donnell of the US for the championship of the world, and this was also refused.)

Pembroke may have been denied a world title but his title to the affection of Irish handball followers was never disputed.

PADDY PERRY   1911 - 1983

Paddy Perry's name is often mentioned when people talk of John Joe Gilmartin, and I, too, think of him when speaking of Gilmartin and with some reason, as I refereed them when first they met in a singles match. That was in

October 1937, and the venue was Clogh, County Kilkenny.

Like the meeting of two great players in any sport, the match did not answer all the questions. It showed Perry at his masterly best. It showed a Gilmartin who had still some way to go before he would attain the same mastery. Perry was then a commanding figure, fast-moving with a deceptively easy way of hitting a decisive 'kill'. His beautiful service that ran only inches below the board at the top of the side-walls meant that Gilmartin rarely put him out on the return of service.

While I had seen Perry play before that day, Gilmartin was but a name to me. He was ideally built for distinction in any sport demanding relentless concentration and it was no surprise when in later years he became a low-handicap golfer. He seemed far less relaxed than Perry but his breath-taking speed and rapier drives down the side-walls must have taken Perry by surprise.

Perry came out the winner by the odd game in five and on the homeward journey, none of us had any doubt but that we had seen a match that would not be surpassed in our time.

Perry was then in his 10th year of first-class handball. John Casey of Boyle had coached him for the 1927 Roscommon junior title which he won, and every honour in the softball game followed during eight unbeaten years.

But if he was supreme in singles play, he was somewhat less effective in doubles. His partner, Alfie Mullaney wrote of him that 'he was so anxious to hit *every* ball that he was blind to the fact that he had a partner'. Mullaney knew this and was, in many respects, the best partner Perry ever had. Reid, who came in on his right in later years, was too good a player to be left out of the game and, for that reason, I rather think that Perry played his best ball with Mullaney.

While I will always remember Perry the handballer, there are others who will remember him as the player who won three Dublin senior championships in one day – football, hurling and handball!

TIM TWOHILL 1872 – 1934

Tim Twohill I never met, though I knew his sister and nephew, also named Tim, and often talked of him to Christy Guiney and Dan Singleton both of whom saw him play.

His career may be said to have begun when he was matched with Jim FitzGerald in 1891. Not surprisingly, he was not yet ready for the great Tralee man and was well beaten, winning but one game of the twelve played. He then had a series of challenge matches against such good players as Carver of Kanturk and Roche and Tobin of Fermoy.

When he had beaten these he was ready to bid for the Irish title left vacant after FitzGerald had emigrated to the USA. As usual it was the winner of the Cork Tournament who was hailed as champion and in August 1898, at the Old Market Place, Twohill beat O'Herlihy by the odd game in eleven to win his first title. He withstood a challenge from the ageing Lawlor and another from

O'Herlihy and it was as Irish champion that he was matched with Egan in 1903.

While it is as a ballplayer he is best known, he played for his native Cork in football and took part in one of the most dramatic of All-Ireland finals – that of 1897. In those days championships were not always completed within the year and, in fact, it was not until two years later that the final against Dublin was played and lost.

Appendix C

Great Partnerships

P. BELL AND J. DOYLE, MEATH

When on winter nights talk turns to handball, old players will recall the great names from Kilkenny and Carlow, from Cork and Kerry, and almost certainly from Kells. For there were born the Bells and the Doyles, the O'Reillys, the Tormays and McCabes – all great names in the world of a game now dying, hardball.

All these played ball in the old Foresters' Court. It was not a big ballcourt by modern standards but it was true and the gallery usually held good judges who wagered freely on the results of the Sunday morning matches.

Joe Doyle and Paddy Bell had gone to school together, kicked football for Erin's Own in the meadows beside the Blackwater and, finally, won for Royal Meath three senior All-Ireland titles. Rubbers were long and hard in those days and Bell went the whole 13 games with Ormonde in 1932 before winning by 5 aces. But it was a year later, in September 1933, that they played the match for which they will long be remembered. Ormonde and Maloney were 3 games clear and 18 aces in the fourth (only 3 aces from an All-Ireland title) when Bell and Doyle changed places. Bell took all the play inside the short-line while Doyle 'covered' the back wall. In 45 minutes they turned defeat into victory – scoring aces almost at the rate of two a minute!

J. BERGIN AND J. SWEENEY, TIPPERARY

Joe Bergin made his reputation as a doubles player in 1937 and it is as a doubles player with the redoubtable Jackie Sweeney that he is best remembered. Yet he was also the All-Ireland singles champion on two occasions in the 'fifties.

He learned the game in the Shamrock ballcourt in Kenyon Street, Nenagh. He played there with the Hassett brothers, Ned, Mick and Joe, who were possibly the best players and the best sportsmen in the country at the time. In fact, my memory of Nenagh ballplayers is that they all were good – Phil

Ayres, 'Ginger' MacMahon, Micksie Gorman, Paddy Kennedy, Denis Carey, etc.

Bergin's first appearance in an All-Ireland final was in most unusual circumstances. He had declared for his native Sligo and, partnered by his brother, Stephen, they reached the final in which they met two other Tipperary players, Con and Anthony Collins, from Ballina just 12 miles outside Nenagh! For the record, Ballina beat Nenagh by 3 games to 1. Five years later Bergin and Jimmy O'Rourke put the name of Sligo on the championship roll of honour for the first time.

But his greatest days were yet to come. A returned emigrant, Jackie Sweeney, used go in for the odd game in Nenagh. Bergin noticed his extraordinary hitting power and a new partnership was quickly established. Sweeney hit every ball viciously and his service could and often did touch all four walls before hitting the ground. With Bergin beside him to drive home any returns that chanced to reach the front wall, they won every match they played over a period of 30 months, and that included two All-Irelands.

D. BRENNAN AND J. LUCAS, KILKENNY

The first senior softball doubles championship played under GAA rules was won by Behan and Norton of Urlingford, county Kilkenny. That was over 30 years ago. Since then the Kilkenny colours have been carried to victory in all grades and in Gilmartin the county produced the finest player of recent times.

However, I want to mention another Kilkenny pair, a pair who played ball not only in Talbot's Inch but in the City Court beside the Franciscan Abbey and 'down the Canal' – Danny Brennan and Jim Lucas. I don't think I shall ever see a player move to meet a ball like Brennan did in his day. He seemed just a dark, graceful shadow gliding across the floor, and beside him was the imperturbable Lucas who could change the fortunes of any match with his beautifully judged lobs.

Their year of glory was 1929. In that year the championships ran late and it was November before Lucas and Brennan travelled to Westport to win the All-Ireland semi-final. They then faced Flavin and Batterberry from neighbouring Waterford in the final. They lost every one of the six games at Spring Garden Alley, Waterford, but reeled off seven games in a row at Kilkenny in a match which lasted just under four hours!

J. HASSETT AND E. HASSETT, TIPPERARY

Travel Ireland and you will not find any pair of ballplayers as popular as Ned (born 1908) and Joe Hassett! When I first knew them, Micksey Hassett was Ned's partner, but in 1934 Joe came in on the left and from then on, for five years, no pair could 'live' with them. Not that they ever really trained – they enjoyed handball too much to take it seriously. And any ballcourt was good enough for them; they would play an All-Ireland final in the same spirit as they would take on a couple of cattle-drovers at the fair of Roscrea.

They began playing ball in the Shamrock ballalley in Nenagh in the early 'thirties. Now any man who won a Shamrock championship was good because he had to beat good men – Ayres, Bergin, McMahon, O'Gorman – to win through. So when Ned and Joe Hassett stepped into the court for their first All-Ireland final, against the reigning champions, Perry and Mullaney, in 1934, they played and won a match which opened the way to five years of glory.

Glorious years they were, when crowded galleries everywhere gave welcome to them – the greatest partnership in the history of handball. 1934, 1935, 1936, 1937 and 1938 went by and still the newspaper headlines kept repeating, 'Hassett brothers win again', 'Hassetts retain title', etc. Tipperary was proud of them, but they belonged to all Ireland, winning friends as they won matches in every part of the country.

P. PERRY AND A. MULLANEY, ROSCOMMON

'The greatest of all players in the softball code but the most difficult to partner' – that is Mullaney's summing-up of Perry with whom he won the senior All-Ireland titles of 1932 and 1933. It is true that they were wonderfully suited to one another yet completely different to watch. Perry played handball at a pace that was unknown with the softball before his time, yet there was grace in his every stroke and blinding power behind every 'kill'. Mullaney seemed slow-moving in comparison – what partner would not! But it was his 62 aces, scored direct off service, which almost certainly won the 1933 final against Daly and McCoy of Dublin.

Paddy Perry and Alfie Mullaney grew up in a county where handball had long been popular and where village tournaments were numerous and closely contested. I can well remember the workers on a State Forestry Scheme forfeiting a half-day's pay to see a mid-week tournament at Ballincurry in 1932! Johnny Casey of Boyle was always at hand to coach them and tournament matches at Fairymount, Ahascragh, Creeve and Tulsk soon welded them into the best partnership in the country. From the spring of 1932 until the autumn of 1934 they remained undefeated, winning provincial, Tailteann and All-Ireland titles. It was a period of great partnerships – the Hassett brothers, Lucas and Brennan, O'Neill and Sherry – but Perry and Mullaney beat them all.

JOHN RYAN AND JOHN DOYLE, WEXFORD

When John Ryan of Bridgetown and John Doyle of Trinity began to play together in 1952, they had each won a junior title in different years and in different grades. During the next seven years they took on all comers, winning six of the seven senior hardball titles and one softball title.

I saw many of their matches during those years and few will disagree with me when I say that their first victory was perhaps their greatest. The final was played at Talbot's Inch and opposing them were Joe Hassett and Jimmy O'Brien of Kerry. Level scores were called at 20-all in the last game with the score in games standing at 3 games all. Each pair went in twice to toss game ball before Wexford won by one ace.

Long into the night discussion in the bars of Kilkenny centred on which of the two Wexford men had contributed most to victory. Ryan had served hard throughout, taken two-thirds of the play and 'killed' more balls than any of the other players. Doyle had, however, for seven long games, lasting two and a half hours, kept returning the heavy service that both the Kerry players had kept driving down the right. Let the last word rest with the late Jimmy Kehoe of Trinity (himself no mean player), 'Neither of the Kerry pair served a ball that Doyle did not return and Ryan served no ball that I could return!'

They typified the sportsmanship that is so much a part of their county whether in hurling, football or handball and their victories are remembered wherever 'Boolavogue' is sung.

Appendix D

Great Clubs

CORK CITY

One sentence from a letter written to me by Tom Soye, dated 30 November 1954, will serve to introduce the Cork City Club: ' "The Old Market Place" (where the City ballcourt stood) holds very happy memories for me as it was there I met the best sportsmen during my long handball career.'

It boasted of having the largest club membership in the country, and the Cork Tournament was considered the equivalent of the Irish championship. My membership card is dated '1931' and I am immensely happy to recall some of the great players who were still to be seen there when I was a boy: champions like Oliver Drew, Billie O'Herlihy, Matt O'Shaughnessy, Jim Hunt, Mikus Creedon and the O'Mahony brothers – all were members at some time or other. World champions like Fitzgerald and Egan and Kelly had played there, and celebrities in the world of handball like Judge Dunne of Brooklyn and Peter Sastre had stayed in the big four-stories house beside it.

The victuallers were strong supporters of the game and as there were slaughter-houses on all sides, sheep-skins for the making and covering of hardballs were never scarce. I often watched a ball take shape from wood-core to final stitch while, across the way, Shandon had marked little more than an hour on its golden figures. The Coughlans, Looneys, Lenihans and Dillons were butchers and ballplayers, ready to lay a pound or fifty pounds on a game or a rubber. And, at the end of the match, the talk in the Ballcourt Bar – through which you passed to enter the ballcourt – was of drag-hunts and bowlplaying, of pigeon-racing and ballplaying. It was a world that largely vanished with the demolition in 1976 of the ballcourt and the slate-fronted houses that flanked it on either side.

THE METROPOLITAN CLUB, DUBLIN

It is doubtful if any handball club in the country contributed more to the game than this club, yet it never had a permanent home! The first members played in the old Patrick Street court, often referred to as Kenny's Court, which was situated at the back of a butcher's shop. The meetings were at that time held in the Garter Inn in Kevin Street and the members wore the club medal, shamrock-shaped with an Irish harp, embossed on their watch chains.

The club was jealous of the Irish traditions of ballplaying and we find John Lawlor presiding at a meeting of the club on 12 October 1896, when the following resolution was passed: 'That we condemn the action of the American handball players in trying to introduce ace-line tossing and that as Irish handball players, we unanimously agree to uphold the old style of serving i.e. from the base of the front wall'. This decision may have postponed the day when ace-line tossing was adopted, but it was a change that had to come, and by the time Bowles played Kelly in 1908 all tossing was from a centre or ace-line.

With the demolition of the adjoining house about 1907, the Patrick Street court became unsafe and was eventually pulled down. The 'Mets' players moved to Ashtown, to Clondalkin and later to Ballymun. It was in Ashtown that the club champions, Lawlor and Clarke, lost the double-handed championship of Ireland to the holders Aldridge and Robinson of Athy in 1912. The club continued to attract great players, among whom Paddy Lyons, Tim Hurley, Pat McGill and 'Kruger' Fagan were outstanding. In more recent years Paddy Perry and Peter O'Neill played in the club colours and each was elected a life-member for his services to handball. Since 1923 the club is a completely amateur one after its affiliation to the IAHA, and the Clarke family did much to restore the glory of earlier days by their victories and the All-Ireland championship.

TALBOT'S INCH, KILKENNY

In any discussions of handball there will always be widely-different but equally strongly held views on the best handball player and the best handball club. Talbot's Inch will be the choice of many followers, even outside Kilkenny, and it is difficult to oppose it.

There was always ballplaying in Kilkenny, whether at the Ring or at Fennessy's Mill down the canal. The City Club drew for support on the families living nearby, and Danny Brennan, John McGrath, Jim Lucas, Joe Hogan and Paddy Dalton all learnt their handball playing against the Brewery wall in the Ring. A big change came about in 1925 when Michael Davin, who was steward of the Desart Estate, became interested in the game. He spoke to Lady Desart, his employer, of the move to start a new club and not alone did she accept the Presidency of the club but she also gave a site on which to build a ballcourt beside the model village of Talbot's Inch.

The first club members gave voluntarily of their time and labour to build a three-wall court. To this was later added a backwall, gallery and roof. I do not know if any estimate of the number of All-Ireland titles won by the club has ever been made since that summer's day in 1928 when President Cosgrave declared the court open. (On my own count, 28 senior All-Ireland titles have gone to the club in 40 years.)

I have the programme of that July day before me as I write. The first players into the court were Behan and Norton who had brought All-Ireland honours to the little village of Urlingford. Paddy Lanigan, who drew the first cartload of sand, was marker and Sean O'Hanlon, first Secretary of the Irish Amateur Handball Association, was referee. The 5-match programme ran for four and half hours and over 700 people paid for admission.

The amber singlet with the arms of the city in black has since been worn in almost every county in Ireland – usually with success and, during the 'forties, every player taking part in the confined club competitions was an All-Ireland medal holder! To go 'abroad to the Inch' even for a practice game was to share something of the excitement of a full-scale championship.

WESTPORT, COUNTY MAYO

Westport is a town where two very different sports have always been popular: handball and soccer. And, not infrequently, the same players played both.

It was not difficult to see that soccer would gain a footing in an area from which emigration particularly to Glasgow and to other centres of the game in Great Britain, was always high. Handball developed as a country pastime and it was as a three-wall game that it was played throughout county Mayo. At least three of the players who could legitimately claim to be world handball champions were either born in the west or had parents who emigrated from the west. They were Egan and MacDonagh of Galway, and Kelly of Kiltimagh.

There were two ballcourts in the town and two great ballplaying families, the Ruddys and the McNallys. Martin Grealy, the father-in-law of the future All-Ireland champion, Joe McNally, was himself Connacht doubles champion with Pat O'Malley. When Joe won the title in 1928, he had the unusual distinction of losing no game in county, provincial or All-Ireland championship. In the same year Mick Breheny and himself went ten games against Flavin and Batterbeery of Waterford before losing the All-Ireland doubles final.

That was probably the club's greatest year and such names as Paddy Murphy, Paddy Gibbons, Charlie Geraghty and Bruddie Hoban figure in all the championship records of the time. And an indication of how high standards of ballplaying were at the time may be seen from the fact that Canavan and Derrig of Achill met and defeated McNally and Gibbons in a wonderful Westport Tournament final in 1930.

In 1931 when Westport had two interprovincial players McNally and Hogan, on the Connacht soccer team, the club decided to join the IAHU. This brought Westport into competition with such clubs as Virginia, Nobber, Ballymun, etc., but the lack of competition was a handicap and the club returned to the ranks of the GAA. They celebrated their return by winning the junior All-Ireland with MacDonald and Geraghty in 1936.

THE HORSE AND JOCKEY, COUNTY TIPPERARY

On 15 August 1954 the Horse and Jockey club celebrated the golden jubilee of the opening of the ballcourt. To mark the occasion, Austin Clarke and Larry Roe, Dublin met Joe Bergin of Nenagh and Des Dillon of Clare. There was also a junior singles match between Joe Hynes, Dublin, and Michael Shanahan of the Horse and Jockey.

In August 1904 the first ever game of ball was played at the Horse and Jockey. The Rev. John Meagher of Annacarty, who was then a student for the priesthood, used play ball there. He sent a challenge to Tom Price and Dick Breen of Dualla to play himself and Tom Purcell.

The ballcourt was built completely by voluntary labour. Coming from the bog on summer evenings, the men of the district worked on until dark. At least three of the men who worked there were present at the Jubilee celebrations – John Cleary, Michael Caudy and Tom Purcell.

Two of the greatest players of that time were Dick O'Keeffe and Dick Dwyer, who never lost a match at the Jockey. They beat Buckley and Hunt of Cahir, Hurley and Nolan of Dublin, and Molloy and Burns of Cloughmartin.

But, perhaps, the greatest match ever seen there was the junior All-Ireland final of 1926 when 'Shelly' McCarthy and Tom O'Keeffe represented Tipperary against Waterford. It was a home-and-home rubber and Waterford led by 6 games to 0 when the second leg began at the Jockey. For almost two and a half hours the game went on and, at the finish, McCarthy and O'Keeffe had won the 7 games and the title.

In more recent years, the Jockey was the first club in Ireland to introduce a glass backwall, which it did in 1949. It was then decided to roof the court and today it is recognised as one of the finest in the country.

LOUGHMACRORY, COUNTY TYRONE

Not many handball culbs are able to trace their history back over one hundred years as can the Loughmacrory Club in Tyrone. In the early days of the Land League, the MacKernan family, fearing that their land would be confiscated, built a house near Loughmacrory. There is no record of anyone ever living there and local people soon began to use the gable-end for ballplaying. A clay floor was levelled and there to this day the ruins of the old ballcourt may still be seen.

In 1932 a new ballcourt was built for a cost of £8 on the site of the gatelodge to the old MacKernan house. On this historic site the club was established and by 1959 it had become the venue for All-Ireland championships. The Kellys and the Coyles had joined the MacKernans to give Ulster one of its strongest clubs.

What Loughmacrory has so far lacked is the opposition that only other top-class clubs can give. Pomeroy is, of course, an outstanding club and had, in Jimmy Quinn, the most famous figure in the game in Ulster. Cloughfynn is another centre of handball and, as these clubs develop, players like Michael Conway of Loughmacrory will get the competition they need.

Appendix E

Records and Results

Garda and Army Records

A.   The Garda record of All-Ireland handball championships

SSBS   M. Joyce (1925); P. Perry (1930-37)
    SSBD   M. Joyce and C. Ryan (1927);
             P. Perry (1932, 1933)
SHBS   T. Soye (1926); P. Reid (1934)
SHBD   T. Soye and T. J. O'Reilly (1927, 1928);
         T. Soye and G. Browne (1930); P. Perry
         and P. Reid (1937); W. Doran (1969)
         M. Sullivan (1971);

JSBS   P. Perry (1929); R. Walsh (1971)
JSBD   T. O'Keeffe (1928); P. Perry (1929)
JHBS   M. Butler (1939); W. Doran (1957);
         M. Sullivan (1965);

B.   The Army Record

I.   Hardball Singles: Gearoid O'Sullivan Cup

1923 Capt. Brian Whelan – 2nd Battalion	1947 Cpl M. O'Brien – 12th Battalion
1924 Pte J. Delaney – G.H.Q.	1948 Pte J. Merriman – 10th Battalion
1925 Pte J. Delaney – Eastern Command.	1949 Cpl R. Maher – Curragh T. C.
1926 Pte J. Delaney – Eastern Command.	1950 Cpl M. O'Brien – 12th Battalion
1927 Pte J. Delaney – Eastern Command.	1951 Sgt R. Maher – Curragh T. C.
1928 Pte J. Foley – Curragh Command.	1952 Sgt R. Maher – Curragh T. C.
1929 Capt. Whelan – 10th Battalion	1953 Pte Maloney – Southern Command
1930 Cpl T. Doyle – 3rd Battalion	1954 Sgt Maher – Curragh T. C.
1931 Pte F. O'Reilly – 4th Battalion	1955 Gnr M. Redmond – Artillery
1932 Pte Murphy – Supply & Transport	1956 Sgt Maloney – Southern Command
1933 Pte O'Reilly – 4th Battalion	1957 Sgt Maloney – Southern Command
1934 Pte O'Reilly – 4th Battalion	1958 Sgt Geary – 1st Armoured Squadron
1935 Pte O'Reilly – 4th Battalion	1959 Pte M. Hore – Eastern Command
1936 Pte O'Reilly – 4th Battalion	1960 Pte M. Hore – Eastern Command
1937 Pte O'Reilly – 4th Battalion	1961 Pte M. Hore – Eastern Command
1938 Pte O'Reilly – 4th Battalion	1962 Cpl J. Doyle – Equitation School
1939 Pte J. Roche – 2nd Battalion	1963 Pte M. Hore – Eastern Command
1940–2 — No competition	1964 App. T. Geoghegan – Depot Ordnance
1943 Lt. G. Moran – Curragh T. C.	1965 App. T. Geoghegan – Depot Ordnance
1944 Cpl J. Dolan – Curragh T. C.	1966 Discontinued
1945 Pte Molloy – Curragh T. C.	
1946 Tpr R. Maher – Curragh T. C.	

II.   Softball Singles: Sean Quinn Cup

1923	Pte Delahunty – Waterford Command	1948	Pte C. Collins – FCA (Southern Command)
1924	Cpl Scanlan – G.H.Q.	1949	Pte T. Maher – FCA (Southern Command)
1925	Pte D. Brennan – Western Command	1950	Sgt Maher – Cavalry
1926	Pte D. Brennan – Western Command	1951	Sgt O'Brien – Curragh Training Camp
1927	Pte O'Meara – Southern Command	1952	Sgt Maher – Cavalry
1928	Pte E. Hassett – R. & T. D.	1953	Pte Maher – Southern Command
1929	Pte E. Hassett – 4th Battalion	1954	Pte Maher – Southern Command
1930	Pte Murphy – Army Singles Corps	1955	Pte Maher – Southern Command
1931	Pte Murphy – Army Singles Corps	1956	Pte Maher – Southern Command
1932	Pte O'Reilly – 4th Battalion	1957	Sgt Maloney – Southern Command
1933	Pte Hassett – 4th Battalion	1958	Cpl Maher – Southern Command
1934	Pte J. Deane – 4th Battalion	1959	Pte M. Hore – Eastern Command
1935	Pte H Gallagher – 5th Battalion	1960	Pte P. Davin – Southern Command
1936	Gnr Condon (later CQMS) – Artillery Corps	1961	Pte P. Davin – Southern Command
1937	Gnr Condon (later CQMS) – Artillery Corps	1962	Pte J. Doyle – Curragh Training Camp
1938	Gnr Condon (later CQMS) – Artillery Corps	1963	Pte O'Regan – Western Command
1939	Gnr Condon (later CQMS) – Artillery Corps	1964	Sgt P. Cockburn – Eastern Command
1940–2	— No competition	1965	Pte P. Davin – Southern Command
1943	Vol Walsh – First Brigade	1966	Pte P. Davin – Southern Command
1944	Vol Walsh – First Brigade	1967	Cpl J. Doyle – Equitation School
1945	Vol Walsh – First Brigade	1968	Pte Davin – Southern Command
1946	Sgt Merriman – 12th Battalion	1969	Cpl J. Doyle – Equitation School
1947	Cpl Maher – Cavalry	1970	Cpl J. Doyle – Equitation School

Irish Handball Champions; Professional, Amateur, & Intervarsity

I   Irish Champions   —   Professional

1870-80	W. Baggs (Tipperary)	1905-10	J. J. Bowles (Limerick)
1880-85	D. Browning (Limerick)	1910-12	P. Coyne (Carlow)
1885-88	J. Lawlor (Dublin; left for USA in 1888)	1912-20	J. J. Bowles (Limerick)
1888-90	T. Jones (Kerry; entered Maynooth Seminary)	1920-25	M. Pembroke (Dublin)
1890-98	J. Fitzgerald (Kerry; left for USA in 1897)	1925-29	J. J. Kelly (Dublin)
1898-1905	T. Twohill (Cork)	1929-33	T. Leahy (Kildare)

After 1933 the amateur winners of the Canon Cantwell Cup, presented to the Ballymore-Eustace Club, were considered as the Irish champions.

1933-35	J. Byrne (Kildare)
1935-36	M. Dowling (Kildare)

Ballymore-Eustace Club then joined the IAHA and the Dublin championship winners, Ballymun, were recognised as champions of Ireland. At the end of 1937, this club joined the IAHA and the IAHU then ceased to exist.

II Irish Champions — Amateur

Senior Softball Singles

1925 – M. Joyce (Dublin)
1926 – T. Behan (Kilkenny)
1927 – W. McGuire (Dublin)
1928 – J. McNally (Mayo)
1929 – D. Brennan (Kilkenny)
1930 – P. Perry (Roscommon)
1931 – P. Perry (Roscommon)
1932 – P. Perry (Roscommon)
1933 – P. Perry (Roscommon)
1934 – P. Perry (Roscommon)
1935 – P. Perry (Roscommon)
1936 – P. Perry (Roscommon)
1937 – P. Perry (Roscommon)
1938 – J. J. Gilmartin (Kilkenny)
1939 – J. J. Gilmartin (Kilkenny)
1940 – M. Walsh (Galway)
1941 – J. Dunne (Kilkenny)
1942-45 (No competition owing to scarcity of Soft balls)
1946 – J. J. Gilmartin (Kilkenny)
1947 – L. Rowe (Dublin)
1948 – J. Bergin (Tipperary)
1949 – L. Rowe (Dublin)
1950 – J. Bergin (Tipperary)
1951 – L. Rowe (Dublin)
1952 – J. Ryan (Wexford)
1953 – M. Griffin (Cork)
1954 – J. Ryan (Wexford)
1955 – J. Ryan (Wexford)
1956 – J. Ryan (Wexford)
1957 – J. Ryan (Wexford)
1958 – P. Downey (Kerry)
1959 – F. Confrey (Louth)
1960 – F. Confrey (Louth)
1961 – P. Downey (Kerry)
1962 – J. Delaney (Kilkenny)
1963 – J. Maher (Louth)
1964 – J. Maher (Louth)
1965 – D. Lyng (Wexford)
1966 – S. McCabe (Monaghan)
1967 – S. McCabe (Monaghan)
1968 – J. Maher (Louth)
1969 – J. Maher (Louth)
1970 – J. Maher (Louth)
1971 – D. Lyng (Wexford)
1972 – P. Murphy (Wexford)
1973 – J. Maher (Louth)
1974 – P. Kirby (Clare)
1975 – P. Kirby (Clare)　60 x 30
　　　　P. Kirby (Clare)　40 x 20
1976 – P. Kirby (Clare)　60 x 30
　　　　P. Kirby (Clare)　40 x 20
1977 – P. Kirby (Clare)　60 x 30
　　　　P. Kirby (Clare)　40 x 20
1978 – R. Lyng (Wexford)　60 x 30
　　　　P. Kirby (Clare)　40 x 20
1979 – T. O'Rourke (Kildare)　60 x 30
　　　　P. Kirby (Clare)　40 x 20
1980 – P. Ryan (Dublin)　60 x 30
　　　　P. Kirby (Clare)　40 x 20
1981 – P. O'Reilly (Kilkenny)　60 x 30
　　　　A. Ryan (Tipperary)　40 x 20
1982 – O. Harold (Kilkenny)　60 x 30
　　　　A. Ryan (Tipperary)　40 x 20
1983 – A. Ryan (Tipperary)　60 x 30

Senior Softball Doubles

1925 – T. Behan and J. Norton (Kilkenny)
1926 – J. Whyte and C. Barrett (Galway)
1927 – M. Joyce and C. Ryan (Dublin)
1928 – J. Flavin and M. Batterberry (Waterford)
1929 – D. Brennan and J. Lucas (Kilkenny)
1930 – M. O'Neill and L. Sherry (Wicklow)
1931 – M. O'Neill and L. Sherry (Wicklow)
1932 – P. Perry and A. Mullaney (Roscommon)
1933 – P. Perry and A. Mullaney (Roscommon)
1934 – J. Hassett and E. Hassett (Tipperary)
1935 – J. Hassett and E. Hassett (Tipperary)
1936 – J. Hassett and E. Hassett (Tipperary)
1937 – J. Hassett and E. Hassett (Tipperary)
1938 – J. Hassett and E. Hassett (Tipperary)
1939 – J. J. Gilmartin and J. Dunne (Kilkenny)
1940 – J. J. Gilmartin and J. Dunne (Kilkenny)
1941 – J. J. Gilmartin and J. Dunne (Kilkenny)
1942 – J. Collins and C. Collins (Tipperary)
1943 - 45 — No championship.
1946 – L. Rowe and G. Rowe (Dublin)
1947 – J. Bergin and J. O'Rourke (Sligo)
1948 – L. Rowe and G. Rowe (Dublin)
1949 – J. Bergin and J. Sweeney (Tipperary)
1950 – J. Bergin and J. Sweeney (Tipperary)
1951 – J. Hassett and J. O'Brien (Kerry)
1952 – J. Hassett and J. O'Brien (Kerry)
1953 – M. Griffin and M. Walsh (Cork)
1954 – C. Delaney and J. Dunne (Kilkenny)
1955 – P. Downey and J. O'Brien (Kerry)
1956 – P. Downey and J. O'Brien (Kerry)
1957 – J. Ryan and J. Doyle (Wexford)
1958 – T. McGarry and M. Mullins (Limerick)
1959 – T. McGarry and M. Mullins (Limerick)
1960 – P. Downey and J. O'Brien (Kerry)
1961 – P. Downey and J. O'Brien (Kerry)
1962 – P. Downey and J. O'Brien (Kerry)
1963 – P. Downey and J. O'Brien (Kerry)
1964 – P. Downey and J. O'Brien (Kerry)
1965 – J. Delaney and T. Ryan (Kilkenny)
1966 – M. Walsh and P. McGee (Mayo)
1967 – L. Molloy and D. McGovern (Meath)
1968 – T. McEllistrim and M. McEllistrim (Kerry)
1969 – P. Lee and J. Cleary (Wicklow)
1970 – D. Lyng and S. Buggy (Wexford)

1971 – T. McEllistrim and M. McEllistrim (Kerry)
1972 – P. Murphy and J. Quigley (Wexford)
1973 – M. McEllistrim and N. Kerins (Kerry)
1974 – P. Murphy and J. Quigley (Wexford)
1975 – P. Murphy and R. Lyng (Wexford) 60 x 30
         P. Kirby and M. Kirby (Clare) 40 x 20
1976 – P. McGarry and M. Hogan (Limerick) 60 x 30
         P. Kirby and M. Kirby (Clare) 40 x 20
1977 – R. Lyng and S. Buggy (Wexford) 60 x 30
         P. Kirby and M. Kirby (Clare) 40 x 20
1978 – J. Kirby and D. Kirby (Clare) 60 x 30
         P. Kirby and M. Kirby (Clare) 40 x 20
1979 – R. Lyng and S. Buggy (Wexford) 60 x 30
         P. Kirby and M. Kirby (Clare) 40 x 20
1980 – O. Harold and P. Reilly (Kilkenny) 60 x 30
         P. McGee and P. MacCormack (Mayo) 40 x 20
1981 – A. Greene and P. Hughes (Kilkenny) 60 x 30
         P. Delaney and W. Mullins (Offaly) 40 x 20
1982 – R. Lyng and J. Goggins (Wexford) 60 x 30
         J. Fleming and P. Clery (Wexford) 40 x 20
1983 – T. Quish and J. Quish (Wexford) 60 x 30

Senior Hardball Singles

1925 – W. Aldridge (Kildare)
1926 – T. Soye (Dublin)
1927 – T. Soye (Dublin)
1928 – T. Soye (Dublin)
1929 – T. Soye (Dublin)
1930 – T. Soye (Dublin)
1931 – T. Soye (Dublin)
1932 – J. Lucas (Kilkenny)
1933 – P. Bell (Meath)
1934 – P. Reid (Carlow)
1935 – S. Tormey (Meath)
1936 – J. J. Gilmartin (Kilkenny)
1937 – J. J. Gilmartin (Kilkenny)
1938 – J. J. Gilmartin (Kilkenny)
1939 – J. J. Gilmartin (Kilkenny)
1940 – J. J. Gilmartin (Kilkenny)
1941 – J. J. Gilmartin (Kilkenny)
1942 – J. J. Gilmartin (Kilkenny)
1943 – M. Dowling (Kildare)
1944 – A. Clarke (Dublin)
1945 – J. J. Gilmartin (Kilkenny)
1946 – J. J. Gilmartin (Kilkenny)
1947 – J. J. Gilmartin (Kilkenny)
1948 – A. Clarke (Dublin)
1949 – A. Clarke (Dublin)
1950 – R. Grattan (Kildare)
1951 – A. Clarke (Dublin)
1952 – J. Ryan (Wexford)
1953 – J. Ryan (Wexford)
1954 – A. Clarke (Dublin)
1955 – A. Clarke (Dublin)
1956 – J. Ryan (Wexford)
1957 – J. Ryan (Wexford)
1958 – P. Downey (Kerry)
1959 – P. Downey (Kerry)

1960 – P. Downey (Kerry)
1961 – J. Maher (Louth)
1962 – P. Downey (Kerry)
1963 – J. Maher (Louth)
1964 – J. Maher (Louth)
1965 – P. McGee (Mayo)
1966 – P. Hickey (Tipperary)
1967 – P. McGee (Mayo)
1968 – J. Maher (Louth)
1969 – J. Maher (Louth)
1970 – J. Maher (Louth)
1971 – P. Hickey (Tipperary)
1972 – P. McGee (Mayo)
1973 – P. McGee (Mayo)
1974 – P. McGee (Mayo)
1975 – P. McGee (Mayo)
1976 – P. McGee (Mayo)
1977 – P. McGee (Mayo)
1978 – C. Winders (Kildare)
1979 – P. McGarry (Limerick)
1980 – P. McGarry (Limerick)
1981 – P. Winders (Kildare)
1982 - P. McGee (Mayo)
1983 – P. McGee (Mayo)

Senior Hardball Doubles

1926 – J. J. Bowles and S. Gleeson (Limerick)
1927 – T. Soye and T. O'Reilly (Dublin)
1928 – T. Soye and T. O'Reilly (Dublin)
1929 – P. Ormonde and C. Maloney (Tipperary)
1930 – T. Soye and G. Brown (Dublin)
1931 – P. Ormonde and C. Maloney (Tipperary)
1932 – P. Bell and J. Doyle (Meath)
1933 – P. Bell and J. Doyle (Meath)
1934 – J. Lucas and T. Cherry (Kilkenny)
1935 – P. Bell and J. Doyle (Meath)
1936 – P. Perry and P. Reid (Roscommon)
1937 – J. J. Gilmartin and A. Cullen (Kilkenny)
1938 – J. J. Gilmartin and T. Cherry (Kilkenny)
1939 – J. J. Gilmartin and T. Jordan (Kilkenny)
1940 – J. J. Gilmartin and P. Dalton (Kilkenny)
1941 – J. J. Gilmartin and J. Dunne (Kilkenny)
1942 – A. Clarke and J. Clarke (Dublin)
1943 – W. Walsh and D. Keogh (Cork)
1944 – W. Walsh and D. Keogh (Cork)
1945 – J. J. Gilmartin and P. Dalton (Kilkenny)
1946 – J. J. Gilmartin and P. Dalton (Kilkenny)
1947 – J. J. Gilmartin and P. Dalton (Kilkenny)
1948 – W. Walsh and T. Morrissey (Cork)
1949 – R. Grattan and J. Bolger (Kildare)
1950 – A. Clarke and G. Moran (Dublin)
1951 – J. Hassett and J. O'Brien (Kerry)
1952 – J. Ryan and J. Doyle (Wexford)
1953 – J. Hassett and P. Downey (Kerry)
1954 – J. Ryan and J. Doyle (Wexford)
1955 – J. Ryan and J. Doyle (Wexford)
1956 – J. Ryan and J. Doyle (Wexford)

1957 – J. Ryan and J. Doyle (Wexford)
1958 – J. Ryan and J. Doyle (Wexford)
1959 – P. Downey and J. O'Brien (Kerry)
1960 – P. Downey and J. O'Brien (Kerry)
1961 – J. Delaney and C. Delaney (Kilkenny)
1962 – J. Ryan and M. Shanahan (Tipperary)
1963 – P. Downey and J. O'Brien (Kerry)
1964 – J. Maher and P. Reilly (Louth)
1965 – P. McGee and P. Bolingbrook (Mayo)
1966 – P. McGee and P. Bolingbrook (Mayo)
1967 – P. McGee and P. Bolingbrook (Mayo)
1968 – P. Hickey and C. Cleere (Tipperary)
1969 – W. Doran and G. Lawlor (Kildare)
1970 – S. McCabe and L. Gilmore (Monaghan)
1971 – M. Sullivan and J. Doyle (Dublin)
1972 – P. Hickey and C. Cleere (Tipperary)
1973 – A. Byrne and W. Mullins (Westmeath)
1974 – P. McGee and B. Colleran (Mayo)
1975 – P. Hickey and J. Cleere (Tipperary)
1976 – P. Hughes and P. MacCormack (Mayo)
1977 – C. Winders and G. Lawlor (Kildare)
1978 – P. McGarry and J. Bennis (Limerick)
1979 – P. McGarry and J. Bennis (Limerick)
1980 – P. McGarry and J. Bennis (Limerick)
1981 – P. Winders and M. Purcell (Kildare)
1982 – P. Winders and C. Winders (Kildare)
1983 – P. Winders and C. Winders (Kildare)

Junior Softball Singles

1928 – M. Flannelly (Waterford)
1929 – P. Perry (Roscommon)
1930 – J. Hassett (Tipperary)
1931 – P. Delaney (Carlow)
1932 – J. Smith (Wexford)
1933 – P. Murray (Offaly)
1934 – J. Dunne (Kilkenny)
1935 – M. McMahon (Tipperary)
1936 – P. Phelan (Kilkenny)
1937 – W. Delaney (Wexford)
1938 – L. Rowe (Dublin)
1939 – M. Walsh (Galway)
1940 – P. Molloy (Kilkenny)
1941 – E. McMahon (Tipperary)
1942 - 45   —   No championship
1946 – P. Clarke (Mayo)
1947 – J. Ryan (Wexford)
1948 – H. Haddock (Armagh)
1949 – V. Sherlock (Cavan)
1950 – M. Griffin (Dublin)
1951 – C. Delaney (Kilkenny)
1952 – S. Commane (Kerry)
1953 – P. McCarthy (Kerry)
1954 – J. Delaney (Kilkenny)
1955 – J. Lyng (Wexford)
1956 – J. Maher (Louth)
1957 – P. Kirby (Clare)
1958 – F. Confrey (Louth)
1959 – M. Kirby (Clare)

1960 – M. O'Brien (Limerick)
1961 – D. Walshe (Sligo)
1962 – S. McCabe (Monaghan)
1963 – R. Lyng (Wexford)
1964 – W. Kerins (Kerry)
1965 – P. Sheerin (Offaly)
1966 – T. McEllistrim (Kerry)
1967 – P. McGarry (Limerick)
1968 – D. Kirby (Clare)
1969 – P. Davin (Tipperary)
1970 – M. Conway (Tyrone)
1971 – B. Colleran (Mayo)
1972 – P. Reilly (Kilkenny)
1973 – J. Howlin (Wexford)
1974 – P. Ryan (Dublin)
1975 – O. Harold (Kilkenny) 60 x 30
         P. O'Keeffe (Tipperary) 40 x 20
1976 – T. O'Brien (Kerry) 60 x 30
         M. Walsh (Roscommon) 40 x 20
1977 – J. Roche (Limerick) 60 x30
         P. Morris (Cork) 40 x 20
1978 – G. Scully (Galway) 60 x 30
         P. Delaney (Offaly) 40 x 20
1979 – A. Ryan (Tipperary) 60 x 30
         A. Ryan (Tipperary) 40 x 20
1980 – T. Quish (Limerick) 60 x 30
         D. O'Callaghan (Cork) 40 x 20
1981 – P. Mullins (Tipperary) 60 x 30
         J. Fleming (Wexford) 40 x 20
1982 – W. Bourke (Kilkenny) 60 x 30
         G. Coughlan (Clare) 40 x 20
1983 – M. Sweeney (Sligo) 60 x 30

Junior Softball Doubles

1928 – T. O'Keeffe and J. McCarthy (Tipperary)
1929 – P. Perry and T. Gaughran (Roscommon)
1930 – J. Molloy and H. Smith (Cavan)
1931 – C. Darcy and J. Cahill (Kildare)
1932 – W. Doyle and J. Fleming (Carlow)
1933 – T. Cherry and J. O'Brien (Kilkenny)
1934 – A. Cullen and P. Power (Kilkenny)
1935 – A. Roe and H. Gallagher (Dublin)
1936 – J. McDonald and J. Geraghty (Mayo)
1937 – J. Bergin and M. O'Gorman (Tipperary)
1938 – A. Collins and C. Collins (Tipperary)
1939 – W. McDonnell and R. Gibbons (Mayo)
1940 – D. McDonald and P. Ryan (Carlow)
1941 – S. Rice and E. McMahon (Tipperary)
1942 – P. Kennedy and J. Gaughran (Roscommon)
1943 - 45   —   No championship
1946 – W. Buggy and T. Buggy (Kilkenny)
1947 – G. Brogan and C. Donohoe (Dublin)
1948 – J. O'Connell and M. O'Keeffe (Kilkenny)
1949 – P. Kennedy and D. Carey (Tipperary)
1950 – T. McCormack and P. McCormack (Mayo)
1951 – P. Downey and T. Commane (Kerry)
1952 – J. Byrne and P. Sutherland (Wexford)
1953 – P. Munroe and M. Fahy (Dublin)

1954 – P. Hackett and J. Moynihan (Limerick)
1955 – T. Ryan and S. Lennon (Kilkenny)
1956 – E. Connolly and S. Fleming (Mayo)
1957 – T. McGarry and M. Mullins (Limerick)
1958 – J. Clery and W. McKenna (Wicklow)
1959 – T. Reilly and P. Reilly (Louth)
1960 – M. O'Brien and S. Walsh (Limerick)
1961 – J. Coughlan and G. Barry (Offaly)
1962 – M. Walsh and P. McGee (Mayo)
1963 – L. Gilmore and J. Gilmore (Cavan)
1964 – W. Kerins and P. Moriarty (Kerry)
1965 – L. Molloy and D. McGovern (Meath)
1966 – T. McEllistrim and M. McEllistrim (Kerry)
1967 – M. Henry and J. Gaffney (Sligo)
1968 – R. Doherty and P. Clarke (Roscommon)
1969 – N. Cahill and P. Masterson (Dublin)
1970 – R. Walsh and J. O'Brien (Dublin)
1971 – J. Kirby and M. Hogan (Clare)
1972 – P. Reilly and P. Delaney (Kilkenny)
1973 – J. Howlin and J. Goggins (Wexford)
1974 – E. Hannon and P. Walsh (Sligo)
1975 – O. Harold and B. Fitzpatrick (Kilkenny) 60 x 30
            T. Morrissey and E. Farrell (Tipperary) 40 x 20
1976 – G. and D. Sheridan (Cavan) 60 x 30
            P. Kealy and P. Mullins (Offaly) 40 x 20
1977 – P. Winders and T. O'Rourke (Kildare) 60 x 30
            M. Ward and G. Scully (Galway) 40 x 20
1978 – N. O'Brien and T. Morrissey (Tipperary)
            60 x 30
            B. O'Brien and M. Ahern (Kerry) 40 x 20
1979 – J. Molloy and F. Carroll (Meath) 60 x 30
            E. Rabbitte and J. Callanan (Galway) 40 x 20
1980 – T. and J. Quish (Limerick) 60 x 30
            M. Hennigan and M. Sweeney (Mayo) 40 x 20
1981 – F. McCann and M. Porter (Sligo) 60 x 30
            J. Fleming and P. Cleary (Wexford) 40 x 20
1982 – E. Farrell and W. Mullins (Tipperary) 60 x 30
            G. Coughlan and J. Duggan (Clare) 40 x 20
1983 – M. Walsh and E. Downey (Kilkenny) 60 x 30

1945 – M. O'Gorman (Tipperary)
1946 – G. Ryan (Kildare)
1947 – R. Grattan (Kildare)
1948 – J. Bolger (Kildare)
1949 – P. Kennedy (Tipperary)
1950 – M. O'Brien (Kildare)
1951 – P. Downey (Kerry)
1952 – C. O'Brien (Tipperary)
1953 – W. Lawlor (Kildare)
1954 – J. Delaney (Kilkenny)
1955 – M. Redmond (Kildare)
1956 – J. Maher (Louth)
1957 – W. Doran (Kildare)
1958 – J. Ryan (Tipperary)
1959 – D. Downey (Kerry)
1960 – J. Donovan (Kerry)
1961 – J. Cleary (Tipperary)
1962 – P. Hickey (Tipperary)
1963 – T. Dowd (Wexford)
1964 – P. Bolingbrook (Mayo)
1965 – P. Sheerin (Offaly)
1966 – T. McEllistrim (Kerry)
1967 – M. O'Gara (Roscommon)
1968 – A. Byrne (Dublin)
1969 – M. McAuliffe (Limerick)
1970 – J. Hartnett (Limerick)
1971 – J. Quigley (Wexford)
1972 – E. Sheeran (Offaly)
1973 – M. Purcell (Kildare)
1974 – P. MacCormack (Mayo)
1975 – P. Hughes (Kilkenny)
1976 – M. Walsh (Roscommon)
1977 – W. MacCarthy (Tipperary)
1978 – C. Quinn (Mayo)
1979 – N. Ryan (Tipperary)
1980 – E. Quigley (Wexford)
1981 – W. Pratt (Kilkenny)
1982 – W. Bourke (Kilkenny)
1983 – E. Lee (Dublin)

Junior Hardball Singles

1928 – J. Ryan (Tipperary)
1929 – J. O'Mahoney (Cork)
1930 – P. Bell (Meath)
1931 – J. Foley (Kildare)
1932 – J. O'Mahoney (Cork)
1933 – T. Cherry (Kilkenny)
1934 – A. Cullen (Kilkenny)
1935 – J. J. Gilmartin (Kilkenny)
1936 – P. Murray (Offaly)
1937 – W. Butler (Dublin)
1938 – T. Jordan (Kilkenny)
1939 – M. Butler (Dublin)
1940 – P. Molloy (Kilkenny)
1941 – M. Dowling (Kildare)
1942 – P. Murray (Offaly)
1943 – James Gilmartin (Kilkenny)
1944 – C. Drumgoole (Wexford)

Junior Hardball Doubles

1928 – S. Ryan and S. McInerney (Tipperary)
1929 – J. O'Mahoney and D. O'Mahoney (Cork)
1930 – N. Gorman and T. Maloney (Tipperary)
1931 – J. McGrath and J. O'Connell (Kilkenny)
1932 – A. Dalton and C. Baker (Kilkenny)
1933 – S. Tormey and P. Bell Jnr. (Meath)
1934 – A. Cullen and J. Dunne (Kilkenny)
1935 – P. Coyne and J. Purcell (Carlow)
1936 – G. Ryan and H. Costello (Kildare)
1937 – J. Hassett and M. O'Gorman (Tipperary)
1938 – J. Hurley and T. Twohill (Cork)
1939 – M. Butler and J. Roche (Dublin)
1940 – W. Walsh and R. Ward (Cork)
1941 – J. McGrath and D. Brennan (Kilkenny)
1942 – P. Murray and J. McHugh (Offaly)
1943 – Jas. Gilmartin and J. O'Brien (Kilkenny)
1944 – C. Drumgoole and J. Duggan (Wexford)

1945 – W. Grace and C. Murphy (Kildare)
1946 – M. Dalton and J. Dunne (Kilkenny)
1947 – J. McGrath and J. Phelan (Kilkenny)
1948 – W. McCabe and T. Tormey (Meath)
1949 – J. Doyle and P. Doyle (Wexford)
1950 – M. O'Brien and R. Maher (Kildare)
1951 – S. Monahan and J. Doherty (Kilkenny)
1952 – J. Kennedy and M. Heffernan (Tipperary)
1953 – W. Lawlor and P. Monahan (Kildare)
1954 – M. Gleeson and R. Doyle (Dublin)
1955 – M. Redmond and J. Parle (Kildare)
1956 – J. Maher and J. McArdle (Louth)
1957 – W. Doran and J. Curran (Kildare)
1958 – T. Doheny and M. Shanahan (Tipperary)
1959 – A. Daly and P. Winders (Kildare)
1960 – T. Cleere and C. Cleere (Tipperary)
1961 – M. Kelly and G. Connolly (Galway)
1962 – P. Hickey and T. Breedy (Tipperary)
1963 – P. Supple and J. Murphy (Cork)
1964 – G. Mahon and K. Fullard (Roscommon)
1965 – M. Sullivan and J. Doyle (Dublin)
1966 – T. McEllistrim and M. McEllistrim (Kerry)
1967 – G. Lawlor and R. Winders (Kildare)
1968 – N. Kerins and T. Fitzgerald (Kerry)
1969 – E. Deegan and J. Browne (Kildare)
1970 – J. Hartnett and P. Clancy (Limerick)
1971 – P. Murphy and J. Quigley (Wexford)
1972 – T. Geoghegan and C. Winders (Kildare)
1973 – M. Purcell and J. Byrne (Kildare)
1974 – M. Brady and T. Hurley (Dublin)
1975 – P. Hughes and W. Kennedy (Kilkenny)
1976 – G. and D. Sheridan (Cavan)
1977 – V. Mohan and S. Bennis (Limerick)
1978 – G. Scully and G. Rabbitte (Galway)
1979 – T. Ryan and N. Ryan (Tipperary)
1980 – T. Quish and J. Quish (Limerick)
1981 – P. Clery and S. MacLoughlin (Wexford)
1982 – W. Bourke and M. Lawlor (Kilkenny)
1983 – E. Lee and R. Walsh (Dublin)

Minor Softball Singles

1949 – J. O'Brien (Kerry)
1950 – L. Egan (Kilkenny)
1951 – R. Doherty (Roscommon)
1952 – R. Doherty (Roscommon)
1953 – J. Lyng (Wexford)
1954 – E. Horan (Kerry)
1955 – T. McGarry (Limerick)
1956 – J. Murray (Kilkenny)
1957 – M. Mullins (Limerick)
1958 – J. Clery (Wicklow)
1959 – J. Clery (Wicklow)
1960 – T. Ledwith (Westmeath)
1961 – D. Lyng (Wexford)
1962 – J. McEllistrim (Kerry)
1963 – M. Henry (Sligo)
1964 – M. Henry (Sligo)
1965 – P. Clarke (Roscommon)

1966 – P. McGarry (Limerick)
1967 – P. Murphy (Dublin)
1968 – P. Bennis (Limerick)
1969 – M. Brady (Dublin)
1970 – M. Walsh (Roscommon)
1971 – S. McLoughlin (Wexford)
1972 – S. McLoughlin (Wexford)
1973 – T. O'Rourke (Kildare)
1974 – D. Doolan (Roscommon)
1975 – J. Wafer (Wexford) 60 x 30
      M. Maher (Louth) 40 x 20
1976 – M. Maher (Louth) 60 x 30
      M. Maher (Louth) 40 x 20
1977 – S. McGovern (Meath) 60 x 30
      A. Ryan (Tipperary) 40 x 20
1978 – A. Ryan (Tipperary) 60 x 30
      A. Ryan (Tipperary) 40 x 20
1979 – W. Bourke (Kilkenny) 60 x 30
      W. O'Donnell (Tipperary) 40 x 20
1980 – W. Bourke (Kilkenny) 60 x 30
      W. Bourke (Kilkenny) 40 x 20
1981 – W. Bourke (Kilkenny) 60 x 30
      W. Bourke (Kilkenny) 40 x 20
1982 – M. Walsh (Kilkenny) 60 x 30
      J. Duggan (Clare) 40 x 20
1983 – M. Walsh (Kilkenny) 60 x 30

Minor Softball Doubles

1938 – J. Doran and G. Brogan (Dublin)
1939 – A. Kelly and J. Gaughran (Roscommon)
1940 – P. Kennedy and J. Sweeney (Tipperary)
1941 – P. Kennedy and J. Sweeney (Tipperary)
1942 - 45   —   No championship
1946 – J. Ryan and A. Power (Wexford)
1947 – P. Doherty and M. Mulhern (Mayo)
1948 – P. Somers and J. O'Keeffe (Kilkenny)
1949 – P. Bolingbrook and K. Swords (Mayo)
1950 – T. Hughes and J. O'Brien (Mayo)
1951 – S. Commane and M. Dennehy (Kerry)
1952 – R. Tunney and J. Swords (Mayo)
1953 – M. O'Connor and E. Horan (Kerry)
1954 – E. Horan and D. Downey (Kerry)
1955 – T. McGarry and M. Mullins (Limerick)
1956 – M. Sullivan and J. Murray (Kilkenny)
1957 – M. Mullins and G. Mitchell (Limerick)
1958 – W. Mullen and P. Geelan (Westmeath)
1959 – J. Clery and M. Dwyer (Wicklow)
1960 – N. Kerins and J. McMullan (Kerry)
1961 – D. Lyng and P. Lennon (Wexford)
1962 – D. Kirby and J. Kirby (Clare)
1963 – H. Ryan and P. Kavanagh (Wexford)
1964 – W. Myles and M. Fitzgibbon (Kerry)
1965 – W. Myles and M. Fitzgibbon (Kerry)
1966 – V. Grimes and C. Grimes (Meath)
1967 – P. Murphy and P. Domigan (Dublin)
1968 – J. Quigley and J. Sydney (Wexford)
1969 – J. Quigley and N. Quigley (Wexford)
1970 – M. Quigley and S. McLoughlin (Wexford)

1971 – P. McCormack and C. Quinn (Mayo)
1972 – D. Doolan and P. J. Moran (Roscommon)
1973 – O. Harold and J. Barron (Kilkenny)
1974 – P. Hughes and E. Mahon (Kilkenny)
1975 – J. Wafer and J. Goggins (Wexford) 60 x 30
      P. Delaney and B. O'Connell (Offaly) 40 x 20
1976 – J. McGovern and F. Carroll (Meath) 60 x 30
      P. Murphy and D. Neff (Cork) 40 x 20
1977 – S. McGovern and M. McGovern (Meath) 60 x 30
      A. Ryan and G. Walsh (Tipperary) 40 x 20
1978 – J. McGovern and M. McGovern (Meath) 60 x 30
      A. Ryan and M. Dyer (Tipperary) 40 x 20
1979 – W. Bourke and M. Cantwell (Kilkenny) 60 x 30
      W. Bourke and M. Cantwell (Kilkenny) 40 x 20
1980 – W. Bourke and M. Lawlor (Kilkenny) 60 x 30
      W. Bourke and M. Lawlor (Kilkenny) 40 x 20
1981 – E. Jenson and C. McGovern (Meath) 60 x 30
      W. Bourke and M. Lawlor (Kilkenny) 40 x 20
1982 – M. Walsh and L. Law (Kilkenny) 60 x 30
      J. Duggan and P. Clavin (Clare) 40 x 20
1983 – M. Walsh and S. Walsh (Kilkenny) 60 x 30

Minor Hardball Singles

1953 – J. Redmond (Wexford)
1954 – E. Horan (Kerry)
1955 – J. Ryan (Tipperary)
1956 – M. Sullivan (Kilkenny)
1957 – P. Hickey (Tipperary)
1958 – P. McGrath (Wexford)
1959 – J. Clery (Wicklow)
1960 – M. Purcell (Kildare)
1961 – J. Brennan (Kilkenny)
1962 – P. McLoughlin (Tipperary)
1963 – T. Morrissey (Kilkenny)
1964 – P. Cody (Cork)
1965 – T. Geoghegan (Kildare)
1966 – M. O'Gara (Roscommon)
1967 – G. Lawlor (Kildare)
1968 – J. Quigley (Wexford)
1969 – J. Quigley (Wexford)
1970 – M. Walsh (Roscommon)
1971 – P. McCormack (Mayo)
1972 – C. Quinn (Mayo)
1973 – P. Hughes (Kilkenny)
1974 – P. Hughes (Kilkenny)
1975 – P. Finnerty (Galway)
1976 – J. Dinneen (Limerick)
1977 – A. Ryan (Tipperary)
1978 – A. Ryan (Tipperary)
1979 – W. O'Donnell (Tipperary)
1980 – W. Bourke (Kilkenny)
1981 – W. Bourke (Kilkenny)
1982 – J. O'Donoghue (Tipperary)
1983 – J. O'Donoghue (Tipperary)

Minor Hardball Doubles

1953 – J. Redmond and M. Redmond (Wexford)

1954 – M. Sullivan and M. Hayes (Kilkenny)
1955 – J. O'Neill and M. Keyes (Limerick)
1956 – M. Sullivan and J. Murray (Kilkenny)
1957 – M. Mullins and J. O'Connell (Limerick)
1958 – M. Purcell and R. Winders (Kildare)
1959 – C. Cleere and J. Cleary (Tipperary)
1960 – M. Purcell and J. Byrne (Kildare)
1961 – J. Byrne and J. Browne (Kildare)
1962 – P. McLoughlin and A. Murphy (Tipperary)
1963 – G. Lawlor and T. Geoghegan (Kildare)
1964 – P. Cody and N. O'Brien (Cork)
1965 – T. Curley and S. Lynch (Galway)
1966 – G. Lawlor and A. Campbell (Kildare)
1967 – G. Lawlor and C. Winders (Kildare)
1968 – W. McCarthy and S. Halley (Tipperary)
1969 – M. Brady and M. Williams (Dublin)
1970 – M. Walsh and P. J. Moran (Roscommon)
1971 – S. McLoughlin and C. Kehoe (Wexford)
1972 – P. Hughes and J. Barron (Kilkenny)
1973 – P. Hughes and J. Barron (Kilkenny)
1974 – P. Hughes and E. Mahon (Kilkenny)
1975 – A. McConnell and J. Reilly (Meath)
1976 – F. McCann and M. Porter (Sligo)
1977 – A. Ryan and W. O'Donnell (Tipperary)
1978 – A. Ryan and W. O'Donnell (Tipperary)
1979 – M. McGovern and J. Smith (Meath)
1980 – W. Bourke and M. Lawlor (Kilkenny)
1981 – W. Bourke and M. Lawlor (Kilkenny)
1982 – E. Jensen and R. Morris (Meath)
1983 – J. O'Donoghue and E. Corbett (Tipperary)

Inter-club Championships

1969 – **Senior** – Ballymote (M. Henry, D. Walsh, J. Mattimoe, E. Hannon).
1970 – **Senior** – Taghmon (J. Quigley, P. Murphy, G. Mullins, M. Furlong).
1971 – **Senior** – Tuamgraney (M. Kirby, D. Kirby, T. Kirby, P. Ryan). **Novice** – St. Mary's, Kilkenny (P. Reilly, A. Greene, P. Delaney, M. Hayes)
1972 – **Senior** – Shannon (P. Kirby, J. Kirby, T. Kirby, M. Hogan). **Junior** – St. Malachy's, Dublin (P. Farrell, Pat Ryan, Pakie Ryan, P. Murray) **Novice** – St. Mary's Wexford (P. Goggins, P. Clampett, E. Byrne, M. Fenelon). **40 x 20 – Senior** – Shannon (J. Kirby, P. Kirby, T. Kirby, M. Hogan). **40 x20 – Junior** – Talbot's Inch (B. Fitzpatrick, O. Harrold, J. Barron, P. Walsh).
1973 – **Senior** – Shannon (P. Kirby, John Kirby, Joe Kirby, M. Hogan). **Junior** – St. Mary's, Wexford (P. Goggins, E. Byrne, P. Clampett, M. Fenelon). **Novice** – Shamrock's, Limerick (J. Power, R. Carey, C. Dunne, R. O'Connell).
1974 – **60 x 30 Senior** – St. Malachy's, Dublin (P. Ryan, P. Masterson, P. Farrell, P. Murray). **Junior** – St. Mary's, Clonmel (T. Morrissey, M. Tyrell, K. Conway, P. Mullins). **Novice** –

Talbot's Inch, Kilkenny (S. Reade, J. Bourke, M. Wall, P. Brennan). **40 x 20 Senior** – Naomh Pádraig, Dublin (T. Hurley, A. Byrne, M. Brady, N. Cahill). **Junior** – St. Malachy's, Dublin (P. Ryan, P. Murray, E. Smyth, A. Buckley). **Novice** – Naomh Pádraig, Dublin (P. Duignan, J. Warren, W. Rogers, P. Grange).

1975 – **60 x 30 Open** – Ballymacelligott (N. Kerins, T. MacEllistrim, M. MacEllistrim, T. Leen). **Novice** – Ballyanne (J. Doyle, J. Inglis, T. Murphy, M. Breen). **40 x 20 Novice** – Carlow (A. Heffernan, F. Flynn, A. Kelly, J. Kavanagh).

1976 – **60 x 30 Open** – Talbot's Inch (O. Harold, A. Greene, C. Young, J. Barron). **Novice** – Talbot's Inch (R. Lennon, S. Fitzgerald, T. Reidy, S. Hennessy). **40 x 20 Novice** – Enniscorthy (S. O'Leary, P. Walsh, J. Doyle, L. Swan, T. McGrath).

1977 – **60 x 30 Novice** – Moycullen (T. Sherlock, A. Audley, M. Lally, J. Flaherty). **Senior** – Roscommon (M. Walsh, J. O'Brien, D. Doolin, B. Colleran). **40 x 20 Novice** – Capwell (D. Callaghan, B. O'Brien, S. Tanner, J. Cronin).

1978 – **60 x 30 Novice** – Baldonnel (J. Warren, P. O'Reilly, F. Lawlor, T. Carr). **Senior** – Roscommon (M. Walsh, J. O'Brien, D. Doolin, B. Colleran). 40 x 20 Novice – Enniscorthy (N. O'Toole, E. Kelly, T. McGrath, M. Balfe, T. Kirwan). **Senior** – Capwell (D. Callaghan, P. Morris, B. O'Brien, E. Kennedy).

1979 – **60 x 30 Novice** – Garryhill (S. Ryan, J. Rossiter, J. Foley, T. Stapleton). **Senior** – Roscommon (M. Walsh, J. O'Brien, P. Moran, D. Doolin). **40 x 20 Novice** – Garryhill (S. Ryan, A. Ryan, J. Rossiter, R. Fitzgerald). **Senior** – Capwell (S. Oakes, S. Tanner, D. Callaghan, P. Morris, B. O'Brien, E. Kennedy).

1980 – **60 x 30 Novice** – Coolboy. **Senior** – Roscommon (M. Walsh, J. O'Brien, P. J. Moran, D. Doolin). **40 x 20 Novice** – Moycullen (M. Conneely, M. Clancy, M. Lally, J. Faherty, A. Audley). **Senior** – Capwell (P. Morris, D. Callaghan, S. Oakes, E. Kennedy).

1981 – **60 x 30 Novice** – Castlebar (M. Cody, L. Roche, S. Clarke, M. Shannon). **Junior** – Kells (J. Grant, A. McConnell, M. McGovern, S. McGovern). **Senior** – Talbot's Inch (J. Bourke, O. Harold, S, Reade, P. Reilly). **40 x 20 Novice. Junior** – Kells (M. McGovern, S. McGovern, E. Carroll, J. Molloy). **Senior** – Tralee (T. Fitzgerald, M. Aherne, J. Kerins, M. O'Brien).

1982 – **60 x 30 Novice** – Clonmel (K. Mullins, J. Ryan, J. Quirke, F. Scully). **Open** – Clonmel (T. Morrissey, E. Farrell, B. Mullins, P. Mullins). **40 x 20 Novice** – Dunshaughlin (P. Murray, E. Donovan, S. Joyce, J. Burke). **Senior** – Ballymore-Eustace (T. O'Rourke, P. Winders, M. Dowling, A. Campbell).

1983 – **60 x 30 Novice** – Na Fianna, Dublin (Patrick McGrath, Michael O'Brien, Gerry Geraghty, Kevin Caffrey). **Senior** – St Coman's, Roscommon (Michael Walsh, Joe O'Brien, P. J. Moran, Dermot Doolin. **40 x 20 Novice** – St. Peter's, Belfast (T. Maguire, J. Rainey, L. Rainey, G. Nugent). **Senior** – Talbot's Inch, Kilkenny (M. Walsh, A. Greene, M. Reade, T. Reade).

National League

1965 – **Wexford** (D. Lyng, W. Lyng, S. Dempsey, J. King).

1966 – **Sligo** (D. Walsh, M. Henry, E. Hannon, J. Finn).

1967 – **Wexford** (D. Lyng, J. King, J. Howlin, S. Buggy).

1968 – **Wexford** (D. Lyng, J. King, J. Howlin, S. Buggy).

1969 – **Dublin** (J. Doyle, P. Masterson, N. Cahill, A. Byrne)

1970 – **Wexford** (D. Lyng, S. Buggy, J. Howlin, P. Murphy).

1971 – **Clare** (M. Kirby, D. Kirby, J. Kirby, M. Hogan).

1972 – **Div. I** – **Clare** (M. Hogan, P. Kirby, J. Kirby, D. Kirby). **Div. II** – **Galway** (E. Rabbitte, D. Mulhern, M. Ward, E. McDonagh).

1973 – **Div. I** – **Clare** (P. Kirby, J. Kirby, D. Kirby, M. Hogan). **Div. II** – **Wicklow** (J. Clery, P. Lee, J. McMahon, R. Doyle).

1974 – **Div. I** – **Wexford** (P. Murphy, R. Lyng, J. Howlin, J. Quigley). **Div. II** – **Galway** (G. Scully, E. Rabbitte, M. Ward, E. MacDonagh).

1975 – **Div. I** – **Limerick** P. McGarry, M. Hogan, M. O'Brien, J. Power, R. O'Connell, R. Carey. **DIV. II** – **Carlow** A. Ryan, S. Ryan, M. Stapleton, F. Flynn, A. Heffernan, J. Lawlor.

1976 – **Div. I** – **Kilkenny** T. O'Brien, J. Burke, S. Reade, R. Lennon, A. Greene, O. Harold. **Div. II** – **Kildare** P. Winders, G. Lawlor, F. Heffernan, S. O'Donnell, T. O'Rourke.

1977 – **Wexford** S. Buggy, J. Goggins, T. Doyle, N. Beaver, J. Furlong, R. Aylward.

1978 – **Wicklow** J. Clery, P. Lee, R. Doyle, M. Dwyer, R. Willoughby, L. Barnes.

1979 – **Div. I** – **Kilkenny** P. Reilly, O. Harold, E. Downey, J. Downey, T. O'Brien, R. Lennon. **Div. II** – **Carlow** J. Ryan, S. Ryan, A. Ryan, T. Stapleton, J. Rossiter, G. Kane.

1980 – **Div. I** – **Wexford** E. Buggy, F. Hillis, P. Lennon, T. Doyle, S. Buggy, J. Goggins. **Div. II** – **Meath** C. Lynagh, J. Murtagh, C, Grimes, A. MacDonnell, J. McGovern, M. McGovern.

1981 – **Div. I** – **Wexford** R. Lyng, P. Murphy, J. Fleming, P. Cleary, F. Hillis, E. Buggy. **60 x 30 Div. II** – **Carlow** J. Rossiter, F. Flynn, A. Ryan, T. Stapleton, S. Ryan. **40 x 20 League** – **Clare** J. Kirby, D. Kirby, G. Coughlan, M. O'Hanlon, P. Devanny, N. Breen.

1982 – **Div. I** – **Wexford** E. Buggy, F. Hillis, J. Fleming, P. Cleary, P. Murphy, S. Buggy. **Div. II** – **Wicklow** M. Barnes, P. O'Donnell, R. Aylward, M. Dwyer, R. Willoughby, L. Barnes.

Willwood Tailteann Competitions

1966 – **Under-14 Singles:** M. Walsh (Roscommon);
Doubles: M. Walsh, A. Jameson (Roscommon)
Under-16 Singles: A. Carey (Tipperary);
Doubles: A. Carey, P. Kelly (Tipperary).
Senior Doubles: P. Hickey and J. Clery
(Tipperary) after extra time.

1967 – **Under-14 Singles:** A. O'Shaughnessy (West-
meath); **Doubles:** W. Long and J. Geary
(Galway). **Under-16 Singles:** M. O'Connor
(Kerry); **Doubles:** N. McKenna and S. Smith
(Meath). **Under-21 Singles:** P. McGarry
(Limerick); **Doubles:** V. and C. Grimes
(Westmeath). **Senior Doubles:** T. and J.
McEllistrim (Kerry). **Masters:** M. and J. Walsh
(Mayo).

1968 – **Under-14 Singles:** S. McLoughlin (Wexford).
Doubles: J. Devitt and N. Prendergast
(Dublin).
Under-16 Singles: B. O'Connor (Kerry);
Doubles: S. O'Connor and D. O'Sullivan
(Cork). **Under-21 Singles:** P. McGarry
(Limerick); **Doubles:** W. Myles and M.
Fitzgibbon (Kerry). **Senior Doubles:** T. and J.
McEllistrim (Kerry). **Masters:** M. Walsh and
M. Groarke (Mayo).

1969 – **Under-14 Singles:** O. Harrold (Kilkenny);
Doubles: J. Barron and W. McCarthy
(Kilkenny). **Under-16 Singles:** D. Kelly
(Dublin); **Doubles:** S. O'Connor and D.
O'Sullivan (Cork). **Under-21 Singles:** P.
Murphy (Wexford); **Doubles:** P. McGarry and
P. Bennis (Limerick). **Senior Doubles:** L.
Molloy and D. McGovern (Meath). **Masters:**
J. Doyle and J. Quigley (Wexford).

1970 – **Under-12 Singles:** F. Kerins (Dublin); **Doubles:**
N.Mannion and P. McCrann (Roscommon).
Under-14 Singles: P. Hughes (Kilkenny);
Doubles: J. Hoare and D. Doolan (Kilkenny).
Under-16 Singles: W. Fitzgibbon (Kerry);
Doubles: O. Harrold and J. Barron
(Kilkenny).
Under-21 Singles: J. Delaney (Kilkenny);
Doubles: P. Murphy and J. Quigley
(Wexford). **Senior Doubles:** M. O'Gara and P.
Clarke (Roscommon). **Masters:** C. Delaney
and T. Ryan (Kilkenny).

1971 – **Under-12 Singles:** T. O'Brien (Tipperary);
Doubles: T. Farrelly and D. Gargan (Dublin).
Under-14 Singles: J. Wafer (Wexford);
Doubles: P. McCrann and N. Mannion
(Roscommon). **Under-16 Singles:** J. Molloy
(Meath); **Doubles:** J. Barron and J. Delaney
(Kilkenny). **Under-21 Singles:** M. Walsh
(Roscommon); **Doubles:** M. Brady and M.
Williams (Dublin). **Senior Doubles:** P. McGee
and B. Colleran (Mayo). **Masters:** C. Delaney
and T. Ryan (Kilkenny).

1972 – **Under-12 Singles:** E. Downey (Kilkenny);

Doubles: C. Pratt and M. Kennedy (Tipperary).
Under-14 Singles: S. Morrissey (Tipperary);
Doubles: N. Mannion and P. McCrann
(Roscommon). **Under-16 Singles:** P. Hughes
(Kilkenny); **Doubles:** P. Winders and T.
O'Rourke (Kildare). **Under-21 Singles:**
M. Walsh (Roscommon); **Doubles:** E. Farrell
and J. Ryan (Tipperary). **Senior Doubles:**
P. Murphy and S. Buggy (Wexford).
Masters: J. O'Brien and P. Downey (Kerry).

1973 – **Under-12 Singles;** J. McCarthy (Tipperary);
Doubles: A. Sheridan and M. Pattison
(Dublin).
Under-14 Singles: D. O'Hanlon (Kilkenny);
Doubles: P. Devaney and D. Halton (Clare).
Under-16 Singles: G. Kelly (Offaly); **Doubles:**
N. Mannion and P. McCrann (Roscommon).
Under-21 Singles: W. Fitzgibbon (Tipperary);
Doubles: M. Brady and D. Sheridan (Cavan).
2**Senior Doubles:** P. Kirby and M. Hogan
(Clare).
Masters: M. Walsh and J. Gaffney (Mayo).

1974 – **Under-12 Singles:** W. Burke (Kilkenny);
Doubles: R. Monks and L. de Barra (Dublin).
Under-14 Singles: G. Ryan (Tipperary);
Doubles: M. Pattison and U. O Rodáin
(Dublin). **Under-16 Singles:** L. Leahy
(Kilkenny); **Doubles:** N. Mannion and
P. McCrann (Roscommon). **Novice Singles:**
R. Carey (Limerick); **Doubles:** P. Duignan and
E. Williams (Dublin).
Senior Doubles: P. Kirby and M. Hogan (Clare).
Masters: J. Delaney and T. Ryan (Kilkenny).

1975 – **Under 12** W. Bourke (Kilkenny). P. Hall and
E. MacCluskey (Dublin). **Under 14** M.
Pattison (Dublin). J. Curley and J. Ward
Galway). **Under 16** E. Downey (Kilkenny).
P. Cleary and J. Fleming (Wexford). **Senior
Doubles** P. Murphy and R. Lyng (Wexford).
Masters: J. Maher and J. MacArdle (Louth).
Novice M. Bourke (Limerick). J. Roche and
R. O'Connell (Limerick).

1976 – **Under 12** A. Kenny (Dublin). S. Ryan and J.
Hickey (Limerick). **Under 13** D. Caulfield
(Kilkenny). K. Murphy and E. Cleary
(Wexford). **Under 14** W. Bourke (Kilkenny).
J. Hogan and T. Costello (Limerick). **Under
15** M. McGovern (Meath). P. Whelan and G.
King (Wexford). **Under 16** T. Ryan
(Tipperary). A. Mulhall and M. Cantwell
(Kilkenny).

1977 – **Under 12** J. Fitzell (Tipperary). J. Walsh and
M. Walsh (Kilkenny). **Under 13** P.
O'Donovan (Limerick). F. O'Callaghan and
F. Cunningham (Dublin). **Under 14** W.
Bourke (Kilkenny). E. MacCluskey and A.
Kenna (Dublin). **Under 15** T. Leahy
(Wexford). R. Lynch and J. Lee (Dublin).
Under 16 M. Pattison (Dublin). J. Smith and

M. McGovern (Meath.
1978 – **Under 12** M. Walsh (Kilkenny). P. Maher, M. Knox (Kilkenny). **Under 13** J. Woodlock (Tipperary). J. Doyle, M. Purcell (Kilkenny). **Under 14** A. Kenna (Dublin). M. Spillane, J. Kelly (Cork).
Under 15 G. Coughlan (Clare). D. Lynch and D. O'Brien (Dublin). **Under 16** W. Bourke (Kilkenny). S. Walsh and s. Foskin (Kilkenny).
1979 – **60 x 30 Under 12** F. Kavanagh (Westmeath). T. Sheridan and A. McGovern (Meath). **Under 13** J. O'Connor (Mayo). A. O'Brien and P. Russell (Limerick). **Under 14** J. Woodlock (Tipperary). M. Walsh and J. Walsh (Kilkenny). **Under 15** T. Foley (Wicklow). S. Murphy and L. Cassidy (Westmeath). **Under 16** W. Bourke (Kilkenny). P. Hall and E. MacCluskey (Dublin). **040 x 20 Under 14** J. Woodlock (Tipperary). P. Clavin and J. Duggan (Clare). **Under 16** G. Coughlan (Clare). J. Scannell and J. O'Neill (Tipperary).
1980 – **60 x 30 Under 12** W. O'Connor (Dublin). T. Sheridan, A. McGovern (Meath). **Under 13** T. Hennessey (Kilkenny). J. Walsh and J. Buckley (Kilkenny). **Under 14** M. Walsh (Kilkenny). N. O'Brien, E. O'Neill (Limerick). **Under 15** E. Jensen (Meath). F. MacCarthy and D. Nolan (Dublin). **Under 16** P. Donovan (Limerick). J. Kelly and M. Spillane (Cork). **40 x 20 Under 14** M. Walsh, Kilkenny, N. O'Brien and E. O'Neill (Limerick). **Under 16** L. Law (Kilkenny). J. Kelly and M. Spillane (Cork).
1981 – **60 x 30 Under 12** J. Dwyer (Tipperary). S. White, J. McGeer (Tipperary). **Under 13** J. Byrne (Meath). N. Clarke, P. Garvey (Mayo). **Under 14** E. O'Neill (Limerick). C. O'Reilly and D. Maloney (Mayo). **Under 15** M. Naughton (Westmeath). E. Corbett and M. Kenneally (Tipperary). **Under 16** J. Woodlock (Tipperary). J. Doyle and P. Meather (Kilkenny). 40 x 20 Under 14 E. O'Neill (Limerick). C. Reilly and d. Malone (Kilkenny). **Under 16** J. Duggan (Clare). M. Walsh and J. Walsh (Kilkenny).
1982 – **60 x 30 Under 12** C. Nevin (Westmeath). D. J. Carey and B. Kenna (Kilkenny). **Under 13** M. Hayes (Kilkenny). P. O'Rourke and D. Gough (Meath). **Under 14** W. O'Connor (Dublin). T. Sheridan and A. MacGovern (Meath). **Under 15** T. Shine (Cork). K. Lynch and S. Hegarty (Cork). **Under 16** M. Walsh (Kilkenny). F. Kavanagh and M. Naughton (Westmeath). **40 x 20 Under 14** W. O'Connor (Dublin). T. Sheridan and A. MacGovern (Meath). **Under 16** M. Walsh (Kilkenny). F. Kavanagh and M. Naughton (Westmeath).
1983 – **60 x 30 Under 12** B. Aldridge (Kilkenny). J.

Delaney, S. Kelly (Kilkenny). **Under 13** S. Ward (Westmeath). K. Lyons, P. Galvin (Limerick). **Under 14** P. Kilgannon (Mayo). D. Gough, P. O'Rourke (Meath). **Under 15** G. McCarthy (Cork). D. Hennick, N. Keogh (Wexford). **Under 16** F. Kavanagh (Westmeath). T. Sherridan, A. McGovern (Meath). **40 x 20 Under 14** M. Hayes (Kilkenny). J. Flynn, C. Warnsley (Cork). **Under 16** W. O'Connor (Dublin). A. McGovern, T. Sherridan (Meath).

III   Intervarsity Handball

Winners of senior singles championship:
1975 – Pat Morris, UCC
1976 – C. Quinn UCD
1977 – C. Quinn UCD
1978 – Pat Morris, UCC
1979 – Mick Shiel, UCG
1980 – Mark Patterson, TCD
1981 – Ger Coughlan, UCG
1982 – Ger Coughlan, UCG
1983 – Ger Coughlan, UCG

RTE Top - Ace Competition

1973 – P. Murphy (Wexford)
1974 – P. Kirby (Clare)
1975 – P. Kirby (Clare)
1976 – P. Reilly (Kilkenny)
1977 – J. Kirby (Clare)
1978 – R. Lyng (Wexford)
1979 – M. Walsh (Roscommon)
1980 – **60 x 30** T. O'Rourke (Kildare)
　　　　40 x 20 T. Muck (USA)
1981 – **60 x 30** P. Ryan (Dublin)
　　　　40 x 20 J. Sabo (USA)
1982 – **60 x 30** R. Lyng (Wexford)
　　　　40 x 20 J. Sabo (USA)
1983 – **60 x 30** T. Morrissey (Tipperary)
　　　　40 x 20 N. Alvarado (USA)

Ladies Handball Championship Records: *We acknowledge with gratitude the assistance of Ann Coady, Sec. Ladies Handball Association, in compiling these records.*

1970 _ First Inter-County: M. O'Toole (Na Fianna); H. and M. Flynn (Oldtown).
1971 – *First All-Ireland:* Over 18 M. O'Toole (Na Fianna); E. Nichols and M. Deignan. Minor M. Hoare (Roscommon); M. Carey and K. Igoe (Roscommon).
1972 – *All-Ireland:* Under 14 C. Monks (Oldtown); L. Cox and J. McDermott (Eoghan Ruadh). Under 16 E. Shannon (Na Fianna); B. McAnaney and E. Doyle (Eoghan Ruadh). Under 18 M. Hoare (Roscommon); M. Carey and K. Igoe (Roscommon). Over 18 M.

O'Toole (Na Fianna); E. Nichol and M. Deignan (Na Fianna).

1973 – *First Willwood Tailteann:* Under 16 B. Foy and B. McAnaney (Na Fianna). Under 18 E. Shannon (Na Fianna). *All-Ireland* Under 12 G. Hall (Oldtown) C. Carey and M. Fitzgerald (Roscommon). Under 14 C. Monks (Oldtown); J. McDermott and L. Cox (Eoghan Ruadh). Under 16 M. Hoare (Roscommon); V. Harris and B. Murphy (Eoghan Ruadh); Under 18 E. Shannon (Na Fianna); K. Igoe and B. Hannon (Roscommon). Senior M. O'Toole (Na Fianna); E. Nichol and E. Joyce (Na Fianna).

1974 – *Willwood Tailteann:* Under 13 P. Keogh (Eoghan Ruadh); M. and L. Kilbride (Coolboy). Under 15 S. Carey (Eoghan Ruadh); C. Monks and K. Finn (Oldtown). Under 17 B. McEneaney (Eoghan Ruadh); B. Murphy and V. Harris (Eoghan Ruadh). *All Ireland:* Senior M. O'Toole (Na Fianna); M. O'Toole and E. Nichol (Na Fianna). Junior H. McCabe (Oldtown); P. Kavanagh and A. Henehan (Na Fianna). Novice A. Sherlock (Na Fianna); M. Mullins and J. Byrne (Eoghan Ruadh). Under 18 E. Shannon (Na Fianna); B. McEneaney and E. Doyle (Eoghan Ruadh); Under 16 C. Monks (Oldtown); Doubles - Roscommon. Under 14 S. Carey (Eoghan Ruadh); K. Finn and A. McArdle (Oldtown). Under 12 G. Hall (Oldtown); P. Hynes and C. Byrne (Oldtown).

1975 – Willwood Tailteann: Under 13 E. Hall (Oldtown); C. Madden and B. Reilly (Galway). Under 15 S. Carey (Dublin); J. McDermott and P. Keogh (Dublin). Under 17 C. Monks (Oldtown); V. Harris and B. Murphy (Dublin). *All-Ireland Juvenile* Under 12 E. Hall (Oldtown); P. Hynes and A. Byrne (Oldtown). Under 14 G. Hall (Oldtown); M. Meehan and K. Byrne (Oldtown). Under 16 C. Doherty (Galway); K. Finn and A. McArdle (Oldtown). Under 18 A. Kelly (Falcarragh); B. Murphy and V. Harris (Eoghan Ruadh). *All-Ireland Adult;* Senior M. O'Toole; M. O'Toole and E. Nichol (Na Fianna). Junior M. Nicholson (Arklow); D. O'Shea and G. Gray (Na Fianna). Novice S. Barnes (Arklow); A. Walker and M. Barnes (Arklow).

1976 – *Willwood Tailteann:* Under 13 E. Hall (Oldtown); P. Hynes and F. Carroll (Dublin). Under 15 A. Holden (Kilkenny); M. Ryan and T. Scully (Tipperary). Under 17 C. Doherty (Galway); K. Finn and A. McArdle (Dublin). *All-Ireland Juvenile:* Under 12 E. Twomey (Ballymacelligot); A. Monks and R. Hogan (Oldtown). Under 14 R. Mulligan (Cashel);

B. Reilly and C. Madden (Galway). Under 16 G. Hall (Oldtown); P. Keogh and S. Carey (Eoghan Ruadh). Under 18 C. Monks (Oldtown); M. Gallagher and M. Kelly (Falcarragh). *All-Ireland Adult:* Senior M. O'Toole (Na Fianna); E. Nichol and E. Shannon (Na Fianna). Junior S. Barnes (Arklow); M. Barnes and M. Walker (Arklow). Novice M. McKeever (Oldtown); M. O'Sullivan and C. Vigers (Arklow). Over 30: P. Archbold (Dunlavin); A. Barnes and M. Byrne (Arklow).

1977 – *Willwood Tailteann:* Under 13 E. Hall (Oldtown); D. Twomey and A. Doherty (Ballymacelligot). Under 15 R. Mulligan (Cashel); M. Doherty and S. Leen (Ballymacelligot). Under 17 G. Hall (Oldtown); S. Carey and P. Keogh. *All-Ireland Junvenile:* Under 12 E. Twomey (Ballymacelligot); T. Bonner and A. Buckley (Cashel). Under 14 M. Doherty (Ballymacelligot); D. Twomey and A. Doherty (Ballymacelligot). Under 16 G. Hall (Oldtown); S. Leen and S. Twomey. Under 18 N. Bonner (Cashel); M. Mythen and A. Mythen (Coolgreaney). *All-Ireland Adult:* Senior M. O'Toole; E. Nichol and E. Shannon (Na Fianna). Junior, A. Sherlock (Na Fianna); M. O'Sullivan and C. Vigners (Arklow). Novice S. Ford (Arklow); A. Sheridan and A. Barker (Oldtown). Over 30 M. Lynch (Na Fianna); M. Byrne and M. Ryan (Arklow).

1978 & 1979 – Senior Singles 60 x 30 Mavis O'Toole (other records for these years untracable)

1980 _ *All-Ireland (40 x 20) Juvenile.* Under 12 Bertilla Mythen; Jill Mulvaney and Michelle Kelly (Oldtown). Under 14 Nora Brooks (Taughmaconnell); Teresa Bonnar and Mary Lonergan (Cashel). Under 16 Elizabeth Hall (Oldtown); Elizabeth Hall and Ann Monks (Oldtown). Minor Majella Mythen (Coolgreaney); Majella and Mary Mythen (Coolgreaney). *All-Ireland (40 x 20) Adult.* Novice Pauline Collum (Na Fianna); Pauline Collum and Denise Doyle (Na Fianna). Junior Mary Fitzgerald (Na Fianna); Mary Fitzgerald and Ann Cody (Na Fianna). Senior Elizabeth Nichol (Na Fianna). Over 30 Brídín Uí Mhaolagain (Na Fianna) and Anne Barnes (Arklow). *Willwood Tailteann (60 x 30)* Under 13 Sheena Sharkey (Falcarragh); Triona Bonnar and Deirdre Heelan (Cashel). Under 15 Elizabeth Hall (Oldtown); Margaret Mc Fadden and Rosie Sharkey (Falcarragh). Under 17 Caroline Tierney (Multyfarnham); Colette Barnes and Kathleen O'Reilly (Arklow). *All-Ireland (60 x 30)* Novice Aine

Hayden (St. Comans, Roscommon); Mary Gullane and Aine Hayden(St. Comans). Junior Mary Fitzgerald (Na Fianna); Mary Fitzgerald and Ann Cody (Na Fianna). Senior Mavis O'Toole (Na Fianna); Mavis O'Toole and Liz Nichol (Na Fianna). Over 30 Ann Ralph (Horse & Jockey); Anne O'Rourke and Anne Ralph (Horse & Jockey). *All-Ireland Juvenile (60 x 30)* Under 12 Claudette Forde (Arklow); Caroline Forde and Miriam Forde (Arklow). Under 14 Nora Brooks (Taughmaconnel); Caroline O'Brien and Caroline Kelly (Oldtown). Under 16 Mary McFadden (Falcarragh); Elizabeth Hall and Ann Monks (Oldtown). Minor Majella Mythen (Coolgreaney); Mary and Majella Mythen (Coolgreaney).

1981 – *All-Ireland (60 x 30)* Novice Marion Graham (Horse & Jockey); Marion and Judy Grahan (Horse & Jockey). Junior Susan Carey (Na Fianna); Susan Carey and Pauline Collum (Na Fianna). Senior Mavis O'Toole (Na Fianna); Mairead O'Sullivan and Charlotte Vigors (Arklow). Over 30 Marie Byrne Arklow); Mollie Ryan and Marie Bryne (Arklow). *All-Ireland Juvenile (40 x 20)* Under 12 Jean O'Brien (Oldtown); J. Mulvaney and Jean O'Brien (Oldtown). Under 14 Ester Breslin (Arklow); Ester Breslin and Ann Marie Gilbert (Arklow). Under 16 Elizabeth Hall (Oldtown); Elizabeth Hall and Caroline O'Brien (Oldtown). Minor Elizabeth Hall (Oldtown); Elizabeth Hall and Caroline O'Brien (Oldtown). *Willwood Tailteann (60 x 30)* Under 13 Bertilla Mythen (Coolgreaney); Miriam Forde and Anne Thompson (Arklow). Under 15 Nora Brooks (Taughtmaconnel); Teresa Bonner and Nora O'Dwyer (Cashel). Under 17 Elizabeth Hall (Oldtown); Saidbh Henderson and Ailson Kelly (Na Fianna). *All-Ireland (60 x 30) Juvenile* Under 12 Claudette Forde (Arklow); Caroline Forde and Eileen Thompson (Arklow). Under 14 Bertilla Mythen (Coolgreaney); B. Mythen and Bernie Boland (Coolgreaney). Under 16 Nora Brooks (Taughtmaconnel); Elizabeth Hall and Caroline O'Brien (Oldtown). *All-Ireland (40 x 20)* Junior Susan Carey (Na Fianna); Susan Carey and Pauline Collum (Na Fianna). Senior Elizabeth Nichol (Na Fianna); Mary Fitzgerald and Ann Cody (Na Fianna). Over 30 Marie Byrne (Arklow).

1982 – *Willwood Tailteann (60 x 30)* Under 13 Claudette Forde (Arklow); Ailish Munnelly and Sharon Nealon (Kilalla). Under 15 Bertilla Mythen (Coolgreaney); Geraldine Kilgannon and Mary Durcan (Kilalla). Under 17 Elizabeth Hall (Oldtown); Janice Walker and Kathleen Healy (Arklow). *All-Ireland (60 x 30)* Under 12 Annette McCarthy (Coolgreaney); Michelle Buckley and Tina Keating (Cashel). Under 14 Bertilla Mythen (Coolgreaney; Noelle O'Boyle and Nuala Coleman (Na Fianna). Under 16 Nora Brooks (St. Coman's); Sodilva Smith and Lucy McCabe (Kingscourt). Minor Elizabeth Hall (Oldtown); Elizabeth Hall and Margaret O'Brien (Oldtown). *All-Ireland (40 x 20)* Under 12 Mary Breslin (Arklow); Annette McCarthy and Kay Butler (Coolgreaney). Under 14 Beverly Kelly (Na Fianna); Bertilla Mythen and Frances McCarthy (Coolgreaney). Under 16 Nora Brooks (Taughmaconnel); Sodilva Smith and Lucy McCabe (Kingscourt). Minor Elizabeth Hall (Oldtown); Elizabeth Hall and Margaret O'Brien (Oldtown). Novice Marie Mallen (Sliabh Dubh, Belfast); Marie Mallen and Noirin McAllister (Sliabh Dubh). Junior Majella Mythen (Coolgreaney); Charlotte Vigors and Ruby Vigors (Arklow). *Leinster* Senior Susan Carey (Eoghan Ruadh); Susan Carey and Marion Mullen (Eoghan Ruadh). Over 30 Teresa Kelly (Loughmacrory, Tyrone); Mavis O'Toole and Brídín Uí Mhaolagain (Na Fianna). *All-Ireland (60 x 30)* Novice Kitty Kerwick (Horse & Jockey); Kitty Kerwick and Ann Graham (Horse & Jockey). Junior Majella Mythen (Coolgreaney); Majella and Bernie Mythen (Coolgreaney). Over 30 Marie Byrne (Arklow). *Leinster* Senior Susan Carey (Eoghan Ruadh); Charlotte Vigors and Mairead O'Sullivan (Arklow).

1983 – *Willwood Tailteann (60 x 30)* Under 13 Alison Smith (Kingscourt); Elaine Garvey and Rosemary Mitchell (Kilalla). Under 15 Bertilla Mythen (Coolgreaney); Geraldine Kilgannon and Mary Durkan (Kilalla). Under 17 Nora Brooks (St. Coman's); Sodilva Smith and Lucy McCabe (Kingscourt). *All-Ireland (60 x 30)* Under 12 Orla Garvey (Kilalla); Mary Breslin and Jane Thompson (Arklow). Under 14 Denise Garvey (Kilalla); Karen Johnston and Catherine Curtis (Kingscourt). Under 16 Bertilla Mythen (Coolgreaney); Sodilva Smith and Lucy McCabe (Kingscourt). *All-Ireland (40 x 20)* Minor Elizabeth Hall (Oldtown); Elizabeth Hall and Margaret

O'Brien (Oldtown). Junior Elizabeth Hall (Oldtown); Geraldine and Elizabeth Hall (Oldtown). Senior Susan Carey (Eoghan Ruadh); Susan Carey and Marion Mullen (Eoghan Ruadh). Novice Doubles Ruth Ryan and Kathleen Byrne (Arklow). Over 30 Mary Lyndsay (Belfast).

LADIES SENIOR TEAM *CHAMPIONSHIPS* (Team of 5)

Year	60 x 30	40 x 20
1980	Arklow	Arklow
1981	Na Fianna	Na Fianna
1982	Na Fianna	Na Fianna
1983	. . . .	Oldtown

(The 1983 Championships have not all been completed at the time of going to press)

Gael-Linn

In 1954 Gael-Linn introduced a completely new idea for a handball competition. Instead of deciding the winner of a match by reference to a given number of games, it was to be decided on a time basis, i.e. the winner to be the player in the lead at the end of a certain period of time, usually a half-an-hour. The idea met with immediate success and hundreds of players took part in the competition each year. The competition ended when the eight 'group' winners were brought together at a central venue for the final stages which were played on the one day.

Winners

1954	J. Ryan (Wexford)	1969	J. Maher (Louth)
1955	D. Dillon (Dublin)	1970	R. Lyng (Wexford)
1956	J. Ryan (Wexford)	1971	R. Lyng (Wexford)
1957	D. Dillon (Dublin)	1972	P. Ryan (Dublin & Clare)
1958	T. McGarry (Limerick)	1973	R. Lyng (Wexford)
1959	T. McGarry (Limerick)	1974	P. Ryan (Dublin & Clare)
1960	J. Maher (Louth)	1975	P. Ryan (Dublin & Clare)
1961	M. Kirby (Clare)	1976	P. McGarry (Limerick)
1962	J. Maher (Louth)	1977	P. O'Reilly (Kilkenny)
1963	J. Delaney (Kilkenny)	1978	R. Lyng (Wexford) 60 x 30
1964	J. Maher (Louth)		P. Kirby (Clare) 40 x 20
1965	J. Delaney (Kilkenny)	1979	T. O'Rourke (Kildare) 60 x 30
1966	F. Confrey (Louth)		P. Kirby (Clare) 40 x 20
1967	T. McEllistrim (Kerry)	1980	Abandoned: trophy now given to National
1968	M. Walsh (Mayo)		League winners

Handballer of the Year
B. & I. Award (1975–)

1975 Pat Kirby (Clare)	1979 Pat McGarry (Limerick)
1976 Pat Kirby (Clare)	1980 Billy Burke (Kilkenny)
1977 Pat Kirby (Clare)	1981 Tony Ryan (Tipperary)
1978 Dick Lyng (Wexford)	1982 Dick Lyng (Wexford)

WORLD'S HANDBALL CHAMPIONSHIP RESULTS, 1964

Teams	Won For Singles	Won For Doubles	Lost To Singles	Lost To Doubles	Standings Won	Standings Lost
Australia			Canada Ireland Mexico U.S.	Canada Ireland Mexico U.S.	0	8
Canada	Australia Ireland	Australia Ireland Mexico	Mexico U.S.	U.S.	5	3
Ireland	Australia	Australia	Canada Mexico U.S.	Canada Mexico U.S.	2	6
Mexico	Australia Canada Ireland	Australia Ireland	U.S.	Canada U.S.	5	3
United States	Australia Canada Ireland Mexico	Australia Canada Ireland Mexico			8	0

* Canada won playoff for 2nd place.

INDIVIDUAL RATINGS

Jimmy Jacobs, United States, with 4 wins in Singles is the world's Singles Champion.
John Sloan and Phil Elbert, United States, with 4 wins are the World's Doubles Champions.
Oscar Villareal, Mexico, second with 3 wins in Singles.
Mickey Unreath and Harry Tepperman, Canada, second with 3 wins in Doubles.

NEW YORK ATHLETIC CLUB

WORLD HANDBALL CHAMPIONSHIP RESULTS 1967

The second official world handball championship was held in Toronto, Canada, from November 20-22, inclusive. A total of 4 countries competed – U.S.A., Canada, Mexico, and Ireland. The Irish representatives were S. McCabe (Monaghan) in singles and L. Molloy and D. McGovern (Meath) in doubles. While success was not our lot, nevertheless our players acquitted themselves well despite the handicap of playing in the smaller courts and eventually finished in third place. Details re the singles and doubles championships as follows:-

Singles
Canada (J. Maher) defeated Ireland (S. McCabe) 21-5, 21-10.
Canada (J. Maher) defeated Mexico (I. Hernandiz), 21-4, 21-11.
Canada (J. Maher) defeated U.S.A. (C. Obert), 21-9, 21-9.
U.S.A. (C. Obert) defeated Ireland (S. McCabe), 21-10, 21-2
U.S.A. (C. Obert) defeated Mexico (I. Hernandiz), 21-13, 21-13.
Ireland (S. McCabe) defeated Mexico (I. Hernandiz), 14-21, 21-10, 21-19.

Winner – Joe Maher (Canada). Runner-up – Carl Obert (U.S.A.).

Doubles
U.S.A. (O. and R. Obert) defeated Ireland (L. Molloy and D. McGovern), 21-4, 21-12.
U.S.A. (do.) defeated Mexico (I. Hernandiz, V. Yamer), 21-18, 21-7.
U.S.A. (do.) defeated Canada (M. Unreath, H. Tepperman), 21-12, 21-20.
Canada (M. Unreath and H. Tepperman) defeated Ireland (L. Molloy and D. McGovern), 21-6, 12-11.
Canada (do.) defeated Mexico (I. Hernandiz, V. Yamer), 21-1, 21-13.
Ireland (L. Molloy, D. McGovern) defeated Mexico (do.), 11-21, 21-10, 21-10.
Winner – Oscar and Ruby Obert (U.S.A.).
Runner-up – M. Unreath and H. Tepperman (Canada).

WORLD HANDBALL CHAMPIONSHIP RESULTS 1970

Singles Champion – Patrick Kirby (U.S.A.).
Singles (runner-up) – Joseph Maher (Ireland).
Doubles Champions – Seamus Buggy and Richard Lyng (Ireland).
Doubles (runner-up) – Mel Brown and Bob Wilson (Canada).
Team Championship – Ireland (R. Lyng, S. Buggy and J. Maher).

Singles

Joey Maher (Ireland) bt. Barry Leech (Canada) 21-5, 21-7.

Pat Kirby (U.S.A.) bt. Victor Yanar (Mexico) 21-17, 21-12.

Vic De Luzio (Australia) bt. Leech 21-16, 21-9.

Maher bt. Yanar 21-3, 21-12.

Kirby bt. Di Luzio 6-21, 21-12, 21-3.

Maher bt. Di Luzio 21-4, 21-8.

Kirby bt. Leech 21-2, 21-5.

Leech bt. Yanar 21-3, 21-4.

Kirby bt. Maher 21-19, 21-12.

Di Luzio bt. Yanar 21-14, 21-10.

Kirby – Played 4, Won 4, Lost 0, Points 4.

Maher – Played 4, Won 3, Lost 1, Points 3.

Di Luxio – Played 4, Won 2, Lost 2, Points 2.

Leech – Played 4, Won 1, Lost 3, Points 1.

Yanar – Played 4, Won 0, Lost 4, Points 0.

Doubles

Mel Brown and Bob Wilson (Canada) bt. Ray Neveau and Simie Fine (U.S.A.) 15-21, 21-19, 21-18.

Terry Caplice and Jim Kiley (Australia) bt. Guillermo Correao and Victor Yanar (Mexico) 21-12, 21-14.

Dick Lyng and Seamus Buggy (Ireland) bt. Brown and Wilson 21-7, 21-6.

Neveau and Fine bt. Correao and Yanar 21-15, 21-2.

Lyng and Buggy bt. Caplice and Kiley 21-4, 21-9.

Lyng and Buggy bt. Correao and Yanar 21-7, 21-14.

Neveau and Fine bt. Caplice and Kiley 21-11, 21-12.

Lyng and Buggy bt. Neveau and Fine 21-5, 21-12.

Brown and Wilson bt. Correao and Yanar 21-5, 13-21, 21-12.

Brown and Wilson bt. Caplice and Kiley 21-19, 21-5.

Lyng and Buggy – Played 4, Won 4, Lost 0, Points 4.

Brown and Wilson – Played 4, Won 3, Lost 1, Points 3

Neveau and Fine – Played 4, Won 2, Lost 2, Points 2.

Caplice and Kiley – Played 4, Won 1, Lost 3, Points 1.

Correao and Yanar – Played 4, Won 0, Lost 4, Points 0.

IAHA, 1924-1983

Year	*Counties affiliated*	*President*	*Secretary*
1924		J. Lawlor	Sean O'Hanlon
1925		A. C. Harty	Sean O'Hanlon
1926		A. C. Harty (died)	
		General E. O'Duffy	Sean O'Hanlon
1927		General E. O'Duffy	Sean O'Hanlon
1928		General E. O'Duffy	Sean O'Hanlon
1929		B. Fay	Sean O'Hanlon
1930	21	B. Fay	Sean O'Hanlon
1931	29	B. Fay	Sean O'Hanlon
1932	29	B. Fay	Sean O'Hanlon (Res)
			Martin O'Neill
1933	23	B. Fay	Martin O'Neill
1934	22	B. Fay	Martin O'Neill
1935	21	E. Purcell	Martin O'Neill
1936	20	E. Purcell	Martin O'Neill
1937	18	E. Purcell	Martin O'Neill
1938	14	T. Caulfield	Martin O'Neill
1939	16	T. Caulfield	Martin O'Neill
1940	15	T. Caulfield	Martin O'Neill
1941	13	M. Byrne	Martin O'Neill
1942	15	M. Byrne	Martin O'Neill
1943	9	M. Byrne	Martin O'Neill
1944	8	P. Murphy	Martin O'Neill
1945	10	P. Murphy	Martin O'Neill
1946	15	P. Murphy	Martin O'Neill

1947	13	J. O'Brien	Gerry Moran
1948	13	J. O'Brien	Gerry Moran
1949	20	J. O'Brien	T. J. McElligott
1950	25	P. Caulfield	T. J. McElligott
1951	25	P. Caulfield	T. J. McElligott
1952	30	P. Caulfield	T. J. McElligott
1953	31	J. Bergin	T. J. McElligott
1954	32	J. Bergin	T. J. McElligott (Res)
			J. Lynch
1955	31	J. Bergin	J. Lynch
1956	30	Canon Carroll	J. Lynch
1957	30	Canon Carroll	J. Lynch
1958	30	Canon Carroll	J. Lynch
1959	30	S. Casey	J. Lynch
1960	30	S. Casey	J. Lynch
1961	30	S. Casey	J. Lynch
1962	30	Fr. Neville	J. Lynch
1963	30	Fr. Neville	J. Lynch
1964	30	Fr. Neville	J. Lynch
1965	31	G. MacGowan	J. Lynch
1966	31	G. MacGowan	J. Lynch
1967	31	G. MacGowan	J. Lynch
1968	31	Br. Ó Murchadha	J. Lynch
1969	31	Br. Ó Murchadha	J. Lynch
1970	31	Br. Ó Murchadha	J. Lynch
1971	32	J. J. Jennings	J. Lynch
1972	32	J. J. Jennings	J. Lynch
1973	32	J. J. Jennings	J. Lynch
1974	32	J. J. Jennings	J. Lynch
1975	32	M. Boyce	J. Lynch
1976	32	M. Boyce	J. Lynch
1977	32	M. Boyce	J. Lynch
1978	32	T. Walsh	J. Lynch
1979	32	T. Walsh	J. Lynch
1980	32	T. Walsh	J. Lynch
1981	32	Caimín MacSeoin	J. Lynch
1982	32	Caimín MacSeoin	J. Lynch
1983	32	Caimín MacSeoin	J. Lynch

Cumann Luith-Chleas Gaedheal

GREAT
HANDBALL
CHALLENGE
ARMY v. ULLARD
at ULLARD on
THURSDAY, 19th MAY '55

ULLARD	ARMY
S. Lannon and M. Duggan v. R. Maher and M. Redmond	
J. Gardiner and J. Hennessey v. T. McElligott and C. White	
T. Ryan and J. Kelly v. S. Parle and J. O'Neill	

FIRST MATCH AT 2 O'CLOCK (S.T.)

Admission : : 1|-

BRADLEY, PRINTER, NEWBRIDGE. PHONE 126.

Bibliography

American Handball: A history of the game, (New York, *c*.1894)
The Badminton Library of Sports and Pastimes, (London, 1891)
Carlow in '98, The Autobiography of William Farrell of Carlow, Roger J. McHugh (London, 1949)
Coaching for Handball
Handball, Ray Doherty (Dublin, 1972)
History of the Royal Belfast Academical Institution, J. Jameson (Belfast, 1959)
Liathróid Láimhe: Ladies Action Call, 1970-77, (Ladies Handball Association)
Manual Completo de la Pelota Vasca, Manuel Cercadillo, (Bilbao, 1981)
Official Handbook of the Amateur Athletic Union, (New York, 1950)
Oxford Companion to Sports and Games,(London, 1975)
ApLSINF'A HNSVLL Fuisw, «nwq yoek, 1923)
Sports Illustrated; HANDBALL, Wayne McFarland and Philip Smith (New York, 1976)
The Story of the G.A.A., T. F. O'Sullivan (Dublin, 1916)
Ullard, P. O'Leary (Pamphlet, *The People*, Wexford, 1911)